The Modern Museum

Michael D. Levin

THE MODERN MUSEUM
TEMPLE OR SHOWROOM

Dvir Publishing House, Jerusalem · Tel Aviv

Acknowledgments for Illustrations

The photographs for this book were taken by the
author except for the following:
Alte Pinakothek, Munich, 59
Leonardo Bezzola, 5, 89
Cleveland Museum of Art, 99
Fondation Maeght, Saint Paul, France / Claude
Gaspari, 95
Alexander Gorges, courtesy Philip Johnson, 47
The Solomon R. Guggenheim Museum, 160, 161
Jesper HOM / Delta, courtesy Louisiana Museum, 58
The Israel Museum, 92 / David Harris, 10
Philip Johnson, 116, 117, 118
Keren Or, 206
Ken Kirkwood, courtesy Foster Ass., 144, 145
Kröller — Müller, Otterlo, 154
Kunsthaus Zurich, 199
Yoram Lehmann, cover
Alexander Liberman, 38
The Museum of Modern Art, New York, The Mies
van der Rohe Archive, 93, 136, 137
National Gallery of Art, Washington D.C., 3, 84
I.M. Pei, 84, 85
Pellechia and Meyers Architects, 114
Cesar Pelli & Associates / Ken Champlin, 17
Armando Sallas Portugal, 204
Horace Richter Gallery, 1
Kevin. Roche — John Dinkeloo Ass., 23, 24, 25
Ezra Stoller Associates, ESTO, 170; courtesy Philip
Johnson, 6, 139, 140, courtesy I.M. Pei, 181
Uffizi, 47
Verlag für Architektur (Artemis), 61, 63, 64, 65, 67
Victoria and Albert Museum, 128, 131, 132
Wurts Brothers, 15
Yale Art Gallery / Joseph Szaspari, 111

Book design: S. Zur

ISBN 965—01—0105—5

To my late parents who introduced me to the world of art

Table of Contents

Acknowledgments

This book is the fruit of a long-term interest in the development of the modern museum. To the late Professor Donald Egbert I am deeply indebted. Under his direction I began work on this subject as a graduate student at Princeton University. Some of the results were first presented at the Frick Collection Institute of Fine Arts Symposium in April 1971. I would also like to thank Professor Kurt Weitzmann for his advice and encouragement.

To Professor P. Reyner Banham and Dr. Christopher Green of the Courtauld Institute of Art, University of London, I am especially grateful for their guidance and criticism as supervisors of my doctoral thesis on which this book is based.

The teaching staff of the Department of History of Art and the Institute of Archaeology at the Hebrew University of Jerusalem also have my gratitude, especially Professors Moshe Barasch, Bezalel Narkiss, and Avraham Kampf, Dr. Ziva Meisels, and Dr. Lola Sleptsoff. Professor Edgar Kaufmann Jr.'s seminar at Columbia University was another valuable source of information.

In addition I would like to acknowledge the assistance of the directors, curators, museum staff, architects, and art historians with whom I talked or corresponded: Dr. Louise Averill Svendson, Curator, Guggenheim Museum; Mr. Arthur Drexler, Director, Department of Architecture and Design, and Dr. Ludwig Glaser, former Curator of the Mies van der Rohe Archive, the Museum of Modern Art, New York; Professor Patrick J. Kelleher, former Director of the Art Museum, Princeton University; Mr. Michael Compton, Keeper and Miss Corrine Bellow, Head of the Information Services, Tate Gallery, London; Mr. Michael Brawne (London); Mr. Kevin Roche (Connecticut); Mr. Philip Johnson (New York); and Professor Mathias Goeritz (Mexico City).

I should also like to recognize the help provided by the following libraries and their staff: Courtauld Institute of Art; School of Environmental Studies, University of London; Royal Institute of British Architects; Victoria and Albert Museum, London; Marquand Art Library and Firestone Library, Princeton University; the Library of the Museum of Modern Art and the Avery Library, Columbia University, New York; the United States Cultural Center; the Hebrew University National Library; and the Library of the Israel Museum, Jerusalem.

I wish to thank Princeton University for providing financial support for my graduate studies and to the Central Research Fund Committee, University of London and the Irwin Fund for their assistance.

Finally, I should like to express my appreciation to Mrs. Nancy Dorfman Pressly, Dr. Hugh Davies, Dr. Vojtech Jirat-Wasiutynski, Dr. Barry Harwood, Dr. George Bauer, and my wife, Talma Tchlenov Levin, who read parts of the manuscript and offered their criticism. The final version also benefitted considerably from the editorial assistance of Yechiel Bar-Chaim, and I am also grateful to Gila Brand for typing the various revisions of the text.

Chapter I.
The concept of the modern museum

1. A symbol of civilization

Shifts in the concept of the museum — what it should contain, whom it should serve, and how it should function — reflect changes in society and culture. More so than with other special types of architecture.

Train stations or airport terminals, for example, are erected to meet specific needs. They are an outgrowth of modern technological developments and as such reflect the greater mobility of modern man. Like other building types, their style, form, location, and size reflect the social and historical values of the society in which they were created. Some were designed by great architects and are considered masterpieces in their own right. Yet the museum, almost by definition, does more than express current social values and tastes; it also makes a cultural statement which goes beyond its own place in history. The museum discussed here is a representative of civilization with a capital 'C'.

This book deals only with museums of art, archaeology, and related subjects and not with science, technology, or other types of museums. Thus the social, functional, and formal solutions surveyed here all constitute a response to a set of specific requirements. One of the most recurrent problems in the design of art museums, for example, is that of natural light, which is definitely a secondary factor where science museums are concerned.

Unless otherwise stated, the term museum will be used for institutions with an encyclopedic range, as well as for galleries devoted specifically to painting and sculpture (either privately or publicly owned)[1]. The British distinction between museum and non-commercial gallery is not commonly accepted in the U.S. where the latter term refers mainly to the commercial gallery[2]. Since the ensuing discussion is to be international in scope, we adopt the American usage.

Although it is relatively easy to categorize museums geographically, to do so is of limited significance. Culture is now international, and the various sources of any individual development do not necessarily originate in a single region. Modern architecture is the outcome of an exchange of ideas and a flow of information from one country to another through publications, travel, etc., a factor which lies at the root of the term "International Style." Mies van der Rohe, for example, designed one museum in Houston, Texas and another in Berlin. Where should one discuss other museums influenced by him like the one in Vienna? Should it be found under United States, Germany, Austria, or Belgium, since it was designed for the American Pavilion at the World Fair in Brussels, but later rebuilt with some modifications in Vienna as the Museum des 20 Jahrhunderts?

Are Le Corbusier museums Oriental, just because he was only commissioned to build museums in Japan and India?

In his book, *The New Museum,* Michael Brawne described tendencies which he saw as regional[3]. In Italian museums the singular element was said to be display, a major concern in adapting palaces and castles to museum use. Particular intentions allegedly underlying Italian museum design were also noted. The architects "see themselves not as rebels against history but as part of a continuous tradition, the most marked aspect of which is a simultaneous belief in the present and acceptance of the past."[4]

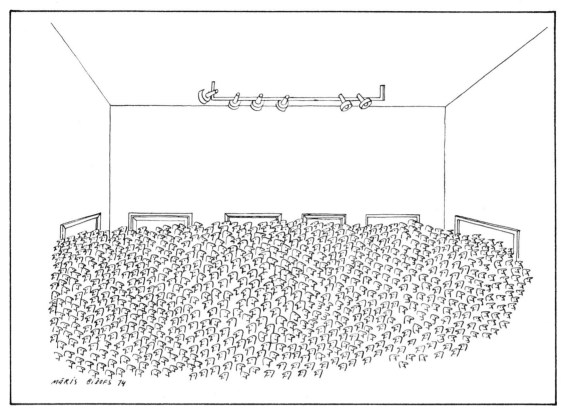

Pl. 1 Maris Bishofs, "Exhibition Within an Exhibition," 1974.

Scandinavian museum design has stressed the achievement of a "complete environment." "It has tried to emphasize the museum as a natural part of civilized life, a place of enjoyment to be visited regularly for a number of activities." The particular attribute of the Scandinavian museum is that it "derives some of its interest from its setting."[5] According to Brawne, "the example set by these museums has not yet been followed elsewhere; like the Italian attitude to display, it has yet to be absorbed into current thinking."

But what about a museum like Fondation Maeght at St. Paul-de-Vence by José Sert, included in Brawne's book in the section devoted to France, Germany, Austria, and Switzerland. Does not this museum "derive some of its interest from its setting?" The museum building is arranged as a small village on the foothills of the Maritime Alps. The main pavilion could be looked upon as the principal public building like a church or a town hall, with the central court serving as a 'piazza', as Brawne himself observed[6].

In most of the recent museum buildings in France, Germany, Austria, and Switzerland, Brawne found that the desire is

> to achieve a rather anonymous, neutral space which would be highly flexible in use. In practice this has generally meant large spaces and controlled toplighting. The emphasis thus differs considerably from the Italian or Scandinavian attitudes except where old buldings were used.[7]

Yet anonymous and neutral space can also be found in museums elsewhere: the Gallery of Modern Art in Milan (1954); the Annex to the Stedelijk Museum, Amsterdam (1954); and the Tel Aviv Museum of Art, Helena Rubinstein Pavilion (1958).

Unique regional features are rare. They can be found, however, in the treasure houses where the architects tried to fit a particular collection to a specific location, like the Tesoro di San Lorenzo in Genoa, designed by Franco Albini, or the Shrine of the Book in Jerusalem by Frederick Kiesler and Armand Bartos. Besides the possible connection to Kiesler's studies for the "Endless House," one of the sources for the dome adopted in the second example is the cover of the terracotta jar in which the Dead Sea Scrolls were found. The Scrolls, the Bar Kochba letters, and related archaeological finds are exhibited in the underground circular room under the dome, in the 'crypt' below, and in the long corridor which leads the visitor from the entrance to the central room. These underground galleries suggest the caves in which the exhibits were found. Here museum form is directly determined by its contents with their strong regional accent[8]. But museum designs stressing regional features remain exceptions to the more general rule.

Our effort is not to examine ten or twenty particular examples of modern museums in order to delineate what they may have in common and where they differ. Rather, the discussion concentrates on the concepts and challenges inherent in modern museum architecture. Examples are cited only to illustrate how different museums embody these concepts; and just how these challenges are met. Other types of museums are mentioned to highlight specific architectural features where they are also relevant to art museums.

Our discussion of modern museum architecture is not organized on the basis of time and place. Certain major developments in the concept of the museum are surveyed, and it is these which have generally inspired changes in architectural form.

2. The impact of democratization on the museum.

Ever since the genesis of the public museum, its development has been characterized by a process of progressive democratization.

The first public museums were conceived as educational institutions for the masses, but because of their limited accessibility they could not fulfill this role. According to Lewis Mumford,

> ...the opening of the British Museum in 1759, after Sir Hans Sloane's bequest, was a landmark in popular culture, for when display ceases to be merely a private gratification of the possessor it has the possibility of becoming a means of public education.[9]

Yet persons intending to visit the British Museum were first asked to give their credentials at the Museum's office. Only after several weeks were they likely to receive a ticket of admission. As a result, during the Museum's first twenty years, an average of only 10,000 visitors were admitted annually[10] (as compared with the 1979 figure of 3,081,141)[11]. The Official Rules and Acts of 1808 concerning the admission of "strangers and artists" show that the Museum was open four days a week and that no more than eight groups of 15 visitors were admitted in the course of one day. To visit the Hermitage, which was in theory ōpen to the public, one had to be dressed in the same outfit required of a visitor to the royal court[12]. The Louvre was declared a public museum by the first republican government of France. As a result of the Revolution of 1789 the royal collection, formerly accessible only to the aristocracy, came under public ownership and was subsequently opened to the populace. In other words, in the late eighteenth century and during the greater part of the nineteenth century, the right to visit a public museum belonged to a relatively select audience.

Only in the late nineteenth century and then in our century, did the great museums become truly public. Attendance at the National Gallery in London rose from 628,548 in 1938 to 1,147,226 in 1960, reaching 2,577,723 two decades later (1979). In the early 1940's there were fifty million visitors to all American museums; in 1960, 200 million; and in 1967, 560 million visitors. The attendance figure of the National Gallery in Washington was below 1,500,000 in the fiscal year ending June 30, 1968. By the end of the fiscal year of 1978, with the East Wing only four months old, Gallery attendance had tripled and stood at 4,500,000 visitors. The estimated audience of the extension service was 6.2 million persons, bringing the Gallery's total audience to over 10 million[13]. Although these figures undoubtedly include repeat visits by many individuals, they do indicate a rapid and undeniable increase of museum visitors during the twentieth century — a dramatic widening of the museum audience.

Notwithstanding this long process of democratization and despite the sharp increase in attendance figures just noted, the question is still raised whether the public museum remains more accessible to the elite than to the masses. Does the astronomical number of visitors really reflect a far-reaching democratization of the great museums or merely an increase in the size and strength of middle and upper income classes?

The question of élitism involves not only the changing functions of the museum and how it is administered, but also the relationship between modern art and the avant-garde, on the one hand, and the masses, on the other.

a. Art for whom? The conflicting views of José Ortega y Gasset and Clement Greenberg.

In his essay, "The Dehumanization of Art," José Ortega y Gasset wrote in 1925 that modern art

> divides the public into two groups, one very small formed by those who are favorably inclined toward it, another very large — the hostile majority. (Let us ignore that ambiguous fauna — the snobs.) Thus the work of art acts like a social agent which segregates from the shapeless mass of many two different castes of man.[14]

New art, he claimed, addresses itself not to every man but to a specially gifted minority, and as a result modern art is inevitably opposed by the masses; it can never be popular art. The problem, he felt, is not that the majority does not appreciate new art, but that they do not understand it. "The masses feel that the new art, which is the art of the privileged aristocracy of finer senses, endangers their rights as men. Whenever the new muses present themselves, the masses bristle."[15] We thus have an art "which can be comprehended only by people possessed of the pecular gift of artistic sensitivity — an art for artists and not for the masses, for quality and not for hoi polloi."[16] It is this "élitist" factor that turned Ortega y Gasset against modern art. He declared himself opposed to art that is not understood by the masses[17].

While art critic Clement Greenberg, writing in 1939 ("Avant-garde and Kitsch"), agreed that modern art can be understood only by the élite, he did not see this limitation as a fatal flaw, since the masses do have access to art they can appreciate[18]. "Where there is an avant-garde," wrote Greenberg, "generally we also find a rear guard. True enough — simultaneously with the entrance of the avant-garde, a second new cultural phenomeñon apeared in the industrial West: the thing to which the Germans give the wonderful name of Kitsch...."[19]

Greenberg used the Russian peasant to illustrate his point:

> Superior culture is one of the most artificial of all human creations, and the peasant finds no 'natural' urgency within himself that will drive him toward Picasso in spite of all difficulties. In the end the peasant will go back to Kitsch when he feels like looking at pictures, for he can enjoy Kitsch without effort.[20]

He maintains that it is not due to

> the social advantage of the avant-garde that it is what it is. The avant-garde's specialization of itself — the fact that its best artists are artists' artists, its best poets, poets' poets — has estranged a great many of those who where capable formerly of enjoying and appreciating ambitious art and literature but are now unwilling or unable to acquire an initiation into their craft secrets. The masses have always remained more or less indifferent to culture in the process of development. But to-day such culture is being abandoned by those to whom it actually belongs — our ruling class. For it is to the latter that the avant-garde belongs. No culture can develop without a social basis, without a source of stable income. And in the case of the avant-garde, this was provided by the élite among the ruling class of that society from which it assumed itself to be cut off, but to which it has always remained attached by an umbilical cord of gold. The paradox is real.[21]

Greenberg felt that the avant-garde was becoming unsure of the audience it depends on — the rich and the cultivated. These same ideas in different guises are still current.

b. The charge of élitism.

Two opposing tendencies can be observed. On the one hand there are serious efforts to transform the museum into an institution open to all segments of society. And in most museums, special educational departments have been erected for that purpose. Thomas Hoving observed in the American museum the presence of a greater desire than ever, with far more effective results than ever, to bring art to the people[22].

On the other hand there is the attitude that the general public is incapable of appreciating art. In 1971 Viscount Eccles told the members of the British Museums Association about a Harris poll of participants at a National Endowment for the Arts conference in Washington at which then-President Nixon urged a major effort to bring the arts to the masses. One of the questions asked was: "Do you feel that most works of art are meant to be appreciated by a small group with some knowledge and background in the discipline or by the general public?" Thirty-three

Pl. 2 The Modern Museum — "Temple" or "Showroom"? Photomontage.

Pl. 3 John Russell Pope, The National Gallery, Washington, D.C., 1937–41.
The National Gallery is not very different from Karl Friedrich Schinkel's museum design of 1800 (Pl. 4).

Pl. 4 Karl Friedrich Schinkel, Museum design of 1800.

percent of them were certain and another fourteen percent nearly certain that the small group was the only audience for most works of art[23].

Michael Compton, Keeper of the Department of Exhibitions and Education at the Tate Gallery, said in a talk to Courtauld Institute Students Union (Autumn 1972) that whether we chose to admit or ignore it, the fact is that the museum today serves mainly the well-educated élite. The Tate collection, in his view, reflects the élite's deep awareness of the avant-garde's historical roots. "Cubism is meaningless without Cézanne."

c. Public access and museum finances.
Another aspect of the problem of élitism within the democratized museum is the question of admission charges, so important in Great Britain at the beginning of the 1970's. Addressing the 1971 Annual Conference of the Museums Association, Viscount Eccles (the member of government in charge of the arts), justified the introduction of admission charges[24]. This was a drastic change in policy since even the first public museum, the British Museum, has not charged admission fees since its opening[25]. Eccles claimed that admission charges would help finance a cultural revolution making it possible to substantially enlarge the number of visitors. According to Eccles the growth of interest in museums "depends on whether we are

Pl. 5 Leonardo Bezzola,
Rolls Royce photomontage, 1981.

Pl. 6 Philip Johnson, Sheldon Memorial Art Gallery, University of Nebraska, Lincoln, Nebraska, 1963.
The Neo-classical idiom was adapted to an endless number of temples of art around the world from America to Russia, using the established classical symbol of cultural heritage and dignity (see Pl. 147). Johnson's Sheldon Memorial Art Gallery suggests strongly a relationship with Schinkel's Classical portico of the Altes Museum in Berlin (Pl. 6).
Pl. 7 Karl Friedrich Schinkel, Altes Museum, Berlin, designed 1823, built 1825—28.

content to wait for visitors to come in increased numbers on their own initiative, or whether we go out after them and attract them as the television attracted the multitudes to the Victoria and Albert Museum to see the dresses of Henry VIII's wives." "We ought not," he continued, "to be asking how fast they (museum attendance figures) could and should rise if, believing that a cultural revolution is round the corner, we did our best to accelerate its arrival."[26]

The question remains, however, how this dramatic increase in museum visitors will come about and what form it will take. The introduction of admission fees may very well exclude many of those whom the museums wish to attract, namely the lower income class, so essential to any prospective 'cultural revolution.'

The Metropolitan Museum of Art introduced admission charges in 1971, but left the exact amount to the visitors' discretion. One drawback to this method is the potential embarrassment of not paying. Many museums do not charge admission for the permanent collection, but do demand an entrance fee for temporary exhibitions, and indeed often these spectacular shows attract large numbers of paying visitors. Meanwhile museum dependence on visitors' fees has increased in recent years.

Exhibitions sponsored by corporations and public institutions such as the Arts Council of Great Britain and the U.S. National Endowment for the Arts (established by then-President Johnson in 1965), also help to cover the chronic deficits of art museums. Further support comes from tax deduction schemes. In the U.S. one third of total taxable income can be given to cultural organizations. Bequests are directly deducted in unlimited amounts from that part of the estate subject to duty. By these means the Internal Revenue Service stimulates further support for museums from individual contributions.

It would be invalid, however, to compare the museum with other art centers such as the opera house, concert hall, or theater where the audience pays a substantial sum in return for cultural entertainment. Even before there were public museums, whenever a museum was accessible to the public, it was almost always free of charge. The performing arts, on the other hand, were always based on admission fees for the simple reason that performers 'have to eat, pictures only need to be dusted.'

The only proper comparison for museums is with public libraries, where the search for knowledge, information, and entertainment is free of charge. Indeed the same impulse motivated the erection of both public libraries and museums in the nineteenth century. They were open free to all parts of society and were intended for the education of the less privileged. Many times the same sponsors established the two complementary institutions, as was the case, for example, with the City Corporation of Birmingham[27].

Yet as museum costs rise and already chronic deficits swell, to the question for whom the art is intended must be added the query who is going to pay. Here there is a need for serious research, using polls as an essential tool, to investigate the social and educational background of museum visitors[28].

d. Who controls the museum?
The charge of élitism laid against the modern museum also concerns the selection of the board of trustees. Protestors and demonstrators in recent years have claimed that the trustees do not represent the different segments of the museum audience. The request for a more balanced representation of the community on boards of trustees is another aspect of the democratization of the public museum.

Even though women are by no means less interested than men in the museum's work, trustees are predominantly male. The elected board of the Metropolitan Museum is largely male, 31 to 5. In 1976–78 there was one woman out of twelve on the Board of the Tate Gallery and three out of fourteen on the Board of the National Gallery in London. Indeed, the express wish of Meyer Schapiro for the second century of the Metropolitan Museum was to have more women among the trustees.

In an article entitled "Democratize the Board of Trustees," Schapiro called for changing the composition of the board of trustees by admitting representatives of the membership, including women; limiting further the present seven-year term of office; and inviting a more active representation of the city. Professor Schapiro is aware that such representation will not by itself generate a better policy in matters of art. But artists, scholars, and devoted public would at least be able to express their opinions more effectively. "It would help," wrote Schapiro, "to remove, or reduce the suspicion of privilege, social exclusiveness, and self-promotion that attaches itself to trusteeship in museums."[29]

Pl. 8 Mies van der Rohe, Neue Nationalgalerie, Berlin, 1962–1968.
This building is self-consciously related to Schinkel's Altes Museum in Berlin (Pl. 7). More than any other building by Mies van der Rohe the museum is an act of homage and rivalry to Schinkel.

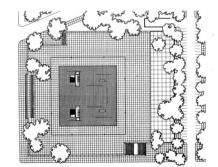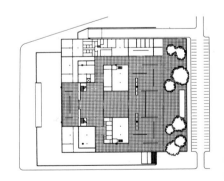

Pl. 9 Mies van der Rohe, Neue Nationalgalerie, Berlin, 1962–1968, plans.
Mies van der Rohe came the closest to realizing the ultimate goal of absolute flexibility in the organization of space. This ideal he approached by designing a single large space within a functional frame which incorporates natural and artificial light, energy outlets, and air-conditioning and which allows complete freedom for the exhibition designer.

In an article on the American scene, Geraldine Norman wrote that élitism was the central theme of protest:

> Museums are run by the rich white establishment for the rich white establishment. Protestors feel that the other ethnic groups, including that paraethnic group the female sex, are not allowed to project their own identity through the museum exhibits and activities. All they can expect from their museums is a neatly packaged dose of traditional, white, masculine culture. The financing of museums has traditionally leaned heavily on the trustees who tend to be drawn from the richest families of the community — for the purpose of leaning on. If the charge of élitism is to be answered this stranglehold must be broken. But could the museums survive?[30]

The situation varies in different countries. The argument presented above refers more to American museums than to European institutions. Since most of the budget of public museums in the United Kingdom, France, or the Netherlands comes from the government or city corporations, the trustees tend to be civil servants rather than rich art patrons.

The professional competence of trustees is also at issue. In 1979 the Tate Gallery had four artists and one art historian out of ten members of the Board. The Museum of Modern Art's Board of Trustees had in 1979 a larger proportion of women (sixteen out of fifty-one members), one art historian, five architects, two Rockefellers, and many other art patrons and donors, but no painter or sculptor[31]. Karl Meyer points out that in its 108 years of existence, the Metropolitan has made room on its board for only one artist of national standing. No professional art historian moreover has ever been invited to serve as a trustee with voting rights.

To professionalize the work of the board of trustees, the American Association of Museums has suggested in recent years guidelines for board procedure. A new phenomenon which points in the same direction is the appointment of a paid president (e.g. Minneapolis Institute of Art, Chicago Institute of Art, Metropolitan Museum)[32].

3. Reorienting the modern museum.

a. Lewis Mumford on the encyclopedic museum.

What still separates the great metropolitan museum from the public? Not élitist art, nor high entrance fees, nor plutocratic boards of trustees. Lewis Mumford put the blame on aimless acquisition, reckless expansion, and progressive disorganization.

In *The Culture of Cities,* first published in 1938, Mumford stated that physical size serves as a substitute for organization. The chaos in the museum reflects the disorganized content of the metropolis itself. "The encyclopedic culture of the metropolis," he writes, "turns the museum into a second metropolis, like the big city, it aims merely at bigness and results in purposelessness and intellectual bewilderment."[33]

The contents of the art museum derive historically

> from the palace and country house displays of loot that mark either ostentatious purchase or military conquest of foreign lands... In time, genuine esthetic and scientific interests develop in these institutions, but the trustees of the museum are more interested in abstract acquisition and honorific display than in matters of truth, taste, and value.[34]

Indeed many museum collections were not formed scientifically, and careful, purposeful reorganization has yet to be imposed. Instead the haphazard principles governing private and royal collections have been allowed to prevail. Whereas private collectors are familiar with their own collections and their few, but knowledgeable, visitors need not be given a clear sense of chronological or other relationships; visitors to a public museum do need guidance. Yet the elegant nonchalance of the private collector has also characterized not a few major public institutions. Until the reorganization begun a few years ago, all the bronzes in the Louvre, from Classical to Hellenistic and Etruscan, were exhibited indiscriminately in the same display cases, which could not help but confuse the inexperienced layman.

Mumford compared the standards of the big metropolitan museum to those of the department store where "the lure of many unrelated articles and their random purchase are all under one roof," and where "culture and knowledge are regarded mainly as means of acquisition and display."

In this the museums are merely bowing to the public will.

> Patrons and public alike, the nouveau riche of the metropolis are culture shoppers. They tend to transform the chief institutions of learning into vast department stores

Pl. 10 Richard Westmacott, The Progress of Civilization, pediment of the British Museum, London.

24

Pl. 11 Frederick Kiesler and Armand Bartos,
The Shrine of the Book, The Israel Museum,
Jerusalem, 1965.
A modern example of the concept of the museum
as a temple, it is neither a Neo-classical temple
nor a Renaissance palace.

of arts and sciences where everything is ticketed and labelled, where the turnover of goods is more important than the ultimate satisfaction of the purchases.[35]

Mumford recommends reorganizing and decentralizing museum collections. Central storage facilities would be established so that objects can be circulated systematically. He would have all specialized museums compressed to conform to a convenient average size (the average size of the encyclopedic museum when Mumford wrote his book); none would expand to outsized proportions. Yet even then MOMA was already organizing travelling exhibitions which had as their nucleus the Museum's own resources.

These ideas reflect a certain state of mind prevalent in the late twenties and thirties. In his article, "Smaller and Better Museums," (The "Atlantic Monthly", 1929)[36], Frank Jewett Mather Jr. criticized the Metropolitan. American museums are growing too large, he declared, and in doing so they are defeating their own purpose. The Metropolitan, which accepted the quantitative ideal long ago, best exemplified the trend and its drawbacks. Mather proposed to eliminate the confusion experienced by the visitor as well as the museum management. His answer: decentralization. Large metropolitan museums would establish branch museums, each of which would specialize in a single field.

Francis H. Taylor, Director of the Metropolitan Museum of Art in the 1940's, had in mind similar solutions. Taylor sought to reorganize the overcrowded and "archaic" Metropolitan into a series of museums of different civilizations and cultures, but his ideas did not materialize, partly because the necessary funds could not easily be raised during and after the Second World War. Only in the master plan prepared by architect Kevin Roche and his associates (1970) has this ideal come to fruition. This plan involved a major reorganization of the museum into smaller, more specialized units with space for visitor orientation, a changing exhibition gallery, and a study collection alongside the principal collection[37].

Not only does Mumford critize the organization of museums and their modes of presentation, he also attacks their relationship with the cultural hinterland. He maintains that museums should grow out of a balanced regional culture. In recent years some museums have attuned themselves to this aim. The museum in Darmstadt, for example, specializes in Jugendstil which flourished locally, while the Neue Nationalgalerie in Berlin features a collection of local painters and art. At the Israel Museum in Jerusalem, the archaeological department concentrates on local finds ranging from the prehistoric period to late Byzantine, while Mexico's Anthropological Museum serves as a center for pre-Columbian archaeology, illustrating the history of Mexico before the Spanish conquest[38].

Although Mumford's ideas partially materialized in the 1960's and the early 1970's, their realization still proved to be only a partial solution to even more complex problems. Meanwhile other creative minds also pondered the future of the museum.

b. André Malraux's Le Musée Imaginaire.

André Malraux outlined his ideas of how the museum should develop in *Le Musée Imaginaire* (translated into English as *Museum Without Walls*)[39]. In his view the limited scope of even the largest museums seemed an insuperable disadvantage.

> After all, a museum is one of the places that show man at his noblest. But our knowledge covers a wider field than our museums. The visitor to the Louvre knows that it contains no significant representation of either Goya or the painting of Michelangelo or even those of Vermeer.[40]

A century ago in order to unite related works of art, one had to memorize the contents of one or more museums. Today one can examine together in a single volume color reproductions of the most important paintings, regardless of where they may be scattered across the globe.

> We have, however, far more great works available to refresh our memories than the greatest museums could bring together. A museum without walls has been opened to us and it will carry indefinitely farther that limited revelation of the world of art which the real museum offers us within its walls: in answer to their appeal the plastic arts have produced the printing press.[41]

Whereas Malraux believed that the illustrated art-book covers a wider field than any museum, the late Rene Gimpel claimed that "the museum is the only good book ever written on art."[42]

Malraux's view could be compared to the predictions that in the next century, records and tapes will replace most live concerts. Records are being made by the best performers and they provide a more precise rendering of the score than most

live concerts can offer. Advanced stereophonic equipment, coupled with the easy, flexible, and relaxed atmosphere of home-listening will gradually oust the concert hall according to this forecast[43].

But Malraux ignored almost completely the unique esthetic experience one enjoys only through direct contact with original works of art. Although Raymond Durgnat observed that the "direct visual experience of originals accounts for a tiny proportion of our participation," these art objects are in fact the only works of art that are not distant and blurred[44]. In this respect neither a record nor a reproduction can replace the original.

Although Malraux felt that the future belongs to reproduced works of art, he still affirmed the place of the museum in this future. He acknowledged, if only in a short paragraph, the validity of the direct esthetic experience:

> The realm of images humanity has known is calling forth its sanctuary, as the realm of the supernatural called forth the Cathedral. But this realm, which makes an island of any Louvre, however vast, is bringing back the faithful to all the Louvres, because their faith is the same. For phonograph records have not destroyed concerts; because we fell a need to rediscover the particular perfection or the irreplaceable texture of flesh, the real or imagined soul that belongs only to the original; because the dialogue between the Avignon *Pietà* and Titian's *Nymph and Shepherd* is not entirely of the same nature as the dialogue between their reproductions.[45]

Yet when he speaks about sculpture he feels that "sculpture can be reproduced in black and white more faithfully than painting, our contemporary art books have found it a realm in which they are entirely successful."[46]

Malraux knew that reproductions cannot replace the museum nor endanger its existence. "We will see — in the museum without walls at first, in exhibitions later, and finally in the real museums — gathered together as a style works that until that time were scattered, considered minor, or linked in our mind to different styles."[47] In the City Art Gallery at São Paolo, Brazil, the exhibits are not compartmentalized by period or school. Paintings from different centuries and countries are exhibited one next to the other so that the curator does not impose his own standards and references on the visitor. Unlike the bronzes at the Louvre, however, the paintings here are carefully labelled to avoid confusion[48].

But one can claim with the same justification that the process starts from the other end — the actual museum and even more so the exhibition create the museum of the mind. The comparisons and juxtapositions that a flexible permanent collection or a specialized exhibition can offer fulfill a powerful formative role. For example, in the exhibition "Fifty Centuries of Masterpieces" at the Metropolitan Museum of Art in New York, the curators compared and juxtaposed the American abstract expressionist Arshile Gorky, the fifteenth century Flemish painter, Master of Flemalle, and a Far Eastern scroll in order to demonstrate different approaches to Symbolism.

It is not only the imaginary museum that shapes the real museum. The museum as it is changes, expands and transforms the museum without walls.

By the time Malraux wrote *Le Musée Imaginaire,* the reputation of MOMA in New York was based as much on temporary exhibitions as on the permanent collection. The printing and distribution of exhibition catalogues, books, reproductions, posters, postcards, and slides, not only of objects from the permanent collection, but also reproductions of art objects from other museums and private collections, blurred the distinction between the museum collection and the works of art outside the museum's walls[49]. These printed images extended the scope of the actual museum.

The "Museum Without Walls" and the real museum continue to change according to Malraux. We have "the feeling of metamorphosis taking place, which we experience in our relation with the museum without walls and, less directly, with our great museums in reality."[50] But is the museum of today the museum without walls of yesterday?

As we shall see the development of the real museum is in fact inseparably linked to that of the museum of the mind. But whereas the preceding discussion has dealt with the aims and ideals which have shaped the modern museum as a social and as an architectural form, it seems more helpful to build the ensuing discussion on those social, functional, and formal elements which define the modern museum. Although the elements to be presented here briefly are more fully treated in later chapters, a complete definition is nonetheless offered so that the various parts of this book can be consistently related to an overall view of the modern museum.

Pl. 13 Philip L. Goodwin and Edward Durrel Stone, Museum of Modern Art, New York, 1939, Extensions by Philip Johnson, East Wing, 1950, West Wing, 1962–1964.
An example of the concept of the museum as a showroom — a commercial type of building as opposed to the temple.

4. The modern museum, a definiton.

The modern museum is characterized by the following six attributes:

a. Multiplicity of function.
The functions of the modern museum are not only to acquire and preserve a collection of art, but also to actively educate the public through temporary exhibits, junior wings, films, and other activities such as lectures and concerts. Not only have new functions been added to the role of the museum, the collection itself has been reorganized into primary and study reserve collections.

b. Expansion and diversification of exhibited material.
The modern museum has expanded its collection to include Primitive, African, Mexican, and Polynesian art, as well as children's art, industrial design, photography, and architecture.

c. A new approach to light.
Artificial light has been introduced into the modern museum, and skylighting has ceased to be the dominant factor in museum design. In the past the use of skylighting led to single story exhibition rooms; any lower floors were used for other functions. Now artificial light has liberated museum design from these strictures.

d. Conservation.
In the modern museum exhibits are protected from air pollution, exposure to direct light, humidity, etc. A conservation department has been set up not as an afterthought within an existing building, but as an integral part of the overall museum plan.

e. Flexibility.
The search for maximum flexibility of space and display methods has led to the design of versatile structures in which the floor space, windows, light projectors, interchangeable partitions and display cases are designed to allow the exhibition designer as much freedom as is technically possible.

f. Expressive form.
Historical styles (the Classical temple, Renaissance palace, or the Medieval church) have been rejected in favor of a new expressive form specifically designed to meet the needs of the museum.

The different components of this definition are discussed in the following three chapters. The multiplicity of function and the expansion and diversification of the collections are examined in the next chapter on the social aspect of museum design, while light, conservation and flexible space and display are studied in the third chapter on the functional aspect. Also treated are the problems of visitor circulation and physical expansion. The fourth chapter on the formal aspect deals with the origin of modern museum styles.

The chronological development of these elements is then traced in a separate chapter. Although one or more aspects of this definition do characterize some early museums, it was not until relatively recently that the modern museum concept was fulfilled in one museum. Yet as this final chapter shows the realization of the modern museum has only sharpened the still developing debate concerning the relation of the museum to the art it displays.

*Pl. 17 Cesar Pelli, MOMA's apartment tower.
The income-producing apartment tower will
emphasize the commercial aspect of the museum
building.*

Chapter II.
The social aspect of the modern museum, "Temple" or "Showroom"?

1. The values a museum expresses.

Built in Neo-classical or Gothic style in the closing years of the eighteenth century and throughout the nineteenth century, the first public museums echoed the spirit of ancient Greek and Roman temples, Renaissance palaces, or Medieval churches. The museum was a monument conveying also a tradition. Even more modern museums have continued to reflect this spirit. The National Gallery in Washington, built by John Russell Pope from 1937 to 1941 (Pl. 3), differs little from Karl Friedrich Schinkel's museum design of 1800 (Pl. 4). Schinkel's "Temple of Beauty," as Professor Rosenblum has observed, was to be located "in a sylvan, Arcadian setting. It is surrounded by figures in antique costumes rather than by Berlin bourgeoisie."[1]

Just as Rolls Royce adopted the Neo-classical facade for its radiator design[2] (Pl. 5), so countless temples of art around the world from the United States to Czarist Russia chose to use this established classical symbol of cultural heritage and dignity. Philip Johnson's Sheldon Art Gallery at the University of Nebraska (1963) (Pl. 6) suggests strongly a relationship with another Schinkel building — the classical portico of the Altes Museum in Berlin, designed in 1823 and built 1825—28 (Pl. 7)[3]. In addition Mies van der Rohe's Neue Nationalgalerie in Berlin (Pls. 8, 9) is self-consciously related to Schinkel's museum[4]. This building, more than any other by Mies van der Rohe, is an act of homage and rivalry to Schinkel, the great Berlin architect[5]. In turn Schinkel's Altes Museum relates to Durand's published plan for a museum which itself refers to Boullée's unpublished (1783) design for a museum[6].

The concept of the museum as a temple necessarily implies that the museum-goer leave the setting of his daily life in order to undergo an esthetic experience. This concept underlies not only Neo-classical temples (Pl. 10) or Renaissance palaces (Pl. 59), but any museum form which is the product of a designer's desire to enshrine art. The museum for Biblical manuscripts, a subdivision of the Israel Museum in Jerusalem, is officially called "The Shrine of the Book" (Pl. 11). Its architects, Kiesler and Bartos, tried literally to enshrine the scrolls and manuscripts in a monumental building. Frank Lloyd Wright wrote of the Guggenheim Museum of Art: "the nature of the building design is such as to seem more like a temple in a park on the avenue than like a mundane business or residential structure."[7] He added that the Guggenheim appears as a temple of adult education and not a profit seeking business venture (Pl. 12).

Opposed to the temple, however, is a concept which views the museum as a commercial showroom. The Museum of Modern Art is an example of the second

Pl. 18 Marcel Breuer and Hamilton Smith, Whitney Museum of American Art, New York, 1963–1966.
The open sculpture court and the storefront windows of the Whitney were designed to attract passers-by and provide contact with the street.

Pl. 19 Robert and Roger Nicholson (interior design) in association with the Council of Industrial Design, Design Center, London, 1965.
The Design Center has an even more obvious storefront.

Pl. 20 Classical columns frame the view of the park in Albright-Knox Art Gallery, Buffalo. Locating the museum outside the course of daily life determines the nature of the museum.

approach (Pls. 13, 14, 15, 16). The glass curtain wall at ground-floor level resembles a shop window. In the Machine Exhibition a remarkable automobile, the Bugatti type 41 "La Royale" of 1931, was placed near the window to attract visitors (Pl. 14), while at all times flags and posters advertise the Museum's activities to the public[8]. To attract passers-by, the Whitney Museum has an open sculpture court next to the sidewalk on Madison Avenue. The entrance bridge as well as the storefront windows — through which one can see the lobby and lower sculpture gallery — give the museum direct contact with the street. Through the strangely shaped windows one can even catch a glimpse of the exhibition (Pl. 18). Not incidentally, both the Museum of Modern Art and the Whitney are located in the downtown business district of New York, where, perhaps between business meetings or while shopping, one can take a "museum break."

In 1956 David Campbell transformed an old row house into the Museum of Contemporary Crafts in New York, a shop-like space on many levels. This museum and the Design Centre in the Haymarket, London, which also opened in 1956[9] (Pl. 18, 19), have even more obvious store-fronts. These museums are no longer temples of adult education but pedagogical showrooms, with locations that underscore their commercial image.

Alternatively a museum may be located outside the course of daily life. Such a placement may in fact determine the entire character of the institution (Pl. 20). The Museum of Anthropology and the Museum of History in the Chapultepec Park in Mexico City or the Cloisters in New York are park museums, undeniably more crowded on the weekend and holidays when a leisurely "pilgrimage" can be combined with a picnic. One has only to compare the banal cityscape seen from the Whitney's windows with the tempting garden outside the New History Museum in Chapultepec Park (Vasquez, 1960)[10] (Pls. 21, 22).

Pl. 21 The banal cityscape seen from the Whitney Museum window, New York (compare with Pl. 22).

Pl. 22 Chapultepec park seen from the New History Museum, Mexico City.

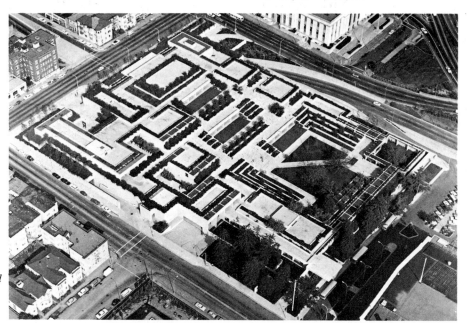

Pl. 23 Kevin Roche and John Dinkeloo, Oakland Museum, Oakland, California, 1970.
The setting of this museum is both park and downtown business area.

The new museum in Oakland, California is a mixed type, which unites a park setting with a downtown-business location. The museum is situated in the center of the city, but a three-level structure bordered by terraces converts it into an urban oasis. Although surrounded by public buildings, the museum is connected on one side to the south shore of Lake Merrit, a nature reserve (Pls. 23, 24, 25). Indeed its architects, Roche and Dinkeloo, originally envisioned a master plan for downtown Oakland with a green corridor from the lake to the town center. Yet for all its park museum appearance, Kevin Roche's own view is that the Oakland Museum is essentially a downtown institution[11].

a. Moving museums closer to the street.
Traditionally museums were elevated on some sort of podium. In many cases a garden was planted in the front, and more often than not a long flight of steps allowed the visitor to approach. Both the podium and the garden placed the museum at a distance from the street[12].

The relation of the museum to the street was changed, however, at the Whitechapel Art Gallery in London, which opened in 1901. Its main facade faces the sidewalk just as any ordinary building with an entrance at curb level; no platform raises the museum from the ground[13], no staircase provides an impressive introduction (Pl.148). At the turn of the century, this was an exception. Exhibitions at the Whitechapel were installed directly at the street entrance; there was no transition area as there is now[14]. It was intended to place a mosaic in the upper part of the facade to attract passers-by to the museum[15].

The Brooklyn Museum, which opened two years before, was designed by McKim, Mead, and White in a Neo-classical style with a grand staircase. But in the mid-1930's the Museum decided to eliminate this baroque palatial feature and the steps were removed. The entrance was relocated with five doors opening directly at street level. The entrance hall was also transferred to the ground level and became the main floor. This large modernized lobby (66 by 90 feet, 25 feet high), which replaced the old auditorium, was also intended to be used for temporary exhibitions. On the same level a new auditorium was built on the south side of the entrance, and new exhibition galleries of primitive art were also connected to the central hall[16]. In this way the Museum tried to break down the division between the temple, with its enshrined collection, and the audience and thus destroy the concept of a shrine (Pls. 26, 27, 28).

The Museum of Modern Art in New York, built in 1939 by Philip L. Goodwin and Edward Durrel Stone, fronted the sidewalk like an ordinary Manhattan office block or apartment house. The busy interior could easily be seen by passers-by. Nonetheless the relation between the Museum and the street remained ambiguous in that while the glass screen opened it to the street, the semi-transparent curtains separated the inside from the outside. At the same time, the additions in 1950 and 1962—64 by Philip Johnson stressed the Museum's storefront character. The later addition has storefront windows that expose the gallery for temporary exhibitions to the street, a fact taken into consideration when displays are being planned[17] (Pl. 29).

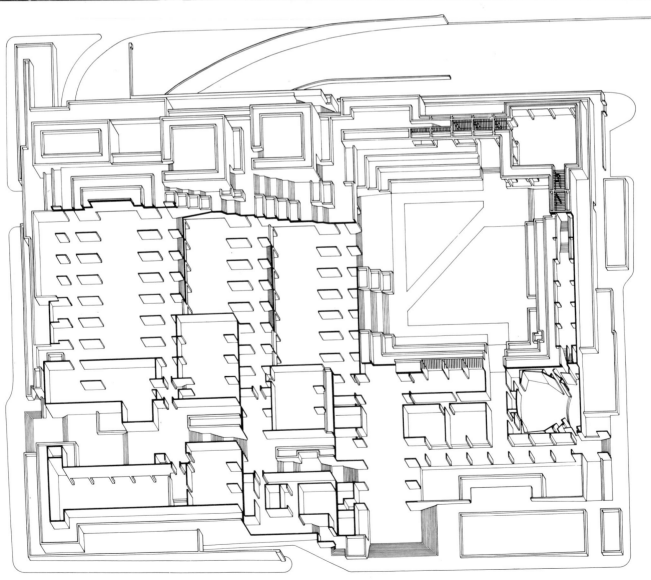

It is interesting to note that Philip Johnson expanded the glass curtain wall of the new wing even though his personal style had turned more solid and tactile by the late 1950's[18].

Laurence V. Coleman has put forward the view that the first museum building with a sidewalk window display was the Grand Rapids Public Museum, completed in 1940 (Pls. 30, 31). It has five windows for the display of small objects, two flanking the entrance and three facing a side street. Coleman feels that this was an influential prototype, but it seems indisputable that the Museum of Modern Art, which was inaugurated a year earlier, is the fundamental "storefront" museum.

The source for the Grand Rapids Public Museum, as Coleman himself suggests, is most probably the public library; that of Grand Rapids itself, for example, while those of Baltimore, Birmingham (Alabama), and Cleveland also "have show windows looking onto the sidewalk."[19] The sources for the Museum of Modern Art are not so much the traditional art gallery or library but the commercial art gallery and major exhibitions like the Armory Show, to be discussed later in more detail. In any event Grand Rapids is a local science museum, while the Museum of Modern Art in New York houses one of the most comprehensive modern art collections in the world and has, since its opening, organized major exhibitions which have attracted international attention.

The new wing of the Boymans-van Beuningen Museum at Rotterdam, finished in the summer of 1972, houses the expanded department of modern art. "The basic premise was that... the new building should be completely open on the Mathenesserlaan side so that the passer-by would be, as it were, drawn in by what was going on inside."[20] This wing has a long glass opening and a canopy reaching the sidewalk (Pl. 32). As such it is dramatically opposed to the distinctly uninviting entrance of the original building designed in 1936 by van der Steur (Pl. 33), where one enters through a small pavilion projecting from the base of the Museum's tall tower which itself possesses a strong traditional character; from a distance it is seen as a church bell tower. The entrance doors to the main building are on either side of this small pavilion, while the pavilion itself has a walled-up front except for a single slot window designed to allow some light in, but not to afford the outsider a glimpse inside.

The Römisch-Germanisches museum in Köln (1963—74) appears at first as an hermetic box (Pls. 34, 35, 36, 37). The architect, Heinz Röcke, did provide contact with the immediate environment, however, by means of apertures in all directions. The museum is open to the plaza, the cathedral, and the Roman street excavated nearby and allows passers-by to glance through store windows at the Museum's most precious treasure, the Dionysius mosaic.

A further development is to take the museum out of its shell and into the streets. In front of Hammarsjkold Plaza in New York, a real estate firm created a sculpture garden (Pl. 38), intended mainly for large scale contemporary sculptures which require a good deal of space in order to be viewed in the proper perspective. Mr. Macklowe of the Wolf and Macklowe real estate firm expressed the hope that "It may tend to break down the wall of the museum."[21]

In the heart of Tel Aviv, wooden partitions were erected in the summer of 1972 for an exhibition of children's paintings of their city, entitled "Museum in the Street."(Pl. 39).

The sculpture exhibition of the Thirty-Sixth Biennale di Venezia (Summer, 1972) was an open air event spread all over the town; part of it was held in the courtyard of the Palazzo Ducale (open free for the occasion to the public); significantly the title of the exhibition was "Scultura nella Città."

More than a decade ago the Louvre even went underground. Its Métro station was remodelled in 1968 with casts of treasures:sculptures, architectural exhibits, small objets d'art, and photographs, all designed to attract subway passengers to visit the museum (Pl. 40). Another ordinary Paris Métro station, St. Augustin, was used in the spring of 1972 to exhibit works by contemporary sculptors and painters.

b. Purity no longer a virtue.

When one examines the "temple" or "showroom" museum it is important to remember that there are no pure examples of either. Although the showroom is a later development, the underlying concepts and forms of most temple museums have also continued to develop. Indeed many temple museums have recently adopted some characteristics of the showroom.

When the Fifth Avenue streetscape of the Metropolitan was redesigned in

l. 24 Kevin Roche and John Dinkeloo, aerial ew of Oakland Museum, 1970.

he Museum is located in the center of the city, ut its three-level structure converts it into a arden; its terraces are transformed into an rban oasis.

l. 25 Kevin Roche and John Dinkeloo, Oakland Museum, Oakland, California, 1970, plan.

Pls. 26, 27, 28 Brooklyn Museum, New York.
26. McKim, Mead and White, 1899.
27. Relocation of entrance and elimination of steps, 1935.
28. The new lobby at street level
Eliminating the steps and relocating the entrance to the ground floor indicated that the monumental, classical order was losing ground.

1968–70, the grand temple staircase was not eliminated (the steps are actually wider and larger than ever), but the entrance's "doghouse" shelter was replaced by an air curtain entrance door (similar to that used by department stores). The other entrance planned by Roche-Dinkeloo will be located at the park side. According to the new master plan, this facade will have a glass wall and green courtyards to serve as relief areas and extensions of the park. They afford a direct visual connection with the park. "It is the museum's stated wish that these new park entrance courtyards will be available to the public as parkland independent of the museum hours,"[22] (as originally planned by Roche-Dinkeloo for Oakland). The works of art will be seen from the park. At night the museum plans to illuminate the new glazed galleries, "opening up the museum visually and in a real sense offering on exhibit some of the Metropolitan's treasures to the public strolling in the park or on Fifth Avenue."[23]

The United States pavilion at the Biennale di Venezia at the Giardini di Castello is a Colonial Neo-classic building with all the traditional attributes of a temple: small dome; classical portico; and symmetrical wings. In 1954 the pavilion became the property of the Museum of Modern Art in New York. Subsequently the wall of one of its side wings was pierced and a large store window with a concrete frame was introduced to allow visitors walking in the park to view the works of art from the outside (Pl. 41).

In general, however, the architectural changes made in the Venice Biennale pavilions should be considered more as stage design than as serious architecture. They tend to reflect changes of fashion and lack the serious motivation which lies behind a fundamental change of style[24]. The face of the main pavilion, the Palazzo dell-Esposizione, has been altered several times during the century. From a Neo-classical facade in 1895 it was changed into the Classical-Baroque of 1914, which was less orthodox in the use of classical elements and designed with more fantasy than the former one. Then in 1932 this facade was replaced by an austere colonnade without pediment or capitals[25]. Finally, the colonnade was concealed behind non-structural brick walls, a new alternative designed by Carlo Scrapa who did not even bother to obscure fully the remains of its Classical predecessor; the tops of the columns are still clearly visible (Pls. 42, 43, 44, 45).

Another transformation of a Neo-classical element can be seen in Kassel. There the Neo-classical frieze of one of the earliest museums, the Fridericianum — now used for Documenta exhibitions — was transformed by Ferdinand Krivet in Documenta 6 (1977) into an electronic teletype for art news.

At the same time various showrooms have absorbed something of the temple. The MOMA eclosed sculpture garden, for example (Pls. 47, 48) has a spiritual affinity with the Cortile del Belvedere in the Vatican (Pl. 46). This link was accentuated by Philip Johnson when he redesigned the garden in 1953 and 1964. Johnson raised the height of the wall, thereby increasing the garden's effectiveness as an enclosed outdoor space. Henry Russell Hitchcock even observes a line of procession for visitors to follow to the sculpture garden, thereby heightening its importance[26].

It is like a paradise garden in the center of town. Only the cafeteria, which suggests more a Parisian boulevard café than a typical New York coffee house, secularizes it. Even so, the iron grill gate facing Fifty-fourth Street reminds the visitor that he is indeed in mid-town Manhattan[27].

At the Whitney, the storefront windows, through which one can see the lobby, the small gallery, and the lower sculpture gallery; the sunken sculpture court; the bridge; and the canopy were all designed to provide contact with the street (Pls. 170–172). An important part of the design, the sculpture court, was to be set alongside the sidewalk. In order to incorporate this feature and provide large flexible galleries, the upper floors had to be cantilevered in a dramatic fashion. Yet the very same sunken sculpture court also acts as a castle moat separating the bastion-like building from the public. Moreover, the enormous concrete walls flanking the Museum isolate the building from its neighbors, so that the commercial art galleries next door on Madison Avenue are clearly cut off from it (Pls. 49). The architect, Marcel Breuer, believes that a museum "should not look like a business or office building... Its form and its material should be an independent and self-reliant unit."[28]

The effect of Louis Kahn's Yale Center for British Art (1969–77), according to its first director, Jules Prown, "...is of traditional, classical order and harmony."[29] The courtyard plan, the room-like space instead of the unarticulated loft-like space of modern museum architecture, the "pewter" quality of the non-reflective steel surface of the building as well as the interior finish create a feeling of classical serenity. Yet the shops at ground level, designed to generate tax revenue for the city, the street-

Pl. 29 Philip Johnson, storefront windows of the gallery of temporary exhibitions, Museum of Modern Art, New York, 1962—1964.
The storefront windows open the gallery of temporary exhibitions to the street.

corner entrance portico, and the windows add a sense of openness as well as a commercial aspect.

The opposing pulls between the temple and showroom museum types continued to preoccupy museum architecture in the late 1970's. The Getty Museum, Malibu, California, is a post-modern version of a Roman villa[30]. Although I.M. Pei's East Wing of the National Gallery in Washington (1968–78) is a building of the 1970's, one is constantly reminded of the Classical esthetic of the temple. Piano and Rogers's Pompidou Center in Paris (1971–77) is a monumental building, but its design was inspired by the showroom type. Instead of Tennessee marble it was built with steel and glass.

2. Changes in museum content.

Along with the change in the form of the modern museum, one can observe a change in content. The material exhibited has been expanded and diversified to cover a broader spectrum of cultural achievements. Not only Western art is considered worthy of exhibition in art and archaeology museums, but also Chinese, Japanese, Primitive, African, Mexican, and Oceanic Art. Temporary exhibitions also widen the scope of museum collections in this respect.

Malraux pointed out that

> It was only yesterday that we discovered the lintel of the abbey church at Cluny, the mosaics of Pella, the real frescoes of Fontainbleau, the Palenque heads, Han-Yung vases, Luristan bronzes, pre-Buddhist Japanese art, Partian statues, Sao terracottas, the Lascaux cave paintings, the rupestral art of the Sahara. The great museum of African art does not yet exist.[31]

What we understand by the term "primitive" has changed radically throughout the last century. This word, which now refers to the art of African and Oceanic cultures, was used before to refer to fourteenth century painters and sculptors like Uccello and Piero della Francesca in Italy or their contemporaries in Northern Europe. Sophisticated works like the Avignon Pieta and the Ghent Altarpiece were labeled as "Primitive Art."

The exhibition of primitive artifacts as works of art and not as exotic curiosities began in art museums and commercial galleries only in the twentieth century. In his pioneer study "Primitivism in Modern Art" Professor Robert Goldwater demonstrated the parallel development of the museum of ethnology and the art museum. Museums of ethnology have been collecting and exhibiting such material in large quantities mainly since the third quarter of the nineteenth century. But only in the twentieth century did scholars and artists as well as the general public begin to regard such works from an esthetic point of view, recognizing in them a different form of art, by no means inferior to the Western traditions. With the growing acceptance of primitive art, as expressed by exhibitions and the transfer of primitive artifacts to permanent collections, ethnographical museums began to view their material less and less from a purely technical and documentary point of view. Museums of ethnology, Goldwater observed, "...while not neglecting documentation and functional considerations have increasingly presented their objects (or at least some of them) as worthy of purely formal study. They have been willing to take the 'ethnographic' risk of making judgments which separate the finer objects from the more everyday ones in their permanent exhibits, and have also organized exhibitions to call attention to these special products of material culture as works of art[32].

Goldwater's "Chronology of Ethnographical Museums and Exhibitions" helps to illustrate this development[33]. A year after Léonce Rosenberg began to collect African sculpture in Paris in 1908, Alfred Stieglitz's gallery at 291 Fifth Avenue organized such an exhibit. And in 1912 African sculptures were shown as works of art at the Folkwang Museum at Essen.

"In 1892 the Leipzig Museum held a special African exhibition, but it was 1921 before there was an exhibition of Negro sculpture."[34] When the Museum of Munich was reorganized in 1926, however, the collection was arranged on the basis of historical and esthetic considerations; certain works were selected for separate exhibition because of their individual excellence[35].

The Museum of Modern Art supplemented its permanent collection of modern art with an exhibition of African Negro art in 1935 and eleven years later organized an exhibition of the Arts of the South Seas. In 1952 the Rietenberg Museum at Zurich was founded. Yet not until 1960 was the Musée des Colonies (de la France d'Outre-mer) reorganized on an esthetic basis as the Musée des Arts Africains et Océaniens.

Pls. 30, 31 Roger Allen, Grand Rapids Public Museum, Grand Rapids, Michigan, 1940. The sidewalk display of small objects was probably derived from public libraries.

The Museum of Primitive Art in New York (originally called Museum of In-digenous Art) was founded in 1954 and opened in 1956. It is now incorporated in the new expansion of the Metropolitan Museum of Art. To house this collection, which bridges a serious gap in the encyclopedic collections of the Metropolitan, Kevin Roche designed a glass pavilion, symmetrical to the glass structure that shelters the Egyptian Temple of Dendur. A few decades ago when the late Nelson Rockefeller considered donating the nucleus of his primitive collection to the Museum, the director felt that it lay outside the Museum's scope of interest. When Rockefeller offered funds to finance the Metropolitan Museum's archaeological expedition to Mexico in 1939, he was turned down by Herbert Winlock. The few pre-Columbian and other primitive works of art that were already part of the collection were given to other museums, like the American Museum of Natural History and the Brooklyn Museum, as long-term loans[36].

The exhibition of children's art within the walls of the museum also reflects a new evaluation of its importance. Educators, psychologists, and artists have become increasingly interested in painting and sculpture made by children[37].

Moreover, the traditional concept of the museum has been widened not only to include the painting and sculpture of other traditions and cultures but also to embrace the whole scope of contemporary visual arts, photography, film, industrial design, and architecture.

MOMA was the pioneer in these fields. In 1932 an architectural department was established and in 1933 industrial art was added to what is now called the Department of Modern Architecture and Design. "The International Exhibition of

Modern Architecture" was the first display of works other than painting or sculpture organized by the Museum. It was also the first show to be circulated (the Department of Circulating Exhibitions was established in 1933, although MOMA had already become active in the field in 1932). The creation of the Film Library in 1935 led to the construction of a film theater-auditorium as an integral part of the building. In 1940 the Museum added the Department of Photography with a collection as well as a reference library; it was the first museum curatorial department devoted exclusively to photography. The Walker Evans Photography Exhibition, the first one-man photography display in a museum, was presented seven years earlier.

A prototype for these tendencies can be seen in the plans for the "Room of our Time" of 1931 initiated by Alexander Dorner, the Director of Landes Museum in Hanover and designed by Moholy Nagy (assisted by Lunderes). "The Room of our Time" further developed ideas embodied in the famous "Abstract Cabinet" of 1925 designed by El Lissitzky (Pl. 50). It was related to Dorner's atmosphere room principle, an attempt to achieve an appropriate environment for different periods and styles (these "atmosphere rooms" should not be confused with "period rooms")[38]. The walls of the "Abstract Cabinet" were covered with metal stripes painted in three different colors: white, black and grey, creating a pattern that changed with any movement (of the visitor). "As one moved along, the walls appeared to change,"

Pl. 34 Heinz Röcke, Römisch-Germanisches Museum, Köln, 1963—74.
Center: The Medieval Cathedral. Right: "the nineteenth century cathedral," (the railway station).
Left: "the twentieth century cathedral," (the Römisch-Germanisches Museum).
Pl. 35 Strong emphasis on education by means of audio visual information as well as clear
organization of the exhibited material.

Pls. 36, 37 Heinz Röcke, Römisch-Germanisches
Museum, Köln, 1963—74.
Although the Museum looks, at first, like a
hermetic box, the architects provided contact
with the immediate environment by means of
openings in all directions. Exposed to the plaza,
the cathedral, and the Roman street excavated
nearby, the Museum allows passers-by to glance
at its most precious treasure, the Dionysius
mosaic.

Pl. 38 Hammarskjöld Plaza, Sculpture Garden, New York, 1971.
Alexander Liberman Odyssey, 1970, painted steel 24'×14'×8'
A sculpture garden in the street created by a real estate firm for
large-scale contemporary sculpture.
Pl. 39 "Museum in the Street," Tel Aviv, Summer of 1972.
"I am for an art… that does something other than sit on its ass in a
museum" (Claes Oldenburg).

wrote Alfred Barr who visited the museum in 1935. He described the "Abstract Cabinet" as "the most famous single room of twentieth century art in the world."[39]

In the "Room of our Time," Dorner and Moholy Nagy intended to integrate photographs, models, and films with paintings and sculpture (Pl. 51).

> When a button was pushed a projector was to show on a screen in the center of the room the newest stage designs including Gropius's design for Piscator's Total Theater and Schlemmer's Triadic Ballet. On another wall two other buttons were installed but proved technically unsatisfactory and the room was opened before it was possible to show films.[40]

Included in the display were many items from the Werkbund Exhibition in Paris in 1930. On the walls there were large photographs illustrating the development of industrial design from the Werkbund to the end of the Bauhaus and the growth of modern architecture. But due to financial difficulties and later the rise of the Third Reich, the plans for the room could never be fully carried out.

Cauman stressed that when architecture, design, photographs, films, as well as painting and sculpture were "brought into a single focus and seen together, they became a critical mass... there was a new visual reality." Dorner's innovations drew many visitors from all over the world, including Alfred Barr, Katherine Dreier (the founder of the Société Anonyme), and MOMA's Philip Johnson.

3. The museum's role in the community.

a. Educational departments and special programs for youth.
Modern museums do not merely collect objects, preserve them, and organize their display. They have, in addition, a multiplicity of other functions.

From its very genesis, the public museum has had an important educational role, a responsibility which has received renewed attention in the twentieth century. Special educational departments, guided tours, lectures, slide presentations, and an orientation gallery have become standard museum features so that the original works of art are no longer the only attraction. Detailed labels, maps, and reconstructions are often designed to help the visitor become oriented. The Römisch-Germanisches Museum in Cologne (Pls. 34, 35, 36, 37), the Anthropological Museum in Mexico City, as well as the Assyrian, Greek and Roman galleries in the British Museum provide excellent examples.

This concern for education led further to the creation of special departments for the young visitor. Later it took the form of autonomous junior wings, aimed at developing art perception in the child, with their own space for exhibitions, studios, class auditoriums, etc. The trend has been particularly strong in the U.S. and Great Britain, paralleling the development of the independent children's museum[41].

Only in the 1940's, under the directorship of Taylor, did the Junior Museum of the Metropolitan Museum of Art expand its educational activities and begin to put on its own special exhibitions.[42]

The Bezalel National Museum in Jerusalem offers a recent example of how the educational program for children has developed. Founded in 1904 and later to become a part of the Israel Museum (1965), Bezalel launched a youth program in 1954. When the Israel Museum building was erected, a large area was designated for a junior wing with gallery space, studios and an auditorium. The aims of the wing were defined in the following terms:

> (a) To guide the child in viewing a work of art and understanding its meaning as an expression of a specific culture and an esthetic entity; in short, an art historical approach with the emphasis on direct perception and discernment of the languages of color, form and matter. This method, we believe, intensifies his esthetic sensitivity and broadens his general education.
> (b) To stimulate the child's growth as a creative human being. The treasures and knowledge stored up in the museum must help to mould the creator and consumer of tomorrow's art.[43]

Over 1500 children now attend the special courses and more than 1600 school classes visit the Youth Wing exhibitions every year. The program expanded so rapidly that it soon outgrew even this building. A new enlarged junior wing was opened in 1977 as well as another branch mainly intended to serve Jerusalem's Arab population, the Paley Center, designed by Moshe Safdie. In addition the Museum has about 25,000 child members out of a total city population of approximately 400,000 persons.

b. Exhibitions.
Another role of the modern museum is to organize temporary exhibits, which

provide an additional didactic tool. They also help to encourage return visits to the museum.

Temporary exhibitions, however, require a space of their own, which must be both flexible and easily accessible. But the British Museum is one public museum without special gallery space for temporary exhibitions. The 1,600,000 visitors to "The Treasures of Tutankhamun" exhibition experienced directly the difficulties such a museum building can impose on visitor circulation (Pl. 52). Ordinary spectators who came to see the rich permanent collection were asked to use the back side entrance. Since then the drawings and prints gallery at the British Museum has been appropriately designed to house temporary exhibitions. Other factors which made this gallery necessary were the immense size of the collection (which simply could not be exhibited in the existing space) and the need to prevent over-exposure.

The organization and loan of exhibitions has become a primary role of the modern museum. Besides displaying contemporary art, temporary exhibits are also arranged to present subjects that are weakly represented, if at all, in a particular museum or to show additional works in a field in which the museum already specializes so as to enrich the public's awareness of a specific artist, school, or culture. The Stedelijk Museum in Amsterdam, for example, offers up to forty exhibitions annually, as does the Museum of Modern Art. E.L.L. Wilde, the Director of the Stedelijk, goes so far as to state that "a permanent stock collection is inconsistent with art-on-the-move; it is a drag on its function. In a museum of modern art only such things are exhibited as relate directly to the present."[44]

The Victoria and Albert Museum's Department of Circulation prepares travelling exhibitions not only for the Museum itself, as most museums do, but also for branch museums and many provincial institutions. Besides exhibition organization on a national scale we now witness an even more complex arrangement on the international scale.

Besides preparing its own temporary exhibitions (almost nine hundred from 1929—69)[45], the Museum of Modern Art in New York also maintains separate departments charged with arranging both the national and international circulation of its exhibits. From 1932, when MOMA began to circulate exhibitions, to 1954, the 25th anniversary year, the Museum sent out almost five hundred displays which had 7,400 showings at more than 3,700 organizations in the U.S. and in thirty-seven foreign countries[46]. In 1976—78 the Museum's New York exhibition program produced nearly ninety exhibitions, fourteen travelling displays in the U.S., and ten internationally circulating exhibitions which had more than fifty showings in twenty-five countries[47]. This pace did not slacken as the 50th anniversary of the Museum approached.

In this respect the Museum carries on the tradition established by the "Museum of Modern Art" of the Société Anonyme founded in 1920 by Katherine S. Dreier with the assistance of Marcel Duchamp and Man Ray (the latter gave the new museum its name). Like its predecessor, the "Museum" of the Société Anonyme (which had loaned it some of its pictures in 1929), MOMA started not by forming a collection or erecting a building but by organizing exhibitions. The displays prepared by the Société Anonyme were designed to stimulate American art-life "...so that it would not sink back into the self-complacent repetition of the past as it was before the exhilirating event of the Armory Show."[48] A collection was only an afterthought, a by-product of the Société Anonyme's activities. Some of the works of art were bought out of consideration for the European artists "who often had to forego sales in Europe for us," explained Katherine Dreier in 1950.

> At this time (the 1920's) Europe was the only market. Often a year or more went by before we could return these loans and so it seemed only right to buy, when we could, examples that would continue the educational work of stimulating both American artists and public.[49]

The 'International Exhibitions' organized by the Société Anonyme were shown at established museums like the Albright Gallery at Buffalo and the Brooklyn Museum, New York. The importance of exhibitions was suggested by the Société Anonyme's interest in new methods of display, an interest conveyed by the model commissioned from Frederick Kiesler for the 1927 exhibition "forecasting the television room in the future museum."[50] In a small dark room an image of the *Mona Lisa* appeared at the press of a button. When pressed again, Velasquez's *Venus* from London would appear or a Rembrandt from Amsterdam. According to Dreier, "people were enchanted playing with this expression of the future." This idea parallels, of course, Malraux's "Musée Imaginaire." It reflects, as Malraux envisioned, a wish for un-

40 The Louvre, Métro Station Paris, *remodelled 1968 (Photographed in 1971). The Louvre has gone underground. Its Métro Station was remodelled to attract the passengers* to visit the Museum.

41 The United States pavilion at the Biennale *Venezia. In 1954 the pavilion became the property of the Museum of Modern Art in New York. Subsequently the wall of one of the side wings of this Colonial Neo-classic temple was pierced and a large store window with a concrete frame was introduced, to allow visitors strolling in the park to view the works of art from the outside.*

conventional exhibitions of unlimited scope, juxtaposing works of art from different collections in various parts of the world and many cultures, superseding the repetitive display of a permanent collection.

From the international exhibition organized by one museum (MOMA) in the 1930's we have witnessed, since the Second World War, the flourishing of international exhibitions sponsored by several museums in different countries, as well as displays organized by two or three museums in the same country. These exhibitions can attain a scale and quality unknown before. In other cases several countries will sponsor an exhibition in one country such as the series of shows organized by the Council of Europe. The fifteenth in this series was "Trends of the Twenties," held in Berlin in 1977. The first was "Humanism in Europe," held in Brussels in 1954—55. Exhibitions of such a scope could hardly be envisioned without such joint sponsorship.

Major East-West art exchanges were also arranged in the 1970's. Soviet and American museums agreed to lend masterpieces from their public collections. (Dr. Armand Hammer, the owner of two art galleries in New York and head of the Occidental Petroleum Corporation served as the intermediary for the first travelling exhibitions.)

In the 1960's, it seemed, in fact, that travelling exhibitions would soon play a dominant role. According to this notion the museum of tomorrow would have galleries mainly for temporary shows, designed to compensate for the lack of a broad permanent collection and the increased dependence on visitors' revenue. It became apparent in the 1970's, however, that the temporary displays will neither eclipse nor replace the permanent collection. Organizing travelling exhibitions has become a complex and expensive operation, due to the rising costs of insurance, the risks for the lenders of art works, and, even more, the difficult problems of art conservation. Packing and unpacking, transportation, and exposure to changes of climate are all hazardous for works of art. Even rich institutions like MOMA were hit severely in the 1970's by rising costs and had to cut down the number of exhibitions drastically. Of course, these considerations will not do away with large-scale, prestigious international exhibitions, but art loans are likely to be cut back and the number and size of exhibitions to be curtailed. The institutions hardest hit will be those which possess only a modest permanent collection. They will find it increasingly harder to borrow major works of art, since they have little to offer in exchange.

One of the solutions hit upon by the large encyclopedic museums is to organize smaller exhibitions which draw from their own reserve collection and on local resources as, for instance, "Florence and the Arts, Five Centuries of Patronage," an exhibition of Florentine art in Cleveland collections organized by the Cleveland Museum in 1971.

Another way to overcome the conservation problems posed by changing temperature and humidity, air pollution, possible damage during handling, and security risks might be to place individual works of art in specially built capsules. In 1971 the *Architectural Forum* reported on a then new scheme for travelling art exhibitions. In the "Art Fleet" devised by architects George Nelson and Charles Forberg, each work of art would be stored in its own controlled capsule

> as sound and self-contained as a space unit. These solid containers... have internal air-conditioning units that would function on the road as well as at the exhibition site. They would be shock-proof, virtually impenetrable, and would even have built-in fire and smoke alarms.

The exhibition visitors and the art capsules would be sheltered by air-supported domes that would be transported together with the capsules[51]. Perhaps because of the expense of implementing such advanced technology, this far-reaching concept has yet to be adopted.

Catalogues from exhibitions offer yet another means to educate the public. In recent years, moreover, many catalogues have been the most up-to-date scholarly reports available. Unlike large well-illustrated "coffee-table" art books, they serve as research tools. Often exhibition catalogues are published in conjunction with commercial publishing houses and are distributed long after the exhibition has been closed. In this way they extend the life of exhibitions.

The first MOMA catalogues were intended to convert the audience to modern art. Alfred Barr introduced the major movements and artists to the Museum's visitors. His texts on Cubism and Abstract Art, Fantastic Art, Dada, and Surrealism as well as on Matisse and Picasso were written in a simple and direct way that had an immense influence on both artists and the general public. In the same way Henry

Pls. 42, 43, 44 The Palazzo dell'Esposizione, Biennale di Venezia in 1895, 1914 and 1932. The facade of the main pavilion has been altered several times during this century, but these changes should be considered more as stage design than as serious architecture.

52

Pl. 45 Carlo Scrapa, Palazzo dell'Esposizione, Biennale di Venezia, the 1968 alteration. In the last alteration of the facade the colonnade was concealed behind a non-structural brick wall; the tops of the columns of its classical predecessor are still visible.

Russoll Hitchcock and Philip Johnson's catalogue of the International Exhibition of Modern Architecture in 1932 was intended to win the public over to the International Style. MOMA's major catalogues have been reprinted several times and are still available, even forty years after some of the exhibitions took place[52]. In fact MOMA's reputation is based as much on exhibitions and publications as on the permanent collection. The museum store now distributes catalogues, books, cards, reproductions, posters, and sometimes even original prints and multiples. A large central space for the museum art shop has become an important feature of nearly all museum planning.

c. Arranging collections for both scholars and the public.

The museum's educational role, as currently interpreted, is more commonly focussed on the general public than on the specialized audience. This attention to the masses is partly a natural outgrowth of the public museum's mission to educate all levels of society; it is also a partial answer to the charge of élitism already discussed.

The democratization of the museum, however, ought not to come at the expense of scholarship. There is a need to make the material in storage more accessible to serious students and researchers. The material selected for exhibition is, after all, already oriented towards the general public. Due to space limitations, only major works of art can be displayed. But for the sake of higher education the museums should transform their storage rooms into study collections and offer researchers a simple and direct approach to the material, without necessitating close supervision by the museum staff.

At any one time, only ten percent of the collections at the Guggenheim or the Walters Art Gallery can be on public display; ninety percent is in storage or on loan. Other museums may exhibit a greater proportion of their collections, yet many works of art still lie in the storage rooms of the great encyclopedic museums. Unless this policy is changed they will remain in partial obscurity.

In the early 1930's the architect Clarence Stein raised the problem of the differing needs of students and the general public[53]. In the *Architectural Record* of January 1930 Stein wrote:

> Art museums appeal to different groups in different ways. The general public visits them for enjoyment or inspiration. Students and craftsmen seek information. In most museums of today exhibits are shown in a manner that serves none of these groups adequately; the two functions of inspiration and education should be separated.[54]

Even if both groups share the educational goal, the public is seeking general information while scholars search for more specific content[55]. In the art museum of tomorrow "the public museum will be selective, the students comprehensive."[56]

Stein felt that a few objects well placed would benefit the general public most. On the other hand, students, scholars, and craftsmen should be accorded easy access to the entire museum collection. "Every authentic work which the museum finds worth

Pl. 46   Cortile del Belvedere, Vatican, Rome, drawing by Giovanni Antonio Desio 1558–60, Uffici, Florence.
The enclosed sculpture garden of MOMA (Pls. 47, 48) has a spiritual affinity with one of the earliest
sculpture gardens, The Cortile del Belvedere.

keeping should be arranged in an orderly systematic manner so as to facilitate research, comparison, and study."[57]

His analogy for the study collection is the public library. "Photographs of related works in other museums should be at hand, as should reference books. It should not be necessary to run from one end of the building to the other to compare two paintings or look up reference material."[58]

Such a reference gallery would also serve as a reserve collection for the primary galleries. With few exceptions the research collection would be open to all. Any casual visitor who wishes to study the collection more closely would be able to do so. Stein prepared diagrammatic plans for a museum that were also discussed at the International Museum's Conference at Madrid in 1934[59] (Pl. 72). His plans, based on the polygonal wheel shape, call for the study collection to encircle the public galleries. These would serve as spokes radiating from the core of the building. Stein suggested that the material exhibited in the inner and outer circles be interrelated. The entrance to the general as well as to the study collections would be from the center. This plan is discussed again at greater length in the third chapter.

Not all museums, however, have as yet adapted themselves to the needs of different publics. The Victoria and Albert Museum is still in the process of reorganizing its collection into primary galleries and study collection. Until 1945 the collection was basically arranged by materials and types of objects. Following the Second World War, the director, Sir Leigh Ashton, decided to reorganize the

Pl. 48 Philip Johnson, The Museum of Modern Art, Abby Aldrich Rockefeller Sculpture Garden, New York, 1953, redesigned 1964.

Pl. 49 Marcel Breuer and Hamilton Smith, Whitney Museum of American Art, New York, 1963–1966.
The storefront windows, the sculpture court, the bridge, and the canopy were all designed to provide contact with the street, but the enormous concrete walls flanking the museum separate the building from its neighbors, clearly cutting off the commercial art galleries next door on Madison Avenue.

galleries "to provide greater attraction for the general public and at the same time safeguard the interests of the scholars."[60] The primary collection occupies about half the museum with the galleries displaying objects from all departments arranged accordingly: architecture, sculpture, ceramics, paintings, metalwork, textiles, woodwork, and so forth.

When the Boston Museum of Fine Arts moved into its present building in 1909, it tried, relatively unsuccessfully, to display the public and study collections separately. The experiment failed, perhaps because both galleries were easily accessible to the public and most of the visitors never became aware of the difference. Even at the Victoria and Albert the difference between primary gallery and study collection is not always clear. Future plans should try to locate them one next to the other. The access to the study collection ought to be simple and direct, but there is a need for a clear transition. In the new wings of the Metropolitan Museum, these requirements are satisfied.[61]

There is, in addition, a growing awareness of the need to transform storage rooms into study collections[62]. In London, the National Gallery partially solved this problem by literally covering the walls of several lower level exhibition rooms with minor paintings that might interest only a specialized audience. The Gallery's northern extension (1975) nearly doubles the space devoted to the reserve collection. The new galleries are also used to exhibit otherwise inaccessible pictures from areas closed for redecoration. (Every year about six rooms are closed.) Furthermore, the additional wall space on the main floor permits a more spacious display of the permanent collection using natural light[63].

Unlike in most museums, the Louvre's new *galerie d'étude* is located neither in the basement nor on the ground floor. Instead it is situated on the top floor, where it benefits from the natural skylight. While the collection was being rearranged the visitor could see there not secondary works of art, but some of the great masterpieces of the Louvre (e.g. Poussin's *Et in Arcadia Ego*), i.e. paintings that had not yet been finally positioned. In addition large numbers of paintings were hung at different levels on movable partitions[64] (Pl. 55).

Reorganizing the museum's collections, however, is not enough. With the growing number of museum visitors the need for special hours or special visiting days for scholars and students has become increasingly important. In the early years of the public museum there were special visiting days for the Academy students, for example, at the British Museum. When the Frick Collection in New York was opened to the public in 1935, a plan was considered to set aside two days each week for the exclusive use of accredited students of history of art[65]. Such special arrangements seem even more essential now to further art scholarship when soaring attendance figures make research and close study of art objects difficult indeed.

Other facilities are also needed to promote art scholarship. The MOMA library and archives are open only to scholars and students, not to the general public, for whom the New York Public Library's services are available. The museum has also tried to encourage research in the International Study Center for training young museum staff and art historians.

In a similar manner, MOMA has demonstrated its concern for the convenience of its 40,000 members. So that members could benefit fully from the Picasso retrospective (April-September 1980), special procedures were adopted. The number of preview days was doubled and viewing hours were extended. On the usual closing day, Wednesday, the Picasso exhibition as well as the rest of the museum was opened to members only.

4. *The museum as a cultural center.*

In order to accommodate their more extensive activities, museums have also had to grow in size. In its 1980's expansion, MOMA will double the present gallery space. The Design and Architecture Department will increase its present space by 140 percent with a study collection and storage archives adjacent to the galleries. The temporary exhibition galleries as well as the museum restaurant will be housed in larger quarters. Other space is required for the museum library, the archive of visual material on modern art, the film library, the publication department, the art lending service, and the circulating exhibitions service.

The transformation of the museum into a cultural center can also be illustrated by the Education Wing of the Cleveland Museum. Designed especially to handle functions not considered part of the museum's role in the nineteenth century, or in

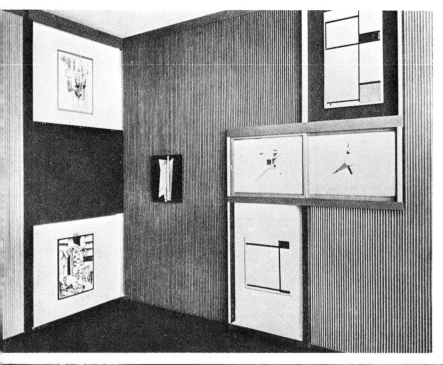

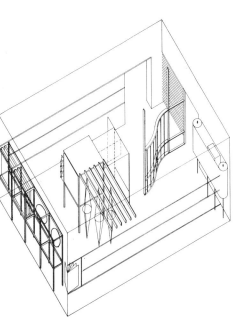

this case, of the original museum erected in 1916, the building, inaugurated in 1971, includes an auditorium for concerts and lectures with film and audio-visual facilities, a special exhibition gallery, education department offices, teaching space for school children, a university art history program, and even a special dining area. It also houses the Extension Exhibition Department which serves the Cleveland Library and the region's school system. In addition it has a new enlarged entrance lobby to serve the growing number of visitors (Pls. 100, 101).

Most modern museums also have an auditorium for lectures and symposiums. Yet the museum auditorium also serves as a lieu for concerts, films and other activities not necessarily directly connected with the other functions of the museum. In addition outdoor grounds offer another multipurpose area for cultural activity; MOMA organizes lively summer concerts in the garden.

One can in fact observe parallel developments. On the one hand there is the multifunction museum containing all under one roof, so to speak, and on the other hand, there is the separate exhibition pavilion, serving as a distinct component within a broader cultural complex, for instance, the Hayward Gallery in London (Pl. 168). In addition to three concert halls and the National Film Theatre, the Arts Council has also included an exhibition building. It was planned as a gallery for temporary exhibitions with only a small storage area provided for current use. The subsequent growth of the Arts Council's permanent collection, however, has created difficulties, limiting the storage space available for current exhibitions[66].

In the same way the Helena Rubinstein Pavilion of the Tel Aviv Museum is attached to the F. Mann Auditorium of the Israeli Philharmonic Orchestra and Habimah, the national theater.

The cultural center at Le Havre (1961) houses the first public museum in France built since 1937, but the exhibition area is only one of the ways in which the center's space is used. As in Atlanta, all the different components are located in the same building.

In the museum the display of art is the prime objective and all the other activities are complementary. In a cultural center, however, the museum section or exhibition pavilion houses just one of the many, more or less equally important activities.

The modern museum is a different social animal from its predecessor and its function has entirely changed. It shares very little with the original functions of the first public museum. To the traditional temple, which has also been transformed and updated, an alternative museum form has been added: the showroom. Not only has the form of the museum changed, but also its content. The material exhibited has been extensively expanded and diversified. Within the community the modern museum fulfills an active and varied cultural role. Its educational function has been emphasized in the twentieth century, moreover, through special educational departments, orientation galleries, slide presentations, detailed explanatory labels, catalogues, posters, and other museum publications. The museum also organizes exhibitions as a new way to attract visitors. Although the size and scope of these temporary exhibitions may change in the future due to financial, conservation, and political considerations, their primary importance as an educational tool remains unquestioned. They are a measure of the museum's continued vitality as a social institution.

Pl. 50 El Lissitzky and Alexander Dorner, Landesmuseum, Hanover, "Abstract Cabinet". 1925.

Pl. 51 Laszlo Moholy-Nagy and Alexander Dorner, Landesmuseum, Hanover, "The Room of Our Time," 1931. In this room Dorner and Moholy-Nagy intended to integrate photographs, models and films with painting and sculpture. Left: two permanent installations to show abstract and documentary films; Center: Moholy-Nagy's Light Machine; Right foreground: rolling screen; Right rear: entrance to "Abstract Cabinet."

Pl. 52 The 1,600,000 visitors to the Treasure of Tutankhamun exhibition demonstrated the difficulties a museum building without special space for exhibitions impose on circulation. The visitors to the permanent collection of the British Museum were asked to encircle the building and enter form the smaller back entrance. The three-year American tour (1976—79) began at the National Gallery in Washington and was described by Newsweek as "Tut-o-mania."

Pl. 53 Temporary shed for the queue for the Treasures of Tutankhamun exhibition, British Museum, London, 1972.
The twentieth century witnessed a dramatic widening of the museum audience. But does the astronomical number of visitors really reflect a complete democratization of the museum?
Pl. 54 British Museum, London, 1972. Treasures of Tutankhamun exhibition.
With the growing number of museum visitors the need for special hours or special visiting days for scholars and students has become increasingly more urgent. In the early years of the public museum, there were special visiting days for Academy students, for example, in the British Museum.

Chapter III.
The functional aspect of museum architecture

So far we have dealt with the social facet of the museum, its design and role in the community. The following chapter discusses the functional aspect of museum architecture, concentrating on visitor circulation, expansion, lighting, conservation, and flexibility of design. Although obviously interrelated, these different functional considerations are treated separately for the sake of clarity.

1. Visitor circulation schemes.

The growing number of temporary exhibitions and museum visitors emphasize the need for an effective circulation scheme. Anyone attempting to visit a particular section in the Metropolitan Museum of Art has been faced with this problem. If one is interested, for example, in the American Wing, one first has to pass through many rooms of European masters. As mentioned, at the time of the Tutankhamun Exhibit (1972), those wishing to view the British Museum's permanent collection were asked to encircle the building and enter from the smaller back entrance (Pl. 52). And before reaching the lecture hall of the Victoria and Albert Museum, the prospective audience must review a large part of the Museum's possessions. Not surprisingly in this museum the word "circulation" refers not to the movement of visitors but to the department which organizes travelling exhibitions.

The circulation problem does not exist, of course, in a private collection or if museum attendance is limited. For small collections, even a great many visitors do not create the severe problem inherent in large museums (Pl. 56). According to the architect Kevin Roche, if the problem of visitor circulation can be solved, there need be no limit on museum size.

The circulation scheme is more important for the encyclopedic institution than for a major museum specializing in one period or type of exhibit, such as contemporary art. On the other hand, an inflexible, predetermined circulation pattern is less annoying in a small museum than in a larger one. The closed circuit of the Louisiana Museum offers one example. Situated in an old park near the Danish coast about 14 miles from Copenhagen (1958, Jorgen Bo and Vilhelm Wohlert), this museum specializes in twentieth century art. From an old villa which serves as an entrance pavilion, the visitor proceeds through glazed walkways protected by projecting roofs into the new structures. Although the circulation is preplanned, the transparent walkways open the museum to the landscape and prevent claustrophobia. These side-lit connecting corridors create a feeling of openness and freedom (Pls.57, 58). In a large museum such a scheme can cause considerable irritation.

Three main patterns of circulation found in the museums of the nineteenth century continue to be applied in twentieth century museums of various architectural styles: continuous flow, gallery and corridor movement, and the "basilica" approach.

The continuous or 'en suite' form offers a sequence of galleries one after the other. This scheme provides for simple circulation and saves space at the same time. Rooms can be added in single, double, or triple file, most often symmetrically, by joining wings around courts. The general shape of the museum building is E, H, L, T, or U. This pattern's main disadvantage is that it forces the visitor to pass through several rooms in order to arrive at a specific gallery. When one room is closed, moreover, for repairs or a change of display, the flow of circulation may be disturbed.

Alternatively the gallery and corridor circulation plan permits the visitor to approach any room directly. In addition, one or several rooms can be blocked off without troubling the circulation of visitors. It is also easier for the visitor to orient himself here than in a museum based on sequential continuous circulation.

The third scheme is the 'basilica' type or 'nave and aisle' room arrangement. Doors on the sides of the main hall open to smaller galleries which are in most cases interconnected. This method allows important exhibits to be organized in the center with related material easily accessible in the adjacent smaller galleries. In this case, however, some space will be wasted in the event of expansion, as the architect Rich Lorimer has pointed out[1].

Pl. 55 The Louvre, Paris, galerie d'étude. Some of the storage rooms were transformed into study collections. Unlike most museums, the Louvre's new galerie d'étude is not located in the basement or on the ground floor. Instead, it is situated on the top floor where it has the advantage of natural skylight.

"A museum should be so arranged that only those who have some interest in a given section will have occasion to enter it," stated Benjamin Gilman in 1909. He found the germ of this arrangement in Munich's Alte Pinakothek (1836) where paintings, of the same artist, country or school were displayed "...in one section consisting of a top-lighted gallery for the large pictures and side-lighting cabinets for the smaller." The architect Leo von Klenze is quoted as saying, "I wish to allow the possibility of arriving at any particular school without going through the building, which communicates with each separate room."[2] (Pl.60)

In improving on nineteenth century circulation patterns and searching for new solutions, twentieth century museum staff and architects have sought a preplanned circulation scheme which would, on the one hand, provide a viewing sequence and, on the other hand, leave the visitor free to approach specific parts of the collection without being forced to go through the entire museum.

a. Resorting to the spiral.

The spiral[3] is perhaps the major schematic, although mainly theoretical, *new* approach to visitor circulation in the twentieth century. Widely discussed in the early part of the century, it has been exploited as an image of movement and growth by both artists and architects. The spiral appears in Boccioni in the early teens of the twentieth century and in Tatlin's monument of the Third International in 1920[4]; Laszlo Moholy-Nagy's Nickel Construction of 1921 at the Museum of Modern Art, New York and his kinetic construction system of 1922 are also important spiral images. The latter even had a definite architectural purpose, being thought of as a structure for sports and recreation with paths of motion. The ramp here was to end

PEINTURE ITALIENNE
XVII⁰/XVIII⁰ siècles

Pl. 56 The Louvre, Paris, Circulation sign. A circulation scheme is crucial for the encyclopedic museum. Lewis Mumford feels that "the worst feature of the old fashioned museum was the continuous corridor..."

at the top near what was to be an elevator shaft[5]. At the International Theater Exhibition at Vienna in 1924, Fredrick Kiesler's spiral model for a continuous stage of 1923 was exhibited; and it reached Paris as an image of movement in architecture when illustrated in the "Bulletin de l'Effort Moderne" in 1925[6]. In America Frank Lloyd Wright used the spiral in a project for a planetarium in 1925[7].

As Christopher Green has observed, Naum Gabo's Construction of the Spiral Theme of 1941 corresponds to the structure of the sea shells he probably examined at this time. In the same year an X-ray photograph of a Molluscan shell (*Nautiles Pompeius*) was republished (in the second edition of D'Arcy Thomson's *Growth and Form*, first published in 1916)[8]. It is a fascinating comment on the importance of the spiral as an image of movement that this same X-ray photograph or a drawing of it had already appeared in the Le Corbusier's *City of Tomorrow* (1929)[9] and again in Mumford's *Technics and Civilization* (1934)[10].

As early as 1929 Le Curbusier had designed a square spiral for the World Museum of the Mundaneum for the League of Nations in Geneva. It was shaped in the form of a stepped pyramid, like a Mesopotamian ziggurat. The visitors were to be lifted by elevators to the upper part of this Tower of Babel as Francis H. Taylor called it[11]; from there they would descend following the widening spiral (Pl. 61). Yet al! of Le Corbusier's later museum projects were designed not as rising pyramids but as flat spirals. Unlike the rising spiral which emphasized only viewer circulation, the flat spirals were also based on a preplanned expansion scheme. Nonetheless the idea of an entrance in the heart of the museum and a square spiral still served as the nucleus.

In Le Corbusier's Paris project for a contemporary art museum (1931), the visitor is led through an underground tunnel to the central entrance (Pl. 62). Eight years later in his plan for "The Museum of Unlimited Extension" at Philippeville, the structure was to be erected on piloti with the visitor entering the center of the museum at ground level. From the central hall a passage was to lead through the spiral in two directions: one to the garden, the other to the exit. This passage was to connect the different rooms and sections (Pls. 63, 64). Although the three museums which Le Corbusier actually did construct used only a single spiral, they theoretically can be extended by employing additional spirals in the future (Pl. 65).

Of all Le Corbusier's museum designs the first to be executed was the cultural center of Ahmedabad, Pakistan (1954) (pl. 66). The second, the National Museum of Western Art, Tokyo (1957–59) is also a version of the spiral museum (Pls. 67, 68), as is the third, the Museum and Art Gallery of Chandigarh, India, which was designed in 1964 and finished only in 1968, three years after Le Corbusier's death. It should be remembered, however, that these single spiral museums represent but a partial expression of Le Corbusier's method of organizing circulation and space[12].

A prototype for Le Corbusier's ideal spiral circulation scheme seems to have been the Paris Universal Exhibition of 1867 (Pls. 69, 70, 71). Instead of a square spiral, the Exposition building was composed of concentric galleries. Originally these

Pls. 57, 58 Jorgen Bo and Vilhelm Wohlert Louisiana Museum, Humlebaek (Denmark), 1958, and future extension.
Although the circulation is preplanned, the glass-enclosed walkways and the upper exhibition room with its large window open the museum into the landscape and prevent claustrophobia.

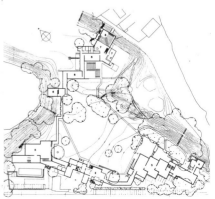

galleries were to be circular, but the narrowness of the location, the Champs-de-Mars, forced them to be designed as ellipses. The visitor could go around these ellipses from the outer and largest gallery, the Galerie des Machines, to the smaller galleries exhibiting other subjects from clothing to furniture, from raw materials to the history of work and the fine arts. At the same time the visitor could also examine any single country's development by making a transverse walk. From the French section of the Galerie des Machines he could pass on to see French clothing and so on until he reached the palm garden at the center which served as a rest area[13].

As his 1937 project for the 1938 French Pavilion at San Francisco or Liège indicates, Le Corbusier, while critical of more recent efforts, was probably familiar with the nineteenth century tradition of international exhibitions with their complex circulation problems. Max Bill, the editor of the third volume of the *Le Corbusier: Oeuvre Complète,* wrote:

> Dans l'idée de Le Corbusier et Pierre Jeanneret, les expositions de ces derniers temps sont tombées dans une architecture 'en toc' cherchant à limiter la réalité des maisons ou des palais contruits 'en vrai'. Leur idée, au contraire, de reprendre plutôt la grande tradition des expositions universelles du XIX siècle (fer et verre) et de créer des 'lieux d'exposition' favorable à la visibilité à la circulation et une émotion architecturale venue de la franchise de solution proposée. Tel était le projet présent exécuté, en tôle d'acier soudée a l'électricité.[14]

Clarence Stein's diagrammatic plans for the "Museum of Tomorrow" also recall the circulation scheme of the 1867 Paris World Exhibition. His designs called for separating the main collection from the study reserve. As in Le Corbusier's schemes the entrance to both collections was to be from the center and they were to be displayed in two concentric galleries shaped like a wheel. The study collection on the rim would encircle the smaller display of the primary collection, itself organized around the hub or core. The spokes of the wheel, so to speak, connect the two (Pl. 72). This circulation pattern enables the visitor to follow the art of the same period in different countries by going around the circle or follow the art of one country from one period to another by transverse walks from the primary collection to the study reserve and vice versa (like the Paris Exhibition of 1867). On every floor the primary collections (Stein had in mind multi-story buildings) would be directly accessible from the museum's central core; the visitor would not have to pass through other collections to examine them.

Twenty years after Stein's proposal, the Director of the American Museum Association, Laurence Coleman, suggested in 1950 that even the primary collection for the general public should be arranged for different kinds of audiences. The outer circuit of rooms would be for everyone, while the inner space would be utilized for orientation and the display of special interest exhibits[15].

For the World Museum of the Mundaneum (1929), Le Corbusier had thought of separating the galleries without resorting to the use of partitions. He had envisioned three parallel naves. The first would contain the objects; the second, historical documents; and the third, information on the geographical background of the object[16].

b. The solution at the Guggenheim.

Although similarly based on a circular spiral, the Guggenheim Museum (1943—59) probably does not stem from Le Corbusier's snail-shell museums. As previously mentioned, Wright was interested in the relationship between circular forms and movement as early as the 1925 project for the Gordon Strong Automobile Objective, Sugar Loaf Mountain, Maryland, which featured ramps for ascending and descending traffic[17] in the form of a double helix, and later, in the Morris Gift Shop, his son's house, and many other projects.

Many critics and art historians have commented on the formal aspect of the Guggenheim Museum[18], but the building also offers an interesting solution to the circulation problem that has not received sufficient attention[19]. A double spiral staircase and a similar skylight dome can be found in the entrance hall of the Vatican Museum, completed in 1932. The spirals at the Vatican, however, only lead the visitor in and out of the museum; they do not serve as display areas. At the Guggenheim Museum, the visitors are lifted by elevator to the top of the spiral and then walk down the widening ramp. This solution to the circulation problem encourages the exhibition designer to arrange the works of art chronologically or in any other logical or instructive sequence[20]. To arrive at a specific point of the spiral the visitor does not have to pass through the entire museum — he can reach it by using the elevator or staircase core. Although the museum was originally planned for a

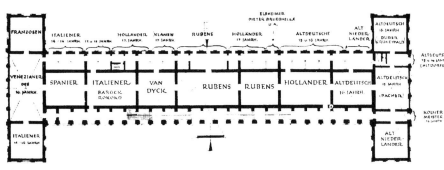

Pl. 59 Leo von Klenze, Alte Pinakothek, Munich, designed 1823–24, built 1926–36. South facade.
The facades and the principle rooms were inspired by Italian High Renaissance.
Pl. 60 Leo von Klenze, Alte Pinakothek, Munich, designed 1823–24, built 1926–36, (floor plan).
The most important innovation was the planning of the upper floor. Three parallel strips were constructed: the south one for the loggia giving access to every hall, the skylit central strip with halls for the large paintings, and the north one for cabinets with windows for small paintings. The paintings were arranged chronologically by shcool. The circulation scheme provided a viewing sequence with some freedom to approach specific parts of the collection.
According to Nikolaus Pevsner this was the most influential museum plan of the nineteenth century.

specific permanent collection, it also functions well for temporary exhibits.

Even so, many critics feel that the building itself attracts too much of the visitor's attention, and thereby distracts from the contents. "You may go to this building to see Kandinsky or Jackson Pollock, you remain to see Frank Lloyd Wright," remarked Mumford[21]. Yet, as visitors return and become accustomed to the building, they can direct their attention to the works of art. Furthermore, the spiral is so designed that one either looks at the entire inner space or concentrates specifically on a particular work of art. Both views cannot be experienced simultaneously. In such an environment, a three-dimensional work of art exhibited in the central space is freed from any encumbering relationship to the walls as is generally found in rectangular commercial galleries or in an ordinary museum space.

As many critics have noted, the visitor can see most of the paintings on display at once; in this respect the element of surprise is eliminated. But having an overall view allows the museum-goer to orient himself between what he has already seen and what is left to be studied (Pls. 73, 160, 161).

c. Adaptations and alternatives.

Other museum designers responded sympathetically to Wright's design. In Mexico City Pedro Ramirez Vasquez and Rafael Mijares arrived at a variation of the Guggenheim in their circular New History Museum of 1960 (Pls. 74, 75). Although they designed a wider spiral and used a glass curtain wall instead of concrete, Vasquez and Mijares retained the basic idea of starting the visit from the top and having the viewer descend the spiral. In this case, moreover, an elevator was unnecessary, as the museum is built on a hillside with the entrance at the upper level[23].

Ten years after the Guggenheim, the New England Aquarium in Boston was opened to the public. From the outside the rectangular building, designed by Cambridge Seven Associates, Inc., (Ivan Chermayeff, principal-in-charge), does not suggest any resemblance to the earlier building, but the circulation scheme is another variation of that used by Wright[24]. A one-way route along straight ramps, bridges and galleries around the reinforced concrete walls of the rectangular building slowly leads the visitor to the top. The quicker descent back to the ground floor follows a steep spiral ramp around the central giant ocean tank (Pl. 76).

The Hirshhorn Museum in Washington (Pls. 78, 79), designed by Gordon Bunshaf of Skidmore, Owings and Merrill, was completed fifteen years after the Guggenheim (1967—1974). Although the external monumentality, the blank wall, and the circular shape suggest the Guggenheim, the changes and modifications are illuminating. Escalators replaced the ramp; the inner central space became an external open court; and the wider circumference solved the problem posed by installing large flat paintings against curving walls. But the unique qualities of the central area as an integral part of the museum's space and the continuous movement along the ramp of the Guggenheim are missing. The strong sense of spatial movement, the surprise and magic vanished as a result of these improvements. For Suzanne Stephens the essential architectural element missing in the Hirshhorn building is scale[22].

Le Corbusier's museums have also been influential in this respect. His museums in Ahmedabad (1954) and Tokyo (1956—59) serve as the starting points for the quite different design of Philip Johnson at Utica (1957—60) and I.M. Pei's Everson Museum of Art, Syracuse, New York (1961—69), which in turn influenced the Tel Aviv Museum (1964—71).

While Philip Johnson's debt to Mies van der Rohe is obvious in the Museum of Art of the Munson-Williams-Proctor Institute, Utica, New York, it is interesting to note that the organization of long narrow galleries along the walls of the square building and the two-story high central court have something in common with Le Corbusier's museums (Pl. 141).

I.M. Pei also assimilated the square spiral circulation scheme attributed to Le Corbusier. The galleries at the Everson Museum are cantilevered from all sides and connected by narrow bridges and ramps (Pls. 180, 181). Pei substituted a round spiral ramp ascending from the central sculpture court to the first floor for the straight one used by Le Corbusier.

In Tel Aviv the architects Itzhak Yashar and Dan Eitan adopted Pei's system for organizing the galleries, introducing different floor levels to add variety, and returned to Le Corbusier's original straight ramp. In addition, they "filled in" Le Corbusier's ground floor piloti or the space under Pei's cantilevered galleries with additional exhibition space around the central court (Pls. 80, 81).

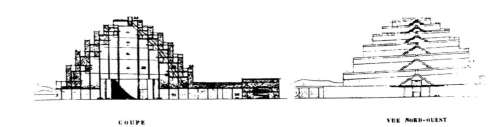

COUPE

VUE NORD-OUEST

MUSEE MONDIAL

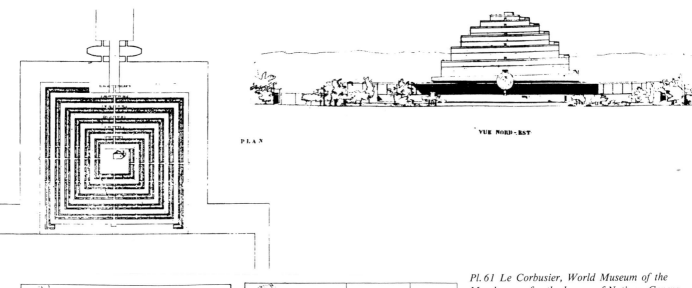

PLAN

VUE NORD-EST

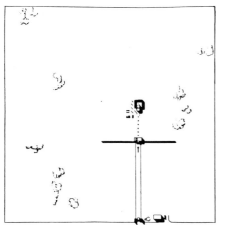

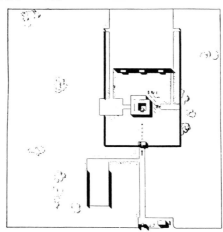

*Pl. 61 Le Corbusier, World Museum of the
Mundaneum for the league of Nations, Geneva,
project, 1929.*
*The visitors were to be lifted by elevators to the
upper parts of the stepped pyramid; from there
they would descend following the widening
spiral.*

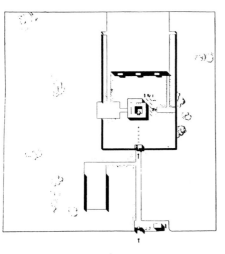

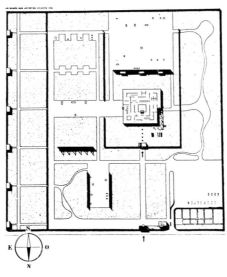

*Pl. 62 Le Corbusier, a project for Museum of
Contemporary Art in Paris, 1931.*
*The first of Le Corbusier's designs to suggest, in
addition to a circulation scheme, a basic solution
to the problem of preplanned growth.*

The circulation problem of a large museum like the National Museum of Anthropology in Mexico City is much more complex. Designed by Vasquez and Mijares in 1962 and inaugurated in 1965, this museum was constructed as a rectangle with a patio partially sheltered by a huge mushroom-like form (Pls. 82, 83). The rectangular exhibition halls run around three sides of the rectangular patio on two levels above a basement. Although built on a much larger scale, it is nonetheless quite similar to the other museums just mentioned in Ahmedabad, Tokyo, Utica, Syracuse, and Tel Aviv: two levels of exhibition halls situated around a central court. As in Ahmedabad, the central court is not covered. Irene Nicholson has suggested, on the other hand, that the adoption of the patio as a central architectural element derives from ancient Mexican, as well as colonial Spanish design[25].

The ground floor halls of the Anthropological Museum are dedicated to anthropology, while the upper ones display ethnographic materials and exhibit the contemporary culture of Mexico's Indians. The visitor can either follow the planned circulation pattern throughout the rectangle, starting at the right hand side from the gallery which introduces the anthropological section and continuing counter-clockwise to the last gallery on the left, or enter only an independent unit of the museum — for example, Mayan culture or Aztec art. By crossing a central courtyard, he can observe single sections without having to pass first through the entire museum. These small "museums" have their own circulation pattern, as sub-units within the overall scheme. A glance through the large glazed opening to the courtyard also helps orient the visitor in relation to the entire collection. This solution offers a flexible circulation scheme that leads the museumgoer in a certain order but allows him to skip sections or to visit only a specific department by taking a short cut across the courtyard. Similarly, the gallery for temporary exhibits and the auditorium can be reached directly from the entrance hall.

It is now common in museum design to locate the exhibition gallery as well as the auditorium next to the entrance in order to allow their use when the rest of the museum is closed. In the new wing for the Cleveland Museum of Art (1967–71), for example, Marcel Breuer and Hamilton Smith designed a new entrance lobby to serve the temporary exhibitions gallery, the auditorium, and the educational department.

The transparent Perspex external escalators of the Pompidou Center (1971–1977) provide magnificent views of Paris and a dynamic solution to the circulation problem. The system exposes the endless upward and downward flow of visitors (6,000,000 in the first year) to public view and allows for maximum flexibility in the exhibition galleries (1,000,000 visited the New York–Paris show in 1977) (Pls. 188, 191, 192).

2. Possibilities for museum expansion.

A concurrent functional aspect of museum design is to create the possibility for expansion. Often, funds are insufficient to finance a full-scale museum immediately as, for example, with the Museum of Fine Arts, Houston, or the Israel Museum, Jerusalem. In other cases, it is impossible to predict what funds or collections will be donated to the museum in the future. This was the case, for example, with the Yale Art Gallery to which Paul Mellon gave his important collection of English painting. Because of the lack of free space next to the present museum, itself an addition to the initial structure, the University had to plan another wing across the street, designed by Louis Kahn, the architect of the original extension. Other sources of pressure for expansion are the growth of the permanent collection, the need for adequate space for temporary exhibits, and the increase in the number of visitors, as was the case with the National Gallery in Washington.

a. The need for harmonious integration.
To expand an existing building, to combine and fit the new to the old, one has to confront one of the principal dilemmas of modern architecture: the need for harmonious integration. In the design of new buildings to be juxtaposed to older ones, Michael Webb has identified two approaches. In the first aproach, "the architects responded with strong characterful buildings that respect the proportion of the old but refuse to be cowed by it." According to the second approach, "there is also a place for new work which, without lying about its age, consciously subordinates itself to the existing building or environment."[26]

The East Wing of the National Gallery in Washington, designed by I.M. Pei between 1967 and 1971 and completed in 1978, could serve as an example for the

Pls. 63, 64 Le Corbusier, The Museum of Unlimited Extension, Philippeville project, 1939. The Museum is built on piloti and the visitor enters at ground level in the center. In the event of expansion the present external wall would become an internal wall of the new gallery and the external wall of the new addition to the spiral would serve as a temporary facade.

first approach. Pei had to design a building located on an awkwardly shaped site, a trapezoidal plot at the junction of Pennsylvania Avenue and the Mall, between the existing symmetrical Neo-classical museum and the Capitol (Pl. 84). One of Pei's major problems was "the difficulty of building a structure that relates to the main gallery and other Neo-classical buildings, yet for our time."[27] According to Carter Ratcliff, "The trouble is that the East Building addresses the future only with its 'conservativism', its 'classicism'". Ratcliff believes that the acclaim generated by the East Wing's "classicism" is owed in part to the skill with which it detaches modernism from whatever terrors loom beyond the immediate present (Pls. 184—187).

In order to adjust the extension to the main Neo-classical temple, Washington's monumentality, and the difficult site, Pei designed a separate building connected to the first only through an underground passage. The impressive new wing consists of two triangles with opposing apexes, one devoted to exhibition space and including a large skylit sculpture area, the other for the new study center, library, and some of the museum's departments. The height of the structure's lower level is coordinated with that of the buildings along the Mall, while the upper level relates to the taller structures along Pennsylvania Avenue (100 foot cornice height). The use of the same pink Tennesee marble also helps harmonize the new wing with the main building (Pl. 85).

The Albright-Knox Art Gallery exemplifies another solution to the problem of designing a modern addition to a temple-like museum. In this case the architect succeeded in enlarging the museum without isolating the old from the new. He respected the proportions of the original building yet created a distinctly modern design (Pl. 86).

In 1958 Gordon Bunshaft of the architectural firm Skidmore, Owings and Merrill was asked to design the additions to the art museum of Buffalo, the "Athens on the Niagara." The Buffalo Arts Academy was founded in 1862, but its first building was not designed and erected until the twentieth century between 1900 and 1905 by a local architect Edward B. Green. Then called the Albright Art Gallery, it was renamed the Albright-Knox Art Gallery in 1961 in honor of the donor who financed most of the expansion as well as the modern collection[29]. For the Greek Revival temple with two symmetrical side pavilions, native son Bunshaft had to design an additional 6,000 square feet of galleries for the contemporary collection and an auditorium seating 350 persons. His solution was to continue the high podium of the main building. All the new galleries are located in this "basement" and face an internal sculpture court. On the edge of the elongated stone-covered podium, he designed a Miesian cube with a tinted glass screen housing the auditorium, which somewhat balances the weight of the large white Greek Revival structure[30].

The new extensions for the Tate (the first phase) offer an example of a new structure which, "without lying about its age, consciously subordinates itself to an existing building and environment." In 1964 the Gallery considered a plan for a new extension along the front of the old building which would mask the whole of the present facade. The northwest corner of the site would have been left free for a gallery park and for future extensions of the collection. This would have solved possible circulation problems and provided one main entrance for the increasing number of visitors.

It is generally accepted that the original building is far from being an architectural masterpiece. Even the Tate's director, Sir Norman Reid, found it "...hard to disagree with the excellent opinions which have found Sidney Smith's frontage undistinguished."[31] His other arguments for a masking facade were:

> The fact that many of us have become attached to it (the old facade) is due as much to the site as to the design. It is probably due still more to the associations of the building which one can hardly think of without remembering some of the more formative artistic experiences of one's life. The old facade is rather like the massive frames of the period. It pays impressive tribute to art, yet emotionally becomes a burden to it. It is hardly more considerable in its own right. In fact, the fulsome entasis of the columns and the coarse detail that surrounds them betray a certain falseness; they blunt the very senses that the Gallery exists to sharpen. The sentiment that is felt for the place and its purpose deserve something better. It can hardly weigh against the urgent need of the Gallery work.[32]

Yet public pressure and sentiments forced the Gallery and the government to reconsider this plan. The Gallery managed to persuade the government to secure space for future expansion by removing an adjacent military hospital. On the cover of the Tate Gallery Report of 1969—70, the museum published a photograph of the Britannia which surmounts the pediment "...to celebrate her survival together with

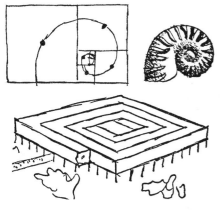

Pl. 65 Le Corbusier, sketches of a shell, an abstract diagram of growth curves and an "Unlimited Extension Museum", 1938. Preplanned circulation as well as expansion are solved by the design of flat spirals. The spiral is associated with movement and growth.

the whole of the Tate Portico."[33] Meanwhile the other additions planned for the vacant corner site went ahead, enabling the existing building to meet the urgent needs of the Gallery. The pamphlet prepared by the Department of the Environment for the corner-site extension stressed that "...while taking advantage of modern techniques of construction and servicing, the design should have a sympathetic relationship to the scale and massing of the old building."

In the extension completed in 1979, a simple, blank Portland rock-bed stone wall matches the height of the existing building. Besides the smaller temporary gallery on the lower floor, the new exhibition space is also top lit. The conservation studios and workshops occupy the three upper floors of the new glazed structure. This taller block is located on the central axis of the five-story building, at the rear, corresponding in bulk with the entrance rotunda and the central octagon.

b. Expansion in practice.

An example of a two-phase addition to an existing museum is Mies van der Rohe's design for the Museum of Fine Arts in Houston. The first construction stage, opened to the public in 1958, encloses a court between two wings, themselves previous additions to the museum (Pl. 87). The first wing was added in 1926, whereas the second was not finished until 1953. As in Cleveland, the entrance was reversed by Mies van der Rohe; it is now located in the new extension. The main floor of Cullinan Hall is devoted chiefly to temporary exhibitions. A thirty-foot high column-free space, it encloses ten thousand square feet within a steel frame.

For the second phase of the expansion project (completed in 1974), the glazed side of the hall was opened and the hall became an enclosed sculpture court. Mies also proposed an open air sculpture garden at the back of the museum which was formerly the main entrance. Mies completed the design of the second expansion phase shortly before he died. The second level of the new Brown Wing consists of a single gallery, and, aside from two small service shafts, it is column-free. Some critics object to the immense size of the display gallery, saying that it dwarfs the exhibits, large however they may be.

This expansion materialized not only as a result of the expanding collection, the growing audience, and the existence of patrons in a location far from East and West coast art centers[34]. It was also intended to counter-balance the erection and growth of other museums in Texas. The opening of the Brown Wing doubles the present 70,750 square feet of exhibition space, thereby enabling the Houston Museum to retain its place as the largest in Texas.

Alfred Mansfeld and Dora Gad solved the problem of expansion in Jerusalem by designing a museum consisting of several pavilions connected to each other to create a continuous flowing space. The idea was to erect the nucleus necessary for the Israel Museum and then add pavilions as more material became available for exhibits and funds permitted further construction. When Mansfeld and Gad won the 1959 competition, they planned a minimal first stage and several successive phases of expansion. But when the museum was opened to the public in May 1965, it included many more pavilions than were originally intended. In the following years, a large library, an auditorium, period rooms, a design wing, cafeteria, additional galleries, and a new junior wing were completed (Pls. 88, 89, 90).

The museum design is based on a space unit of 36 × 36 feet. The shape of the roof and its central supporting column suggests a mushroom or an umbrella turned upward. The roof is formed as a hyperbolic paraboloid shell supported on a central column. This reinforced concrete hollow column holds all the services: air conditioning, electrical conduits, and rain water drainpipes for the roof (Pls. 91, 92). The design combines one or several "mushrooms" together with column-free spaces which serve in most cases as connecting elements[35].

Whereas the expansion scheme proved to be successful, the units with the central column raise serious problems for interior and exhibition design. Because of the column the center cannot be used as a focal point for the display. Nor can the space be seen in its entirety. In addition it is difficult to control the light coming in from the ribbon windows in the upper part of the wall.

The umbrellas of the Punjab University Teaching Museum suggest those of the Israel Museum. Sixteen interconnected galleries, each twenty-five feet square, are arranged around a courtyard with pools. In each gallery the hyperbolic paraboloid roof is supported by a single column. This arrangement leaves the walls free of column support and allows a continuous strip of clerestory windows beneath the roof[36]. Although the Israel Museum might be the sole source for this solution, it

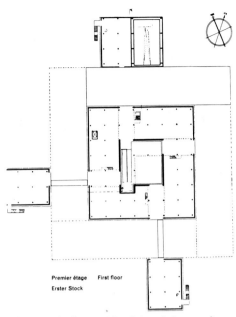

Premier étage First floor
Erster Stock

Pl. 66 Le Corbusier, The Cultural Center of Ahmedabad, Ahmedabad, 1954.
The executed designs of Le Corbusier museums are single spiral museums which represent only a fragment of Le Corbusier's method of organizing circulation and space. Theoretically they can be extended by other spirals in the future.

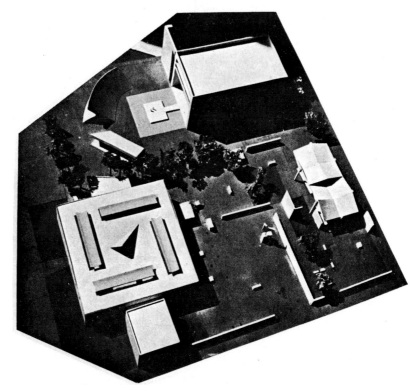

Pl. 67 Le Corbusier, National Museum of Western Art, Tokyo, 1957—1959. The starting point of the design is the functional aspect; the form has only a supplementary role.

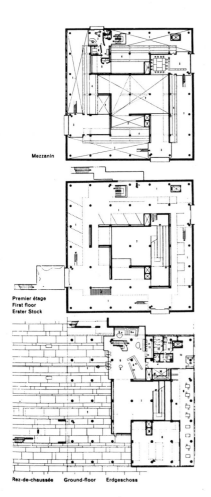

Pl. 68 Le Corbusier, National Museum of Western Art, Tokyo, 1957—59, plans and section.

should be noted that the designer of the museum, Bhanu Mather, was one of Le Corbusier's associates in the development of Chandigarh. The design could relate to Le Corbusier's roofs for exhibition pavilions such as the sketches for Exposition a la Porte Maillot of 1950, the project for a pavilion for the National Gallery of Western Art in Tokyo, 1957, and the Centre le Corbusier in Zurich, 1963—67, or even the project for the French Pavilion at San Francisco or Liège of 1937—38.

The Israel Museum shows an integration of landscape and structure recalling a Mediterranean village, like Sert's grouping of the different pavilions at the Fondation Maeght (Pls. 94, 95, 96). The design allows for the Israel Museum's organic growth on the crown of the hill and the surrounding slopes. The views from the central plaza and several large windows help to orient the visitor. They integrate the museum with the Valley of the Cross below and the monastery situated on a straight axial line from the central plaza. Although this idea for creating a harmonious extension recalls the massing of volumes in Mediterranean hill-villages, it is worth noting that the result also recalls Mies's project for a Brick Country House of 1923 (Pl. 93).

c. Unplanned-for expansion.

There are many examples of chaotic expansion, including the rather interesting case of Cleveland, but the most elaborate example is the Metropolitan Museum, New York.

In erecting a new wing in 1958, the Cleveland Museum of Art left room for the future construction of a symmetrical wing to the west. Yet less than ten years later the museum architect chose to ignore this plan and decided instead to mask the undistinguished 1958 east wing by a new wing on the same side along the latter's north and east flanks. The extension was attached to the 1916 Neo-classical structure so that the three sections would interlock[38]. According to the *Architectural Forum*, the architect did not blend the new wing with the Neo-classical facade of the original building and its 1958 extension for two reasons: first, "because the site with its nice trees tended to separate the old from the new — visually at least — so it seemed unnecessary to make an effort to relate the two." Second, "...because he rather enjoys the tensions that are created between old and new things. To him such contrasts enrich rather than deplete the scene."[39]

The new Education Wing provided the Museum with a modern and dramatic entrance sheltered by a long canopy (115 × 26 feet) with a spacious lobby and a direct approach to the temporary exhibitions gallery, auditorium and classrooms (Pls. 97, 98).

The Metropolitan Museum of Art in New York, on the other hand, always had a master plan which provided for orderly expansion whenever funds were available or collections added. The Metropolitan's main problem has been its several master plans, five in all, none of which has ever been carried out completely. Only a fraction

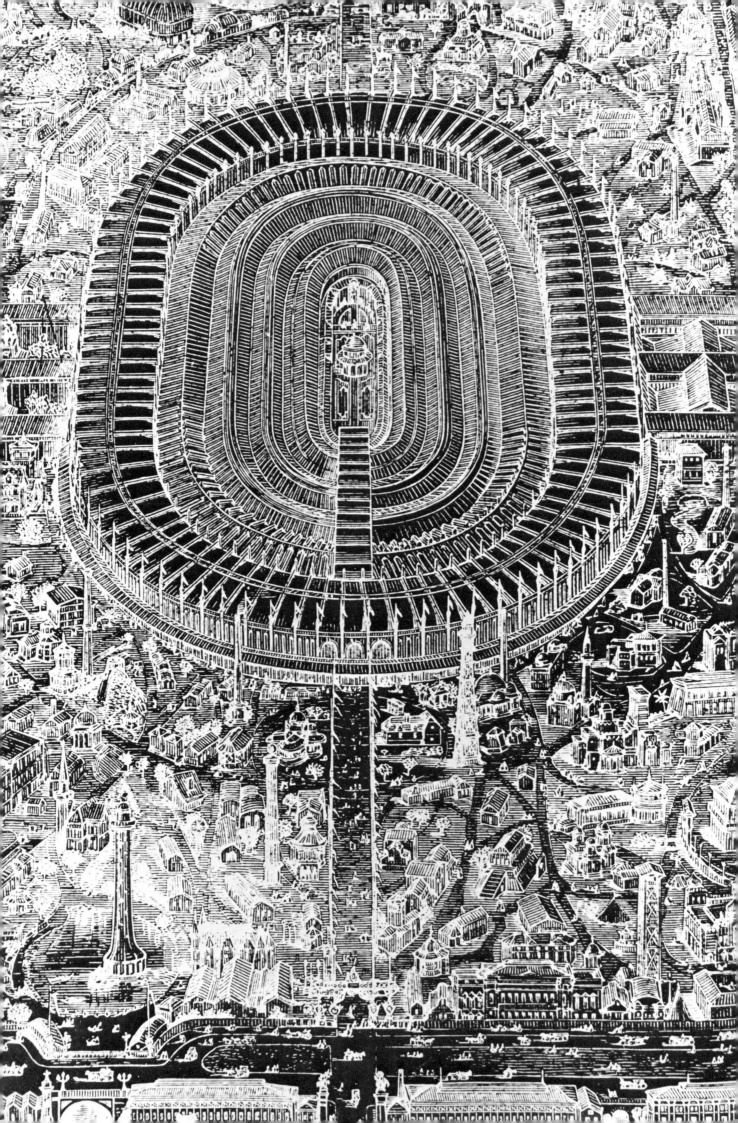

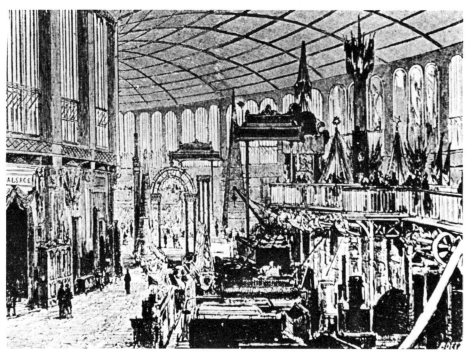

Pl. 70 International Exhibition, Paris, 1967.
Galerie des Machines.

Pl. 69 International Exhibition, Paris, 1867.
The visitor to the exhibition could go around
these ellipses from the outer and largest gallery,
the Galerie des Machines, to the smaller
galleries exhibiting other materials from clothing
to furniture, from raw materials to the history of
work and the fine arts. At the same time the
visitor could also examine any single country's
development by making a transverse walk. This
exhibition building seems to be a prototype for
Le Corbusier's ideal spiral circulation scheme.

of the first three was ever realized, and none of the fourth. In between, there were occasional haphazard additions in violation of the then existing master plans. It still remains to be seen how much of the fifth master plan will materialize. These different plans represent shifts of style, of approach to the park and street, and consequently have led to changes in the siting of entrances.

When one approaches the present museum from the south side, the park front, for instance, one sees a haphazard conglomeration of structures and styles. Facing the parking lot are the red brick walls of Wing B, build by Weston in 1888 as an addition to Vaux's original structure. A modern Miesian addition connects this building to the brick back walls of the Fifth Avenue Neo-classical main structure of which a few decorated marble-faced corners can be seen. Before the new Sackler Wing was completed, the disorder of this arrangement was further magnified by a temporary inflated bubble storing the Dendur Temple. A large entrance sign helps to orient the confused visitor (Pl. 100).

The first building of the Metropolitan was Wing A erected in 1881. Conceived by Calvert Vaux, one of the designers of Central Park, it was the only section of his comprehensive architectural plan to be executed. He had in mind long galleries which would surround a series of open courts. This building was designed in Ruskinian Gothic style. Its entrance faced the west side and looked out toward the Central Park reservoir.

"Wing B" by Weston and Tuckerman was added in 1888 in sixteenth century Italian Revival style. The entrance still faced the park but was shifted from the west side to the south.

The shift of approach from park to street orientation is a result of Richard Morris Hunt's master plan. Hunt, of World Columbian Exposition fame, designed a colossal Neo-classical structure. The only part of his master plan that materialized was the marble-faced Great Hall (1902), which masks the red brick building behind it. A long structure with narrow side galleries and staircase leading to the upper gallery connect the two.

The 1904 McKim, Mead and White master plan was similar to Hunt's symmetrical rectangular mass with extensions to the grandiose Fifth Avenue facade and a series of internal courts. The Fifth Avenue front was constructed between 1911 and 1926 in Roman-Italian Renaissance style which blended with the exterior of the central hall. Yet this master plan was ignored in 1924 when the American Wing was added by Grosvenor Atterbury, an extension which still raises grave circulation problems. In 1931 the van Rennsslaer Period Rooms were added piecemeal.

The next master plan was never carried out at all. Undertaken by the museum director, Francis H. Taylor, and the architect, Robert O'Connor, with the idea of reorganizing the institution into a series of museums, it did not feature an innovative style. They had envisaged a monotonous, standard, Federal structure; no entrance at all was planned for the park side.

The fact that the Metropolitan has had a master plan or even several such plans

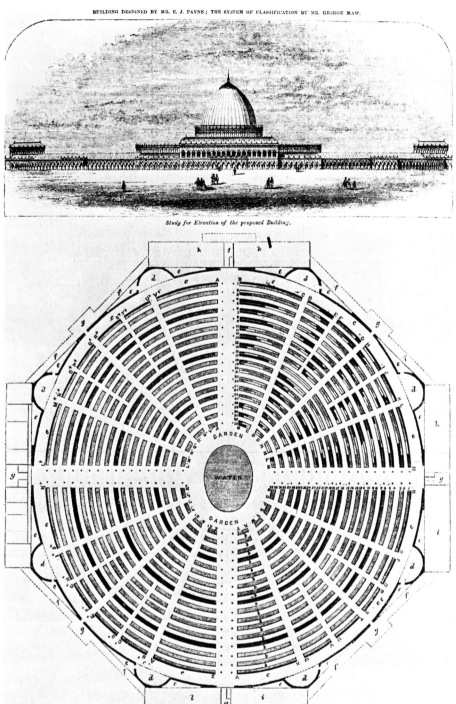

BUILDING DESIGNED BY MR. E. J. PAYNE; THE SYSTEM OF CLASSIFICATION BY MR. GEORGE MAW.

Study for Elevation of the proposed Building.

Pl. 71 E.J. Payne and George Maw, design for an exhibition building for the exhibition of 1862, The Builder, 1861.
A scheme for circulation and space organization similar to that of the Paris International Exhibition of 1867 can be found in a project for the earlier London exhibition of 1862. It was proposed in The Builder *by E.J. Payne who designed the building and George Maw who suggested the system of classification. The suggested circulation patterns were circular (or elliptical, according to the chosen form) together with a double system of intersecting avenues. The organization of exhibited material received more emphasis than circulation. As such, the plan is closer to library designs.*

since its foundation has not ensured preplanned expansion. The intent at least of the new master plan is to combine the different wings into a workable superstructure. The Roche-Dinkeloo master plan of 1970 will return to the first master plan by offering a park entrance from the west side. The park aspect of the museum will be stressed by two enclosed, year-round garden courts, attached to the park entrances. The glass curtain wall of the new side wings on the south and north sides will open the museum to the park and afford a glimpse of the exhibits even from the street. The architects also had to solve the complex problems of circulation and thus provide a clear traffic pattern for the increased museum audience (Pls. 101, 102).

d. Le Corbusier's theoretical expansion scheme.

Le Corbusier too was preoccupied with the problems of expansion. Preplanned expansion went with circulation as one of the two most important features of his museum designs. Whereas the 1929 project for Geneva suggested the basic circulation pattern he was to use for the rest of his life (Pl. 61), the 1931 design for a museum of contemporary art in Paris was the first of his designs to solve the problem of preplanned growth (Pl. 62). The solution was based on an entrance placed at the museum's center. In the event of expansion the existing external surface

Pl. 72 Clarence Stein, diagrammatic plan for a museum, 1932.
The main and study collections were to be displayed in two concentric galleries with the study collection encircling the smaller display of the primary collection. The exhibited material in the inner and outer circles would be related to each other.

76

would become an internal wall of the new gallery and the exterior of the new addition to the spiral would serve as a temporary facade. When the last spiral had reached the exterior gate, the museum would have attained its maximum size.

Le Corbusier's 1939 project for a museum in Philippeville, Algeria was called "Musée à croissance illimitée" (Pls. 63, 64). This museum of unlimited extension was designed to be built on columns so that the central entrance could be approached at ground level and not through an underground passage as in his 1931 project. The main hall was to serve as a starting point for the visit.

As previously mentioned, the spiral is associated not only with movement, but also with growth, and it is known that forms expressing measured growth fascinated Le Corbusier. His sketches from 1938 include a shell, an abstract diagram of curves of growth, and an unlimited extension museum with several spirals (Pl. 65)[41]. Already in 1914 Sir Theodore Cook's "The Curves of Life" had concentrated on the spiral alone. "Its fascination," he wrote, "lay in the fact that in almost perfect mathematical form it seemed to underlie the growth of an unparalleled variety of things both animate and inanimate and when it occurred, growth could be reduced to an abstract idea..."[42]

Yet in the three projects for museums which actually materialized — Ahmedabad, Tokyo, and Chandigarh — only one spiral was built. The plans for the museum in Ahmedabad included three annexes: one housing a lecture hall and workshop for preparing exhibitions, another for anthropology, and a third for archaeology. The plans left a space between the museum and the annexes for future extension through an additional spiral. The 50 meter by 50 meter external walls could be extended to 84 by 84 meters, providing an expansion from 2,500 square meters to 7,000 square meters (Pl. 66). Were another spiral added, however, the large side window would have to be blocked off. In Tokyo the project included a lecture and cinema hall next to the first spiral external wall, but these were not built (Pls. 67, 68). In Chandigarh an independent structure for a lecture hall was built on the north side, while on the ground floor archive-rooms were attached to the east side of the museum. Here the solution did not, in fact, encourage future expansion since any extension would have to take into account the ground floor structure; it might even necessitate demolition of the lecture hall.

3. Lighting the museum.

One of the most important features of museum design is light, and until artificial illumination was introduced, providing for natural light was a dominant factor in museum planning. Skylight is the most common method of furnishing natural light, but clerestory and side windows are also used frequently. One has now become

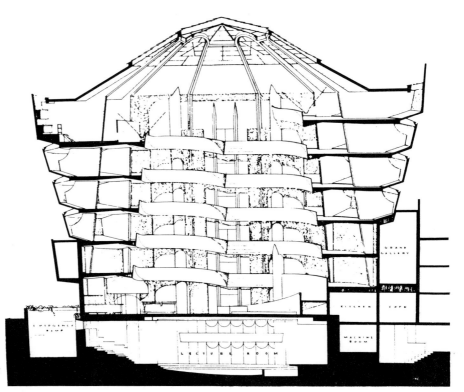

Pl. 73 Frank Lloyd Wright, the Solomon R. Guggenheim Museum, New York, 1943–1959, Section.
The visitors are lifted by elevator to the top of the spiral and then walk down the widening ramp. To arrive at a specific spiral the visitor does not have to go through the whole museum; he can reach it by using the lift or staircase core.

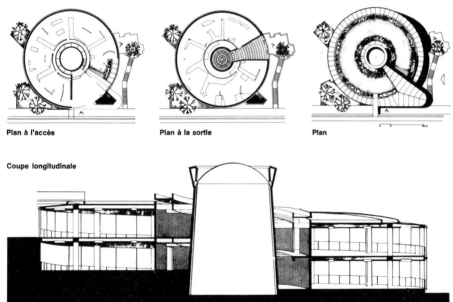

Plan à l'accès

Plan à la sortie

Plan

Coupe longitudinale

Pls. 74, 75 Pedro Ramirez Vasquez and Rafael Mijares, New History Museum, Chapultepec Park, Mexico City, 1960.
This museum is a variation of the Guggenheim Museum. The architects designed wider spirals and used a glass curtain wall instead of concrete, but the basic idea of starting the visit from the top and making the viewer descend the spiral was not changed. The wider spiral is not used for a more flexible display than at the Guggenheim. In this case the central space is walled up and is used as a separate conical space framing dramatically the Mexican constitution. The comparison between this museum and the Guggenheim demonstrates how much more successful, as well as more impressive, is the manipulation of space at the Guggenheim.

accustomed to a combination of natural and artificial light. In some cases natural light is given the major role; in others artificial illumination takes precedence. A natural source is often used to light general space rather than particular objects, but even then, general artificial illumination can be given a share. Unlike science museums which do not require natural light, art museums without natural illumination are a recent phenomenon.

The traditional means of natural lighting is skylight (Pl. 127). Hubert Robert's paintings of the Louvre's skylit galleries are the only evidence of his 1780's project for remodelling the museum in accordance with plans provided by several architects. This idea was partially carried out in the nineteenth and twentieth centuries, but in fact the Grande Galerie received skylighting only in 1938 (Pl. 104)[44].

One of the first museums actually to be built with skylight was Sir John Soane's Dulwich College Picture Gallery, 1814–16, following the pattern of the Royal Academy in Somerest House (about 1780)[45]. Klenze's Alte Pinakothek in Munich of 1826–36, which proved to be very influential in museum design, was also top lit[46]. According to Coleman, "...it may have been suggested by little overhead openings in Italian palace galleries like the Museo Chiaramonti of the Vatican."[47] A century later the design of the National Gallery in Washington was determined to a large extent by skylight, and Aalto's most recent museum is still dominated by natural light.

The main advantage of skylight is that it supplies more or less sufficient light,

Aquarium Floor Plans

1ST LEVEL

2ND LEVEL

3RD LEVEL

4TH LEVEL

Pl. 76 Cambridge Seven Associates, New England Aquarium, Boston, 1969.
The aquarium "...is like putting the Guggenheim spiral inside the Corbu scheme and filling the center space of the Guggenheim with water," observed the architect.

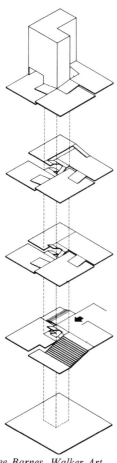

Pl. 77 Edward larrabee Barnes, Walker Art Center, Minneapolis, 1970.
According to Barnes, "It is flow more than form that has concerned us. The sequence of space must be seductive. There must be a subtle sense of going somewhere, like a river. At the same time the architecture must be relatively uneventful and anonymous."

leaving the walls of the gallery free for display. The main disadvantage is that it dictates a low building with only one or two stories available for display. The other functions of the museum are relegated to the basement. It thus determines as well the space proportion given to museum services. In a skylit museum space organization as a whole is so dominated by the need for this light that from the outset other functional considerations must play a secondary role.

Windows as the source of natural light raise other difficulties. They set up far more reflections and glare, especially where glass is used to protect exhibits. To paraphrase Mumford, when you visit the Wallace Collection you may come to see Boucher or Fragonard, but you end up seeing your own reflection. In addition, windows can be effective only up to a certain width according to their size, and the spaces around the windows cannot be used for display at all. Even so, by locating the windows near one of the long walls of a medium-size gallery most of the glare and reflection can be eliminated, and where these problems are solved the advantages in freedom of space organization are great, since side lighting allows the construction of multiple story museums without any single dominant floor.

The disadvantage of clerestory windows is that they can be used only in high galleries over the roofs of the lower adjacent rooms. In addition, unlike normal windows, they do not provide any view of the outside. Their main advantage, according to Coleman, is that the central court no longer need be treated as a high skylit space. Yet, on the other hand, a high ceiling is required to keep the light out of the visitor's eyes, and a good deal of space between the high windows and the exhibits is wasted.

Other methods of lighting are monitors and inverted monitors, variations of the usual skylight system. The monitor is a large lantern formed by raising the central part of the upper gallery ceiling above a band of windows. Each wall recieves natural light from the opposite windows of the monitor[48]. In the inverted monitor the box with windows around is hung from the ceiling, each side illuminating the wall on the same side of the gallery. An elaborate inverted monitor system of top side lighting in which only one side is lit is attributed to S. Hurst Seager who coined the term in British journals during the 1920's. The disadvantage of his system was that it left one side of a gallery fairly dark, wasting possible exhibition space[49].

In many cases more than one system of natural lighting is used. In the Israel Museum, Jerusalem, for instance, each of the pavilions with a central column supporting an inverted umbrella ceiling is lit by clerestory windows which use the peculiar properties of the ceiling shape as an aid (Pls. 91, 92). The light filters through glare-absorbing glass and is then reflected into the building by the inward inclined curve of the roof. To these clerestory windows the architects added in some galleries large windows or glazed doors which allow the visitor to see the surrounding landscape. In addition, skylight is also used in several picture galleries. In this case, however, the natural light itself caused difficult problems, so that curtains had to be added to cover the large windows and some of the ribbon ones as well. The most successful use of natural illumination in the Israel Museum is in the

new Impressionist and Post-Impressionist gallery inaugurated in 1979.

One of natural light's main advantages is the variety it offers in the quality and quantity of light. From season to season and hour to hour, the light becomes softer, stronger, or sharper, thus renewing the esthetic experience as intensity and color change. Windows also provide contact with the outside world; they counteract feelings of claustrophobia, refresh the visitor, and help to orient him. Moreover, natural light allows the visitor to view works of art in conditions more nearly similar to those in which they were painted or intended to be seen. Yet the limitations imposed by skylighting, monitors, and windows on the organization of internal space and on the size or placement of exhibition walls are significant, and even in the most successful examples, natural light is difficult to manage.

a. Combining natural light with artificial illumination.
Laurence Coleman objects strongly to using natural light as the only or main source of illumination, preferring instead to combine natural with artificial sources. He disdains skylighting because it limits building height and suppresses essential functions to the basement, as discussed above. Skylighting is also the most expensive way of capturing natural light due to high installation and maintenance costs. The wasted space of the tall gallery, the large attic, and the expensive special glass above and below the light mixing chamber count against the skylight, while the significant cost of cleaning, replacing breakages, stopping leaks, and ventilating or heating the attic depending on the season, are in Coleman's view prohibitive. "...The cost of skylighting is far beyond the means of every museum that has work to do with its money."[50] Coleman prefers corner or end lighting to top illumination. He is also against all-purpose lighting and differentiates between room and object illumination.

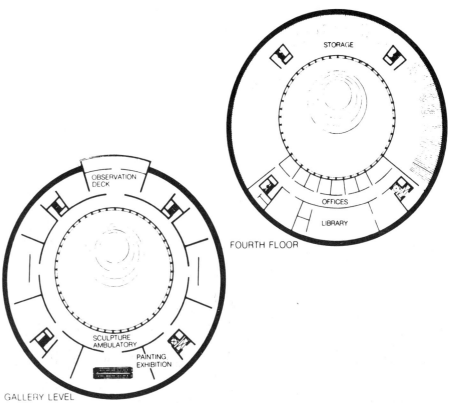

STORAGE

OFFICES

LIBRARY

FOURTH FLOOR

OBSERVATION DECK

SCULPTURE AMBULATORY

PAINTING EXHIBITION

GALLERY LEVEL

Pls. 78, 79 Skidmore, Owings, and Merrill (designed by Gordon Bunshaft), Hirshhorn Museum, Washington, D.C., 1974.
The external monumentality, the blank wall, and the circular shape suggests the Guggenheim Museum completed fifteen years before.

The room may be lit by indirect artificial light, by natural means, or by a combination of the two "to make people feel at ease and to provide conditions under which object lighting can be carried out successfully."[51] Objects, he maintains, should be lit artificially so that the visitor will be able to see them clearly at all times.

Clarence Stein rejected skylights not only because of their high cost but also because of what he considered the "depressing flatness and evenness of their light."[52] In the early thirties Stein suggested that all museum exterior walls be made of glass screens to provide for complete flexibility in the use of natural light. At the very least the two long sides of the structure should be made of glass to allow sufficient flexibility. It should be possible to cover up sections of the glass wall and rearrange the location and size of the windows according to the light requirements dictated by different arrangements within. Stein envisioned a double glass wall: from the outside there would be a uniform appearance while on the inside the use of interchangeable solid and glazed panels would allow the amount and direction of light filtering in to be controlled. In this way the temporary surface behind the external glass walls would furnish the fenestration required for the optimal illumination of the exhibits. Stein's idea was the natural outcome of the free plan developed by the International Style, and it reflected his emphasis on the flexible use of space.

Nine years after Stein made these suggestions the Museum of Modern Art was built with two long glazed facades, and about a decade after Stein's second article Mies van der Rohe designed a project for a Museum in a Small City which was to have walls entirely of glass (Pl. 137). Only thirty years later a museum with all four walls of glass was in fact designed and built by Mies, the Neue Nationalgalerie, Berlin, 1962—68.

The application of glass screens for the MOMA's two long walls made it at least theoretically possible for the museum to have flexible natural light in a multistory structure. (In his diagrams of the "Museum of Tomorrow", Stein envisioned 17 stories.) To block off, reduce, or adapt the size of the light opening according to the needs of the exhibition, special panel boards of cement asbestos composition can be employed. MOMA was also the first museum to adopt insulating glass for its external wall. The specific material used, "thermolux," has a double pane with an intermediate packing of spun glass: it is therefore a diffusing medium as well as a heat and sound insulator. Its disadvantage is that it delivers a cold light since it filters out a disproportionate amount of the red end of the spectrum[53].

The narrow sculpture gallery on the third floor is the only room at the Museum of Modern Art which receives top light as well. From the fourth floor (offices and services) upwards, the building is stepped back on the side facing the garden[54].

Almost a decade before MOMA was opened to the public in its present building, in the same year that Stein first suggested glass screen walls for the "Museum of

THE TEL AVIV MUSEUM | מוזיאון תל אביב

Tomorrow," George Howe and William E. Lescaze proposed several schemes for a "Museum of Contemporary Art for New York City" (the Museum of Modern Art). Important pioneers in applying International Style principles in America, they prepared in 1930 six preliminary schemes for a multi-story museum building[55]. Each plan offered a different solution to the lighting problem, for them the most vital factor in museum design. Scheme number four which combined top side lighting with skylight was developed in greater detail. In addition to skylight, each gallery was to be illuminated from north and west, or east and west. The building is composed of an arrangement of horizontal blocks placed one above another and at right angles to each other[56] (Pls. 105, 106), and in the second and sixth schemes (Pl. 107), the facade is entirely made of glass. Externally it suggests the Museum of Modern Art as built by Goodwin and Stone. Also similar are the elevator and staircase solution to the circulation problem as well as the penthouse and the restaurant at the top. But by allowing natural light to dictate the design and by keeping most of the museum services in the basement, the Howe and Lescaze project more closely resembles the traditional museum than its modern appearance would suggest.

b. Artificial illumination preferrd.

At MOMA the free space and movable partitions were matched by glass screen walls in the two long facades which made it possible to illuminate the galleries with flexible natural light. At the Yale Art Gallery (1951—54), however, Louis Kahn blocked the front facing the street (Pl. 108); glass screen surfaces are used only for the back wall facing the sculpture garden, the narrow side of the building, and the entrance section which is set back at right angles to the street facade. As a result, artificial means provide most of the light; natural sources have only a supplementary role. Moreover, the traditional attic or lightmixing chamber (Pl. 126) has been reduced to a concrete frame, a few inches deep, which supports a flexible light system. It also contains the exposed pipes and ducts of the ventilating system (Pl. 109). This functional frame is given a strong sculptural shape which in some way takes the place of the attic, so characteristic of traditional museums and such a waste of space[57].

Since the 1950's museums have also adopted the commercial gallery's use of spot lights. Spot lights constitute a highly flexible system by which one can dramatically emphasize certain objects and change the illumination level at will.

At the museum for the Gulbenkian Collection in Lisbon, natural light was given an even more limited role. As a result of Garry Thomson's research in 1961, which demonstrated the relation between the amount of light and the deterioration of organic objects[58], the Museum decided to strictly control the daylight admitted through windows. Although the building was initially planned to be top lit, W.A. Allen advised the foundation to follow Thomson's recommendations in order to protect the Collection's many sensitive objects[59]. He suggested abandoning skylighting, which he regarded as a device for general illumination, unsuitable for creating selective lighting levels for individual displays. To preserve the generally low balance of brightness in indoor views, the brightness of the outdoor views was reduced by grey glass with light transmission of about 30 percent. The shape, size, and location of windows and curtains were also planned to control light penetration. To help the visitor's eyes adjust to the low level of illumination, the first exhibition hall was designed for dark adaptation. It is lit only by the exhibits. From there the planned circulation scheme in the shape of the letter Z (within a rectangle), leads the visitor to galleries with limited supplementary natural light in daytime. The adaptation of the eye to bright or dim illumination is a most important consideration, according to Thomson.

> The response of the pupil of the eye to the strength of the light is well known. Because of this, objects can be satisfactorily viewed in a very wide range of illumination levels — provided the eye has been given time to adapt itself. For proper adaptation, we must avoid rapid transitions from light to dark between rooms and also within a room. Even a white wall will cause the pupil to close in response to it, so that a picture looks darker on it than on a lower level-toned wall.[60]

In the Hayward Gallery, designed by the Greater London Council for the use of the Arts Council, supplementary natural lighting is used only in the upper floor. The highly complicated system of skylighting was designed to screen out ultra-violet light, and through light-sensitive cells it automatically controls the level of illumination. Originally all the galleries were to be artificially lit, but the Arts Council Committee, under the influence of Henry Moore, asked for natural lighting. From the exterior one can see the steeply sloped structure of self-cleaning glass pyramids designed to admit maximum light (Pl. 168). Baffles under these pyramids cut off direct sunlight, while horizontal blinds controlled by photocells are motor operated to maintain acceptable daylight intensity. This system is further supplemented by color-corrected fluorescent tubes which are also automatically controlled. An egg crate baffle ceiling covered with double-skin, translucent panels is suspended below the light fittings to provide diffusion and an ultra-violet filter. Spot lights can be plugged into the ceiling to illuminate the side walls and help avoid too even a level.

As early as 1968 Thomson, then the scientific advisor to the Trustees of the National Gallery, London, and editor of *Studies in Conservation,* rightly predicted that

> as times goes by the level of operation of automatic control in galleries four and five will by degrees be raised from the hoped-for 150—200 lux to somewhere around 400, where the average viewer will be satisfied. Even so the glare from the east-facing picture window will dim the pictures on sunny mornings.[61]

A later review of the building confirmed his forecast. Instead of being automatically controlled up to the recommended illumination level of 150 lux, the system tends to be manually switched even higher. According to the reviewer for the *Architect's Journal,* the management's experience with the light system is that

> in summer it works, but from September to March there might as well be a solid roof. On 15 December there was no visible sun, but the sky was far from its wintry greyest. As a test the fluorescent light was turned off and the result was like being under the most aged and dirt-encrusted factory roof — impossibly gloomy.[62]

At the Whitney Museum, Breuer and Smith did not consider natural light to be worth such an elaborate and complex solution. The windows at the Whitney serve only for contact with the outside world. While they help the visitor avoid a feeling of

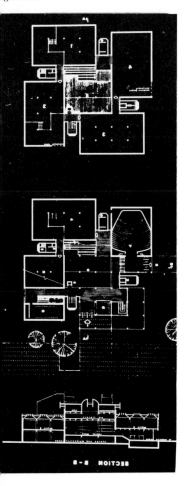

Pl. 81 Itzhak Yashar and Dan Eitan, Tel Aviv Museum, Tel Aviv, 1964—1971, plans and section.
The architects adopted I.M. Pei's organization of the galleries at the Everson Museum of Art, Syracuse, New York, introduced changing levels to some of the galleries, and returned to Le Corbusier's original straight ramp to the galleries.

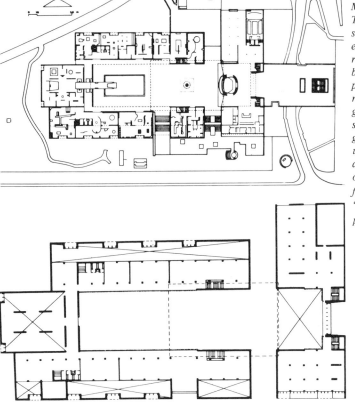

Pls. 82, 83 Pedro Ramirez Vasquez and Rafael Mijares, The National Museum of Anthropology, Mexico City, 1962–1965.

This museum offers an interesting circulation solution for large museums. The rectangular exhibition halls run around three sides of the rectangular patio on two levels above a basement. The visitor can either follow the planned circulation pattern throughout the rectangle, starting at the right hand side from the gallery which introduces the anthropological section, continuing counter-clockwise to the last gallery on the left, or enter only an independent unit of the museum, e.g. Mayan Culture or Aztec art. By crossing the central courtyard, he can observe single sections without having to pass first through the entire museum. These small "museums" have their own circulation pattern, as sub-units within the overall scheme.

claustrophobia and assist in his orientation, these openings hardly serve as a supplementary source of light (Pl. 174). In their later museum building for Cleveland, even the windows were eliminated. These architects believe that artificial light makes exhibition space more flexible; windows in a museum are functionally disadvantageous[63].

Another windowless museum building is the Walker Art Center, Minneapolis, designed by Edward Larrabee Barnes in 1971. The exterior appears as a virtually unbroken sculptural mass. Orientation to daylight is provided occasionally mainly to reduce museum fatigue[64].

The impression of enclosed space at the Museum of the Treasury at the Cathedral of San Lorenzo, Genoa (1956), was intended by the architect, Franco Albini. The underground cylindrical rooms are almost completely artificially lit. For the sake of dramatic effect the light comes from projectors and lamps placed on top of the display cases, while an opaque screen limits the light diffusion. The only natural light filtering in comes from the glazed occulus in the center of each flattened 'dome', but these occuli can hardly be considered as even a supplementary source of light, since they provide only a vague contact with the outside world (Pl. 115).

Artificial light permits a more flexible use of space and at the same time reduces construction and maintenance costs. The comparison here is not between free daylight and costly electricity, however, since both skylighting and windows entail the relatively high costs of heat loss in winter and ventilation in the summer, as well as cleaning and repair year-round[65]. With that, artificial illumination cuts off contact with the outside world, and lacks all the variety of natural light provided by changes in weather, season, and the time of day.

c. The return to natural light.
Side by side with the tendency to rely increasingly on artificial illumination, numerous museums emphasize the use of natural light.

Philip Johnson believes that natural light is unsuitable for exhibiting paintings, and he has designed his many museums accordingly. The art gallery (1966) in his Glass House estate is not an underground building, but a structure erected aboveground and then covered with earth so as not to change drastically the view from the Glass House (Pls. 116, 117).

But where sculpture is to be displayed, Johnson takes an opposite view. The sculpture gallery which was added in 1970 was the antithesis, the negative of the art gallery. Instead of covering the building with earth and green grass, Johnson had the structure whitewashed. The semi-mirrored glass roof of the sculpture gallery provides natural light, while the glass frames of the roof cast strong shadows on the sculpture. The artificial sources of illumination — cold cathode light strips — were designed to reduce the contrast created by the strong shadows, but they were not intended to illuminate the works of art, at least not in daytime[66] (Pl. 118).

In the design of the Civica Galleria d'Arte Moderna in Turin (1954—59) (Carlo Bassi and Goffredo Boschetti), the introduction of natural light to all galleries seems to be the starting point. To provide zenith lighting to the two exhibition floors of the permanent collection, the walls of the superposed galleries were placed at an awkward angle: the walls of the first floor incline inwards, while those on the upper floor tilt outwards (Pl. 120). Special wooden display panels with iron supports were built for the pictures. Hung on metal wires, they seem to float uncomfortably in the air (Pl. 122). At the same time, the rest of the collection is attached to temporary screens: hardly any picture is displayed against a conventional straight wall. The ground floor of the temporary exhibitions wing is laterally illuminated, while the upper floor is lit like the main building, by skylight. Even so, the manneristic result is hardly justifiable on functional grounds. In this case, the introduction of natural light has distorted the building in an unprecedented, almost grotesque, way.

The means of providing natural light dwarf the exhibits in the North Jutland Museum of Art, in Aalborg, Denmark. The architects, Elissa and Aalvar Aalto and Jean Jacques Baruel did achieve a luminous interior. Not only the large central hall for temporary exhibitions, but also several long galleries receive natural light through a series of asymmetrical monitor lights. Unlike the glazed monitors designed by Le Corbusier for Tokyo, they allow some direct light and even occasionally a glimpse of sunlight. "What one sees," wrote Michael Brawne, "is unmistakably daylight." Writing in *The Architectural Review,* he pointed out that in the central gallery,

> the visual emphasis which exists above the level of the top of the wall, indeed the proportion of the total volume which is contained in the upper part, makes the wall surfaces dwindle to insignificance. Yet it is on those walls that the exhibits have to

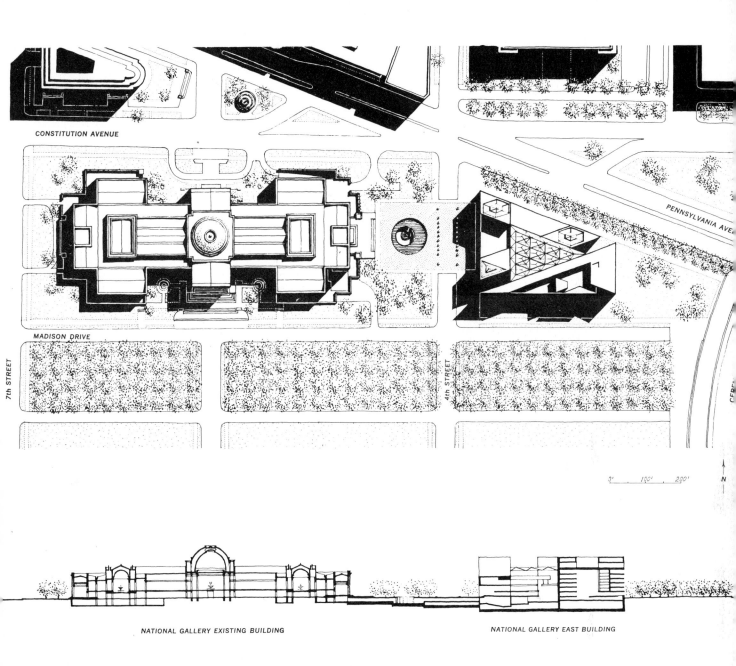

CONSTITUTION AVENUE

PENNSYLVANIA AVE.

7th STREET

MADISON DRIVE

4th STREET

N

0'   100'   200'

NATIONAL GALLERY EXISTING BUILDING

NATIONAL GALLERY EAST BUILDING

Pls. 84, 85 I.M. Pei, The National Gallery, Washington, the East Building, designed 1967–71, completed 1978.
Pei adjusted the extension of the National Gallery to the main Neo-classical temple, Washington's monumentality, and the difficult site by designing a separate building which consists of two triangles with opposing apexes, connected only through an underground passage beneath 4th Street. The two levels of the structure relate to the nearby buildings. The use of the same pink Tennessee marble helps to harmonize the new wing with the main building.

be shown. Not even the monumental and vibrant canvasses of Rothko could come into their own in such a setting.[67]

Pl. 86 Skidmore, Owings and Merrill (designed by Gordon Bunshaft) extension for Albright-Knox Art Gallery, Buffalo New York, 1958–62.

W.G. Quist's top lighting in the extension of the Kröller-Müller Art Gallery, Otterlo (1969–78) enables one to see the sky through the glass instead of cancelling it out above a diffusing ceiling. Richard Padovan considers Quist's lighting system an important breakthrough[68]. Quist illuminated the exhibition areas from above by adopting saw-tooth roofs open only to the north, which produce a light quality described by Padovan as "pure Vermeer-like clarity." (Pl. 123). This lighting system is well suited for sculpture, whereas the strong shadows cast on the walls are problematic for the display of paintings. Manfred Lehmbruck criticizes this principle because one risks dazzling the viewer and exposing the art to oblique and monotonous light. In addition he notes the limited flexibility of display[69]. Artificial illumination is provided by external lamps. In contrast to van de Velde's blank brick walls the new entrance and main circulation areas have glazed walls which offer visitors startling views of the woodlands.

Another successful example of primary dependence on natural light is Louis Kahn's Kimbel Art Museum in Fort Worth, Texas (1972). Like traditional museums, the Kimbel Museum has exhibition galleries on a single story set on top of the storage and office space. This museum's unique feature is the series of cycloid post-tensioned reinforced concrete vaults, each 100 feet long with a 22 foot span. These curved vaults are split at the apex to create a light slot.

In the new wing of the Vatican Museum, designed by Vincenzio Fausto and Lucio Passarelli in 1971 to house the Lateran Museum, natural light is used for effects which could be achieved much more easily by artificial illumination. Besides general lighting from short, slanting barrel-vaults and clerestory sources, funnels from the roof are used to highlight certain exhibits with natural light (Pls. 124, 125). This solution, however, does not allow any flexibility. Were the light sources for special

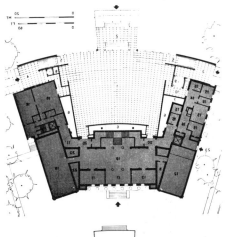

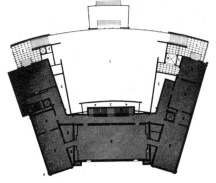

Pl. 87 Mies van der Rohe, extensions for the Museum of Fine Arts, Houston, Texas, Cullinan Hall, 1954—58, Brown Pavilion, 1954—74. An example of a two-phase addition to an existing museum which was carried out.

emphasis spot lights instead of natural light ducts, it would be easy to change the location of the exhibits. The inflexibility of the lighting is matched by fixed rough plaster bases and dividing partitions, as opposed to the changeable steel frame and the movable concrete base.

The general tendency continues to be to combine natural with artificial light as can be seen in Mies's Neue Nationalgalerie, Berlin; Le Corbusier's museum in Tokyo; Piano and Roger's Centre Pompidou; Pei's East Wing of the National Gallery in Washington; Foster Associates' Sainsbury Center, the University of East Anglia, Norwich; and Kahn's Yale Center for British Art, New Haven. The energy crisis is another reason for recent attempts to avoid the excessive use of artificial light.

4. Conserving art treasures.

a. Protecting exhibits.

Museum conservation calls for controlling the following environmental factors: air humidity; temperature; airborne dirt; contaminating gases; ultra-violet light radiation; and illumination level.

There are two reasons to heat and humidify (or cool and dehumidify) museum spaces: one is to ensure the comfort of visitors and staff and the other is to conserve the collection. For staff and visitor comfort, the system need operate only when the museum is open. Conservation, however, requires 24 hour-a-day atmospheric control, the year round. Indeed limiting the air-conditioning to certain daytime hours would accelerate the deterioration of art works due to drastic temperature and humidity changes.

Heating was the first element to be considered in the evolution towards the complete control of temperature and moisture as well as the movement and quality of air. Warmed in winter months from the very beginning, most museums employed one method or another of steam heating such as radiators, heating coils, or unit steam heaters with fan attachments.

Forced ventilation, the supply and removal of air by mechanical means either as part of the heating system or through a complete air-conditioning network, then replaced natural ventilation which brings in unwanted dust from the outside. In addition, sulphur dioxide and other pollutant gases had to be filtered out. At the Museum of Fine Arts, Boston (Guy Lowell, 1909), the dryness of heated air was overcome for the first time in a museum setting. It was not until the 1930's that summer cooling and the attendant removal of excess humidity was introduced to museums.

It is interesting to note that complete air-conditioning with winter heating, summer cooling, and year-round humidity control as well as air purification was first attempted in a museum which was not at all advanced from the point of view of style. Set in a Neo-Renaissance structure, the Frick Collection in New York, opened to the public in 1935, looks more like a private mansion than a modern museum (Pl. 127). The architect, John Russell Pope, more than doubled the exhibition space, but preserved the building's residential character, locating the air-conditioning plant in the basement[71]. The same architect also designed the National Gallery in Washington (1937—41), once more using a traditional architectural vocabulary, but again incorporating an advanced system for climate control.

At the National Gallery, London, only the renovated rooms are fully air-conditioned, while at the Hayward Gallery, the upper galleries alone are so equipped, due to the cost of extending this system to all the galleries as originally planned.

> The result is a paradox: one of the very few galleries in Britain providing full conservation of works of art is also the only gallery where no work stays on view more than a few months. But in the basement store, where works may stay for up to a year, there is no air-conditioning, with the exception of the strongroom, and there only plenum fans, some of which can bring in atmospheric dust... the building-in of service installation appears to make future extention of full air-conditioning to lower galleries difficult.[73]

The air filters used at the Hayward for all exhibition rooms eliminate about 95 percent of all airborne dust, but only in the upper galleries is the relative humidity maintained at a constant level (55 percent). In fact, in the lower galleries the relative humidity can drop to an extremely low level when heating needs are high[74].

"Control of relative humidity to constant level," stresses Garry Thomson, "is very important in maintaining the dimensional stability of all moisture-absorbent material, and in this case we are concerned mainly with wood and canvas." The only major polluting gas in London is sulphur dioxide.

Pls. 88, 89 Al Mansfeld and Dora Gad, Israel Museum, Jerusalem, 1959–1965.
Pl. 88 1965, two exposed mushrooms for the future Junior Wing. Pl. 89. 1980.
The architects' solution to the problem of expansion was to build a museum consisting of several pavilions connected to each other to create a continuous flowing space. It was designed to allow the structure to grow organically on the crown of the hill and the surrounding slopes from the minimal scheme to present and future extensions.
In the first ten years there were six million visitors to the museum. 260 exhibitions were organized, 140 catalogues were published. In the auditorium 400 lectures were delivered, 60 concerts and 200 symposia were held, and 1,000 movies were screened. Exhibition space was doubled and the budget increased more than four-fold.

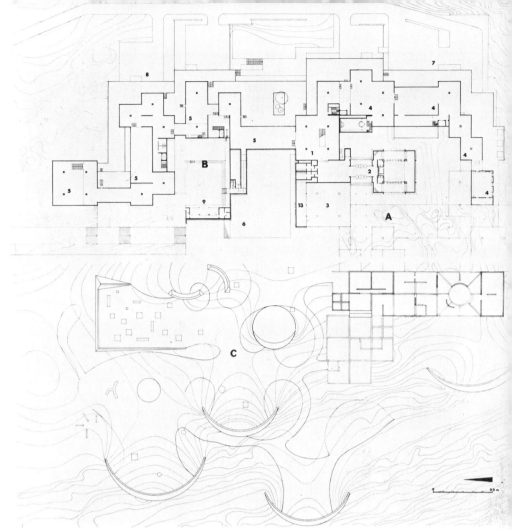

Pl. 90 Al Mansfeld and Dora Gad, Israel Museum, Jerusalem, 1959–1965.
Including the Billy Rose Sculpture Garden designed by Isamu Noguchi and the Shrine of the Book designed by Frederick Kiesler and Armand Bartos.
Pl. 91 Al Mansfeld and Dora Gad, Israel Museum, Jerusalem 1959–1965, Sections.

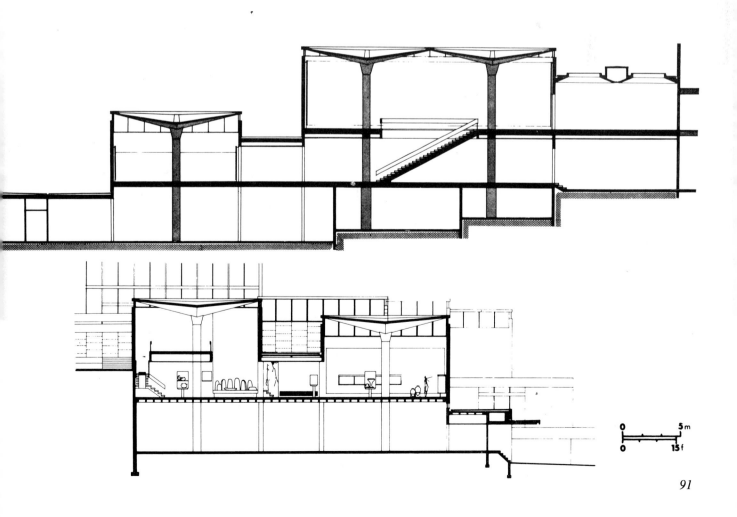

This gas becomes converted to the involatile sulphuric acid in which form it corrodes, rots fabrics, and dissolves alkaline stone. Fortunately, a continuous water spray in the air-conditioning system with frequent changes of water will remove most of the sulphur dioxide and sulphuric acid as well as dealing with humidity. Thus upper galleries get two benefits denied to the lower.[75]

In order to protect works of art, ultra-violet light should be reduced and the illumination level kept as low as possible. In opposition to the then current fashion of excessive lighting, Thomson recommended low illumination levels in 1961. As a result of investigations linking illumination with the deterioration of organic objects, he concluded that for objects insensitive to light, these levels should rarely exceed 300 lux (39 lumens per square foot), except where special emphasis was desired. For most museum objects, including oil and tempera paintings, he recommended the use of automatic shutters for daylight so that illumination would not exceed 150 lux. Nor should there be any sharp transition from high to low illumination in museums, except for special effects. For extremely sensitive objects like watercolors, textiles, and tapestries, the lighting level ought to be at most 50 lux, in which case there is no need to remove ultra-violet light. But for most museum displays, daylight tungsten or fluorescent light can be employed together with ultra-violet filters[76].

According to Thomson,

> The more resistant a material is to deterioration by light, the more its eventual deterioration will be caused by ultra-violet rather than visible light. Put another way, this means that light stable objects will profit more through protection from ultra-violet light than will fugitive material.[77]

Reviewing conservation methods in the Hayward Gallery in 1968 for the *Architect's Journal,* Thomson found that the filters on the upper floor reduced the ultra-violet reading to about three percent of what it would have been without filters[78]. In the lower floor, however, the ultra-violet radiation from the unfiltered tungsten light, though low, was "perhaps four times what it is in the well filtered daylight rooms." With respect to the illumination level, the results were reversed. In the lower galleries the level did not exceed 150–200 lux, whereas in the upper galleries it was twice as high, about 350–400 lux. While the 150 lux downstairs looked light and gay because of the influx of window light, the illumination level upstairs, so near the point of glare, did not seem sufficient.

Adjustable regulating appliances were designed for the new extension of the Tate Gallery completed in 1979. The new gallery space is divisible into twenty-one separate modules and each is covered by a double-layer pyramidal skylight. While the upper layer of louvres is used primarily to prevent excessive heat gain, their precise angle can be adjusted according to the season; the controls for the lower layer of louvres are activated manually or by a photoelectric cell in each bay to maintain the lighting at a pre-set level. Although designed to deal with excessive variation in illumination levels, they have also been calibrated so as not to respond too quickly to slight changes. Critics feel, however, that the system has not succeeded in preventing the shifts in illumination level that are characteristic of

natural light.

According to architect Manfred Lehmbruck, "A choice must be made between a complicated device to provide protection against the sun and an excessively bleak monotony."[79] He believes that differences in the quality of light open up possibilities in the interpretation of objects. Light which always falls on one of the sides is psychologically inhibiting and produces stereotyped patterns of preservation. Lehmbruck recommends combining more than one source of light: light from the north mixed with southern light or light coming from the side facing away from the sun together with reflected light for background illumination. Indirect light alters the colors but avoids the harmful ultraviolet rays.

b. Making room for support services.

In early public museums, small inadequate space in the basement was most often allocated to various museum services. No matter how large the museum, less than one-third of the space was allocated to something other than exhibitions. Conservation departments, now so essential to modern museum management, had no special space of their own. For instance, only in the new extension to the National Gallery in London does the conservation department enjoy naturally lit rooms built especially to suit its needs. Originally the Tate Gallery did not even have a conservation department, since it was connected to the National Gallery and in fact specialized in modern art which did not seem to require such facilities. Only in the new wing will the department have a satisfactory space illuminated by natural light. Here the type of lighting can be critical, since cleaning and retouching paintings in artificially illuminated rooms for eventual display in naturally lit galleries must be extremely difficult.

The MOMA 1939 building opened new perspectives in this regard. Most of the museum's services and workshops were located on the fourth and fifth floors, with only a few services placed in the basement.

In most new museum buildings there is at least as much space for storage, services, curatorial, and administrative purposes as for exhibitions. For example, in the Freer Gallery of Art, Washington, 1923, 57 percent of the total space is allocated to exhibitions, while 43 percent is allocated to all other functions. Approximately the same space distribution is found in the Philadelphia Museum of Art,

Pls. 95, 96 José Louis Sert, Bellini, Lizero and Gozzi, Associated architects, La Fondation Maeght, Saint Paul de Vence, 1959–1964.

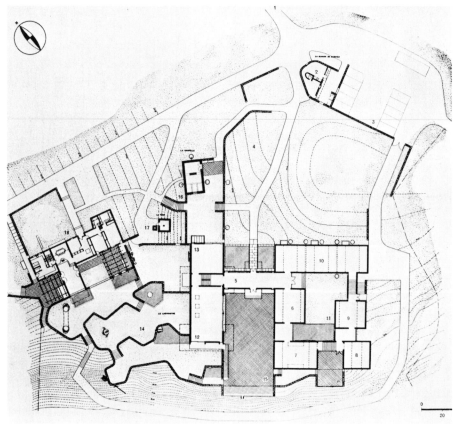

Pl. 97 Marcel Breuer and Hamilton Smith, new wing for Cleveland Museum of Art, Cleveland, Ohio, 1967–1971.
The new wing provided the museum with a modern and dramatic entrance. A long canopy with a spacious lobby offered a direct approach to the temporary exhibitions gallery, the auditorium, and classrooms.
The architects believed that artificial light lends itself to more flexible use of exhibition space. They consider windows in a museum functionally disadvantageous and even eliminated the windows that still existed in the Whitney (Pls. 170–176). The architects tried to compensate for the building's northern exposure by alternating dark and light grey granite bands. The position of the color bands changes from one wall to the other.
Pl. 98 Marcel Breuer and Hamilton Smith, new wing for Cleveland Museum of Art, Cleveland, 1967–71, plan.
Orderly expansion was not ensured by a preplanned extension. The architects ignored the plans for a symmetrical west wing and decided to mask the undistinguished 1958 east wing by a new wing on the same side.

1928 (as rearranged in 1948), the Art Institute of Chicago (as rearranged in 1939) (not including the art school) and at the Nelson Gallery of Art (Kansas City, 1933), whereas only 46 percent of the space is for display at the Metropolitan Museum of Art, New York (1880–1924)[80].

As collections grow and exhibition galleries expand, there is a tendency to provide more space for services in the first phase of museum construction. Some museums have set aside about one-third of the total space for exhibition galleries, leaving the other two-thirds available for curatorial functions, lecture hall, library, conservation department, workshops, plants and administrative offices. Coleman believes in a scheme which splits total space into thirds for exhibitions, curatorial work, and administration including services. He calls it, "...a scheme that would prove itself sound in any growing museum, but that would give most new museums more storage space than they would need right away."[81] Similar proportions characterized museums built as early as the late 1920's and the 1930's: the Detroit Institute of Art (1927); the Fogg Museum of Art (Cambridge, Mass., 1927); the Seattle Art

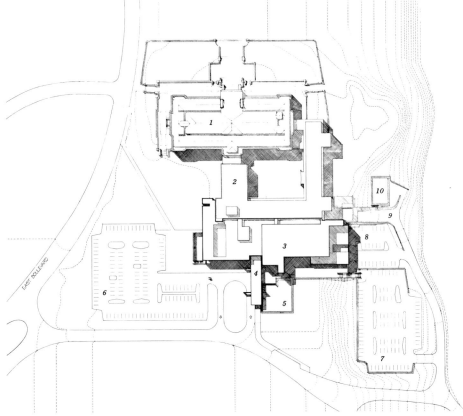

SITE PLAN

1 Original Museum
2 1958 Wing
3 Education Wing
4 Entrance Canopy
5 Sunken Garden
6 East Parking - 148 Cars
7 West Parking - 93 Cars
8 Staff Parking - 26 Cars
9 Truck Ramp
10 Greenhouse

Museum (1932); and MOMA (1939).

In recent years this change in space distribution seems necessary not only for the museum's first phase but also for any later expansion. Every extension of exhibition space should expand the area given to other functions in about the same proportion[82].

5. Flexibility.

Another trend in modern museum design has been to search for maximum flexibility in the use of floor and wall space. Such flexible space for displays has its origins in the nineteenth century traditions of world exhibitions and fairs, market areas, and department stores.

a. The flexibility of nineteenth century world fairs.
The Crystal Palace of 1851 suggested a new kind of architectural space[83]. This gigantic ferrovitreous structure defined a space so large as to be in effect boundless. Framed by a transparent wall, it was articulated by the ironwork and wooden grid of the structural frame as well as by the exhibits and the free-standing screens (Pl. 128). Henry Russell Hitchcock commented that "the predominant pale blue of the metal skeleton — a distance colour must have enhanced the feeling of uncircumscribed space more than colour prints indicate."[84]

The predecessors of this structure were designs for greenhouses, markets, and railway sheds. Out of the 245 entries submitted in an international competition, the commissioners of the Great Exhibition of 1851 selected two glass and iron designs. One ferrovitreous entry was by Hector Horeau (who had submitted an iron and glass design for the Les Halles of Paris) and the second was by Richard Turner (the builder of the Kew Gardens Palm House with Decimus Burton). Once these designs were rejected, the committee prepared its own, which seemed to resemble a railway station[85]. Finally, Paxton's design was approved. His previous experience was in the construction of greenhouses, notably the Great Stove (1836—49) and the Victoria Regis House (1849—50), both at Chatsworth. Assisted by the engineers Fox and Henderson, Paxton proceeded to construct the hall of the Great Exhibition of 1851 which started a long tradition of fair and exhibition halls.

The similarity of the volume of the nave to that of contemporary factories "was actually if negatively recognized in one respect by the critic's remark the Palace was not an "organic whole." He pointed out that it could be enlarged or reduced in size without really affecting its external or internal visual qualities."[86] (Just how modern this concept is can be seen by comparing it to a building like the Stedelijk Museum Annex (1954), where the architects of the Amsterdam Municipality tried to achieve this very kind of flexible space.) The validity of this observation is also underlined by Paxon's 1852 design for enlarging the Crystal Palace[87].

Paxton's influence was widespread. The Crystal Palace in London was followed by many crystal palaces: in Dublin (Sir John Benson, 1852—54); New York (G.J.B. Carstensen and Charles Gildemeister, 1852); Munich (Voit, 1854); and Amsterdam (Cornelis Outshoorn, 1856)[88].

The architectural frame for the main hall of the Paris International Exhibition of 1855 was one of those affected. For the critic of the *Builder* it seemed "...far less striking than the old Crystal Palace," too low for its breadth and much less lofty[89]. The Palais de l'Industrie, however, was in fact wider than the Crystal Palace: its 48 meter span more than doubled the former building's span of about 22 meters, itself the widest span ever to be vaulted up to that time. Besides, in the monumental stonework external frame, "the meaning of the new materials (in the inner space) had been grasped: emphasis rests on opening up of space rather than walling in of a volume," as Giedion commented[90].

Beginning with this fair, France became the center for the most important international exhibitions. The Galerie des Machines of the 1889 exhibition was built by Contamin and Dutert. The photographs of the interior space without the exhibits give a much more impressive view of the immense free space in this glass-walled, 420-meter-long shed than the view of the overcrowded display of machines, which did not match the exceptional versatility the structure offered.

Giedion pointed out that

> the glass end walls do not strictly close up the building: they constitute only a thin transparent membrane between the interior and outer space. And it is not as a building circumscribed within definite limits that the Galerie des Machines is important. The girders in its skeleton could have been either more or less numerous without thereby effecting any distinctive alteration.[91]

Pl. 99 Marcel Breuer and Hamilton Smith, new wing for Cleveland Museum of Art, Cleveland, 1967—71.
The units are modular and tracked for the installation of partitions or lighting.

Pl. 100 The Metropolitan Museum of Art, New York.
A haphazard conglomeration of structures and styles seen from the south side facing the park.
Pl. 101 Kevin Roche and John Dinkeloo, The Metropolitan Museum of Art, New York, 1970, master plan.
The Roche-Dinkeloo master plan of 1970 will return to the first such plan by offering a park entrance from the west side. The park aspect of the Museum will be stressed by two enclosed, year round garden courts attached to the park entrances.

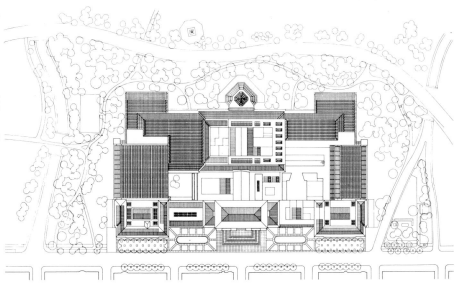

Pl. 102 Kevin Roche and John Dinkeloo, The Metropolitan Museum of Art, The Sackler Wing, 1978.
The glass curtain wall opens the Museum to the park and affords a glimpse of the Temple of Dendur even from the street.

This description could be applied to Mies's Berlin gallery as well.

In the Paris International Exhibition of 1900 designed by Girault, the emphasis was again on "architecture" and not on "engineering." The Grand Palais which replaced the Palais de l'Industrie has monumental walls with large arcades and heavy sculptural ornaments, but the building's interior has an immense open space of dimensions similar to those of the structure it replaced[92]. Since 1900 the building has been used for annual shows of paintings, sculpture, antiques, and so on.

The same kind of flowing space can be found in many later buildings for exhibitions and fairs like the Olympia in London (Pl. 129), although not all the possibilities have been exploited. In his 1932 review of the Annual Building Exhibition, Ian Jeffcott suggested that an architect should be sought to plan the overall design of the exhibition space. Not only the individual pavilions require such professional involvement[93].

The Crystal Palace was criticized in the nineteenth century for being a tent-like structure not a building[94]. Yet tents are still considered suitable for exhibitions. Frei Otto's design, with Rolf Gutbroad, for the West German Pavilion at Expo '67 in Montreal, was a tension net not so dissimilar to a tent. The same applies to the scheme designed by a former associate, Larry Medlin, for an exhibition of photographs and plans of Frei Otto's work at the Museum of Modern Art in 1971. The tension structure for MOMA was developed especially for the Frei Otto exhibition (Pl. 130).

Otto also served as a consultant to the designers of the exhibition structure for "The City of Tomorrow," the International Building Exhibition in the Hansa District, Berlin, 1957. The prestretched roof skin made of resin-impregnated canvas covered two pavilions separated by an open area; the trusses of the roof structure continued through to connect the two halls into a single space[95].

McCormick Place in Chicago also continues the nineteenth century exhibition hall tradition. Designed in 1971 by C.F. Murphy Associates, it has 600,000 square feet of exhibition floor space. It was built in the Miesian spirit, suggesting mainly Mies's unexecuted project of 1953—54 for the Convention Hall in Chicago. The 720 square foot roof shelters a structure free of interior columns, a 'universal space' which can be subdivided and rearranged for different events, like conventions, fairs, and exhibitions. The roof which overhangs all four sides of the hall, the high glass walls, the column-free space, and the platform on which the building is set all recall Mies's Neue Nationalgalerie in Berlin.

b. Museums adapt the new concept.

While it continued to characterize exhibition halls, this concept of flexible space was also applied directly from the Crystal Palace to museums. The South Kensington Museum (formerly the Museum of Manufactures, 1852, later the Art Museum and then the Museum of Ornamental Art), the predecessor of the present Victoria and

Pl. 103 Kevin Roche and John Dinkeloo, The Metropolitan Museum of Art, The Lehman Wing seen from Central Park.

Pl. 104 The Louvre, Paris, the Grand Galerie.

Albert Museum, was founded by the Department of Practical Art, then headed by Henry Cole who had helped organize the Great Exhibition of 1851. This museum was erected in 1857 on a site purchased with profits made in the Great Exhibition. The design for the "Brompton Boilers" as the museum was called, was not the work of an architect or an engineer but of the contractors, D.C. Young and Company, who supplied the columns for Dublin's Crystal Palace. Hitchcock believes that the reason for not employing architects or engineers for the museum was the Crimean War which made monumental construction "difficult or at least unpatriotic."[96]

The Museum included three parallel long galleries, somewhat like the transept of the Crystal Palace with high central nave and upper galleries on both sides of each hall. The cast-iron structure did not frame glass but corrugated iron sheets (hence the name "Brompton Boilers"). The large space defined by simple structural frames provided freedom of display. As in the Crystal Palace, free-standing screens were used to isolate exhibits or helped to focus visitor attention on certain objects.

When a permanent, more monumental, or even palatial building was planned to replace the "Brompton Boilers," each of the naves, instead of being demolished, was offered to North, East and South London as the nucleus of a local museum[97]. Only East London responded and therefore part of the iron structure was transferred to Bethnal Green for a branch of the South Kensington Museum[98]. A more permanent brick frame was planned by Major General Scott and the museum was opened in 1872 (Pls. 131, 132, 133, 134). At its opening the museum exhibited collections transferred from South Kensington as well as Sir Richard Wallace's painting collection. As can be seen in contemporary prints and lithographs the exhibits were displayed on free-standing partitions and in movable display cases (Pl. 131).

The space concept of the Crystal Palace was also applied to the Royal Scottish Museum in Edinburgh, for which funds were first allotted by Parliament in 1854. Prince Albert, the enthusiastic sponsor of both the Crystal Palace and the South Kensington Museum, laid the foundation stone in 1861. The first completed section was opened in 1866, and the original plan was finished in 1888. The space of the central high nave is impressive, but the side galleries are too narrow to provide flexibility (Pl. 135)[99].

Whereas the flexible use of space in the Universal Exhibition was carried on into the twentieth century for fairs and shows, it was applied to museums only in isolated cases in the nineteenth century. When museum staff and designers sought versatility, they had to search in the main outside any existing museum tradition.

c. Other sources of the same idea.
In magazine articles written in the early 1930's and at the International Congress of Museology in Madrid (1934), Clarence Stein argued that a more versatile structure should be developed for the museum of tomorrow. In most museums of his day, the exhibition rooms were divided by immovable masonry walls and the sources of light were fixed. The problems posed by fixed fenestration and the inflexible location of interior walls needed to be overcome, Stein claimed. Recommending that standards of office flexibility be applied to museums, he endorsed the "free plan" advocated by the International Style for museums: "large units of free space, free of all structural or utility impediments such as walls, columns, or pipes."[100] Instead of permanent masonry walls the free plan calls for quickly installed, interchangeable partitions. It should be possible to divide the space and rearrange the display with minimum effort and cost. In addition Stein favored the flexible use of artificial as well as natural light, as has already been discussed.

Ideally the same modules should be used for floor space, windows, light-projectors, partitions, and display cases to allow maximum interchangeability. Partial flexibility can also be obtained in existing museums by using movable or hinged screens, the movable screens being boards set on a heavy stand. The defect of such screens, according to Stein, is that they are "part of the furnishing rather than part of the structure, and they are limited in arrangement."[101] The other type of partition is the hinged screen. Stein was most impressed by the screens in the Hamburg Kunsthalle. Although not part of the structure, they could be arranged in at least four different combinations by swinging them into the desired position[102]. Stein's main objection was that with this system light is admitted at the top and bottom edges of the panels as well as at the screen joints. In other words the screens do not divide the large space into smaller independent space units. In 1932 Stein reported that a new system of interchangeable partitions was about to be put on the market. Made of a steel-stud framework into which sheeting units were set and secured, the

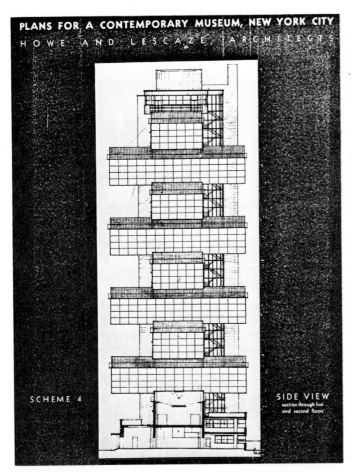

SCHEME 4

SIDE VIEW
section through first
and second floors

SCHEME 6

entire glass front with
alternating strips of
clear and opaque glass

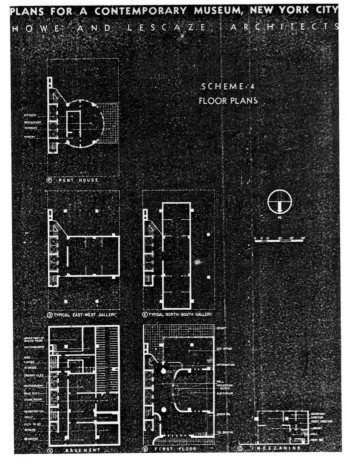

SCHEME 4
FLOOR PLANS

Pl. 105, 106 George Howe and William Lescaze, plans for a Museum of Contemporary Art for New York City, 1930, scheme 4, section and floor plans.

In 1930 Howe and Lescaze prepared six preliminary schemes for a multi-story building for a "Museum of Contemporary Art for New York City" (the Museum of Modern Art). Each one of these schemes offered a different solution to the lighting problem which they saw as the most vital factor in museum design.

Scheme number four which combined top side lighting with skylight was developed in greater detail.

Pl. 107 George Howe and William Lescaze, plans for a Museum of Contemporary Art for New York City, 1930, scheme 6.

In this scheme the facade is entirely made of glass. Externally it suggests the MOMA as built by Goodwin and Stone (Pls. 15, 16). Also similar are the elevator and staircase solution to the circulation problem as well as the penthouse and the restaurant at the top.

partitions could be adjusted according to variations in ceiling height. For complete rigidity they could be drilled into the ceiling and floor.

Built in 1939, the Museum of Modern Art adopted the free plan of the International Style, which it had helped to introduce to the American public in the "Modern Architecture: International Exhibition" of 1932. MOMA applied the principles of office flexibility and subdivided the museum space in ways previously exemplified in private homes like the Schröder house by Rietvelt and in many office buildings and department stores. It is perhaps significant in this respect that MOMA's first headquarters were on the twelfth floor of an office building, the Heckscher Building. This was an open space subdivided into galleries and services, according to the needs of the infant museum. The partitions were from floor to ceiling as advocated by Stein seven years earlier. Such partitions act like permanent walls, except that they can be quickly moved or eliminated (Pl. 16). They not only divide larger spaces into sub-units but also define independent spaces. They are not just "part of the furnishing."

The glass curtain walls for the museum's two long sides fulfill Stein's requirement for a versatile exterior wall. The windows can be relocated, moreover, by placing temporary walls behind those openings not needed to illuminate a specific display.

Edward Durell Stone, who designed the building with Philip Goodwin, wrote that it was the "museum's official concept of open gallery space."[103] It thus answered the requirement "that the gallery space be an open flexible area capable of changes for various kinds of exhibitions."[104]

Partitions used only to subdivide the space can be found in Louis Kahn's first major building, the Yale Art Gallery, in which both the vocabulary and the space concept were influenced by Mies. At Yale the partitions were designed to isolate certain works of art, but not to break the main volume of open continuous space (Pl. 111). Light penetrates from the bottom and top of the partition. The building had to be even more versatile than a normal museum, since it had to serve the Art and Architecture Departments temporarily until Paul Rudolph's Art and Architecture Building could be constructed. Later the museum staff used mainly double partitions which act as flexible walls from floor to ceiling, very much like those at the Museum of Modern Art. These partitions are made of separate side panels with a narrow space in between (Pl. 101).

Interchangeable partitions are now so generally preferred to permanent walls that Roche-Dinkeloo's use of permanent, although non-load-bearing walls in the Oakland Museum is now considered an exception (Pl. 25).

In the 1972 remodelling of the Musée d'Art Moderne de la Ville de Paris, a new dimension of versatility was introduced with the installation of a mobile ceiling[105]. The aluminum ceiling can be raised from $2^1/_4$ meters to more than $5^1/_2$ meters. Partitions can be placed between two ceilings to change the size of exhibition areas. By combining suspended adjustable ceilings with movable partitions, the volume can be controlled both horizontally and vertically. Lowering the ceiling creates an intimate space for small works of art, while raising it to its full height can provide the space needed for large contemporary sculpture.

Another kind of flexibility is exemplified by the Everson Museum of Art, the Hayward Gallery, the Israel Museum, the Whitney Museum of American Art, and the East Wing of the National Gallery, where different display needs are met. Small rooms are provided for drawings, paintings, and sculpture of moderate size, while wide, tall galleries accommodate large scale sculptures and paintings, and carpets. The opinion of Mansfeld and Gad at the Israel Museum was that "instead of creating large anonymous halls which, though theoretically tractable, would forever strain the curator's resources for subdivision and adaptation, we chose to plan a series of interconnected spaces which, by the very fact of being different, would lend themselves to an easy arrangement of exhibits."[106]

Museum exhibition galleries of various sizes were anticipated by the structure for the International Exhibition of 1862, designed by Captain Francis Fowke. As Betty Bradford pointed out on the occasion of the Exhibition's centenary, "Unlike the 1851 Exhibition building it aimed to provide specific conditions suited to the various types of exhibits. This produced a complex group of structures in contrast to the compact, unified design of Paxton."[107] The building of the 1862 Exhibition included skylit galleries designed especially for paintings (the 1851 Exhibition had no art display). These rooms were based on lighting and ventilation experiments for galleries designed by Fowke for the South Kensington Museum (to house the Sheepshanks Collection). The skylit galleries were part of the 'permanent' brick

*P. 108 Louis Kahn, Yale Art Gallery, New
Haven, Connecticut, 1951—54.
Kahn Blocked the front facing the street; glass
screen walls only are used for the back wall
facing the sculpture garden, the narrow side of
the building, and the entrance section which is
set back at right angles to the street facade. As a
result, artificial illumination is the major light
source with natural light fulfilling only a
supplementary role.*

*Pl. 109 Louis Kahn, Yale Art Gallery, New
Haven, 1951—1954, ceiling.
The traditional attic or light mixing chamber
(Pls. 126, 127) has been reduced to a concrete
frame, a few inches deep, which supports a
versatile lighting system. It also contains the
exposed pipes and ducts of the ventilating system.*

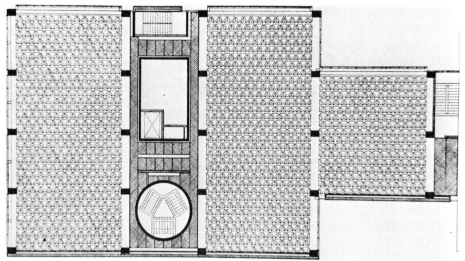

Pl. 110 Louis Kahn, Yale Art Gallery, New Haven, 1951—1954, plan.

Pl. 111 Louis Kahn, Yale Art Gallery, New Haven, 1951—1954, interior.

The partitions were designed to isolate certain works of art, but not to break the main volume of open continuous space. Light penetrates from the bottom and top of the partition which Kahn does not consider as a flexible wall to divide the large space into smaller independent units.

structure intended for future use by the Society of Arts, but unfortunately the building had to be demolished to cover part of the contractor's losses.

This kind of versatility was also suggested by the Universal Exhibition of 1867, in Paris. Here the largest and tallest exhibition hall, the Galerie des Machines, formed the outer concentric ring (Pls. 69, 70).

d. The utopia called utmost flexibility.

It is Mies van der Rohe who most nearly achieved absolute flexibility in the organization of space. By designing a single large space within a functional frame that incorporated natural and artificial light, energy outlets, and air-conditioning, Mies gave the exhibition designer complete freedom. That the display of art preoccupied Mies throughout his career can be seen even in his early work and in his numerous photomontages and drawings (Pl. 136)[108].

For the Barcelona Exhibition of 1929, Mies designed the German Pavilion. The space was defined by its roof slab supported by cruciform columns and the large podium. It was subdivided by opaque and transparent glass panels set in metal mullions and free-standing marble screens. Probably because it was only a temporary building the screens were not intended to be interchangeable, and therefore the space is not completely open and flexible. Yet the horizontals of the travertine elevated base and the thin slab of the roof could theoretically be extended indefinitely: they constitute an impressive forerunner of the Mies space concept which would only be expressed fully nearly four decades later in the Neue Nationalgalerie in Berlin.

In 1942 Mies designed a museum project for a small city (Pl. 137). It offered a free uninterrupted interior space to be defined only by the works of art. Included in his pencil drawing with a collage of the interior were photographs of Maillol sculptures, Picasso's *Guernica,* and a landscape seen through the glass screens against which the works of art are displayed. In this "Museum for a Small City," glass screens would constitute both the external walls and those of the inner court. The columns and roof were to be made of steel; the floor would be paved. Mies described the project in the following words:

> Interior sculptures enjoy an equal spatial freedom, because the open plan permits them to be seen against the surrounding hills. The architectural space thus achieved became a defining space. A work such as Picasso's *Guernica* has been difficult to place in the usual museum gallery. Here it can be shown to the greatest advantage and become an element in space against a changing background.[109]

Mies van der Rohe first demonstrated his concept of flexible space not in a museum but in Crown Hall at the Illinois Institute of Technology (1950–56), in which movable partitions subdivide the space (Pl. 138).

The first museum design Mies carried out was Cullinan Hall, the extension of the Museum of Fine Arts, Houston, Texas (Pl. 87), which he planned in 1958–59. Only at the end of his career did Mies design a complete museum, the Neue Nationalgalerie, Berlin (1962–68) (Pls. 10, 11)[110]. Curiously the museum is directly related to a 1957 project for an open office space. Bacardi Offices at Santiago de Cuba. There the roof and columns were to be of reinforced concrete, a material more readily available than steel in Cuba. The same scheme but in steel was used for the 1960 George Schäfer Museum project for Schweinfurt and at the Neue Nationalgalerie in Berlin.

The upper level of the Neue Nationalgalerie is a large hall for temporary exhibitions. Although the glass-enclosed area, 8.40 meters high, comprises 177 square feet of column-free space, in theory the flat steel roof and the stone paved floor could be extended indefinitely. The lower level conventional space under the concrete podium is used for the regular functions of the museum — the display of the permanent collection, administration, and storage. Unlike the columnless upper floor, the four meter high ceiling of the lower galleries is supported by columns at intervals of 7.20 meters.

Peter Blake, who attended the museum's opening ceremonies in 1968, wrote an enthusiastic review claiming that it is "...the most beautiful building ever created by Ludwig Mies van der Rohe." Unlike Charles Jencks, who felt that "important functions were suppressed and constricted into the basement,"[111] Blake was convinced that:

> Indeed, one of the great surprises in seeing the New National Gallery complete is that the 'basement' — the stuff tucked away in the pedestal — is not just a basement at all: it is full of spacious, beautifully detailed galleries more than 13 feet tall, well lit (regardless of what some of the critics say) and open at one end to a lovely sculpture court.[112]

Commenting on the Berlin Neue Nationalgalerie, Jencks pointed out that "...the same 'perfect' form of a two-way horizontal grid was used indiscriminately for an office project in Cuba, then later on in two different museums... The justification for this repetition was 'that you can do anything you wish in this building' because the form and space were 'universal'."[113] Yet the spaciousness and versatility of the exhibition hall has a very strong functional *raison d'être,* which fits into the manifestly functional tradition of the great international exhibitions which started with the Crystal Palace. For this hall does allow enormous variety in display and is enclosed by a glass wall which could be extended indefinitely. That Mies must have been familiar with this type of structure is indicated by his Country House for a Bachelor, shown in the 1931 Berlin Building Exhibition and located in the center of just such a great exhibition hall[114].

The idea of a free flowing space in which the works of art define the space also goes back to Kiesler's brilliant statement of 1924, the Cité dans l'Espace. The Cité exploited Elementarist ideas of space, although Kiesler's open infinite space was based on esthetic rather than functional considerations.

In an illuminating article on gallery space entitled "Inside the White Cube," Brian O'Doherty wrote that the history of modernism is intimately framed by the gallery space. "We have now reached a point where we see not art but the space first. An image comes to mind of a white, ideal space that more than any single picture may be the archetypal image of 20th century art."[115]

The single flowing space framed only by its functional frame challenges the exhibition designer; it leaves the planning of the display arrangements completely in his hands without any assistance from the architect. Genuinely and consistently imaginative display designers and curators with large enough budgets to plan varied installations should be able to thrive in such a setting.

In recent years, however, it has become evident that utmost flexibility is an utopia.

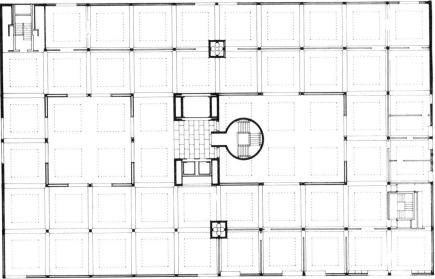

Pls. 113, 114 Louis Kahn, completed after his death, March 17, 1974, by Pellecchia and Meyers, Yale Center for British Art, New Haven, 1969—1977.

The cost of achieving such versatility is so high that it cannot justify the freedom gained. It is easier and cheaper to design a building according to present day needs than to strive for a completely flexible space. The building might not suit future needs, but at least it can serve present day requirements satisfactorily.

The retreat from complete flexibility is for both practical and esthetic reasons. Glass screen walls, for example, raise some difficulties since there are no external surfaces on which to hang the pictures. Although Mies devised a non-glare glass and a projecting roof for the Neue Nationalgalerie. natural light is difficult to control, and curtains made of thin light-gray fabric had to be added to afford protection against sunlight and ultra-violet rays[116]. Alternatively, these glazed walls or part of them can be covered by partitions from floor to ceiling whenever the exhibition designer wishes.

Immense seemingly boundless space also poses difficulties for exhibition

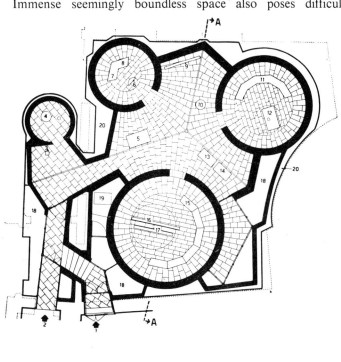

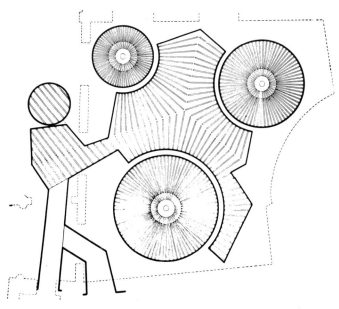

Pls. 115, 116 Francesco Albini, The Museum of the Treasury, San Lorenzo Cathedral, Genoa, 1956.
115. Ground floor plan and plan of roof covering.
116. Section.

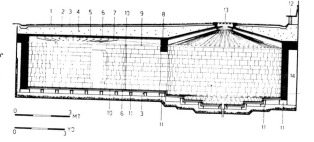

Pls. 117, 118 Philip Johnson, Art Gallery, Glass House Estate, New Canaan, Conn., 1966. Believing that natural light is unsuitable for exhibiting paintings, Johnson has designed his many museums accordingly. The art gallery in New Canaan is not an underground building, but a structure erected above-ground and then covered with earth so as not to change drastically the view from the Glass House.

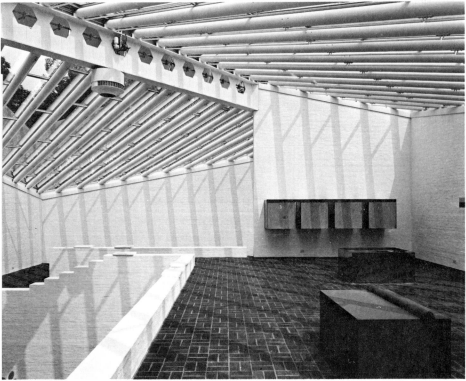

Pls. 119, 120 Philip Johnson, Sculpture Gallery,
Glass House Estate, New Canaan, Conn., 1970.
The sculpture gallery was the antithesis,the
negative of the art gallery. The semi-mirrored
glass roof provides natural light, while the glass
frames of the roof cast strong shadows on the
sculpture. Instead of covering the building with
earth and green grass, Johnson had this
structure whitewashed.

Pl. 121 Carlo Bassi and Geoffredo Boschetti, The Gallery of Modern Art, Turin, 1954–1959.
In the design of the museum, the introduction of natural light seems to be the starting point. To provide zenith lighting for the two exhibition floors of the permanent collection, the walls of the superposed galleries were places at an awkward angle: the walls of the first floor incline inward, while the upper walls incline outwards (see also Pl. 122).
The manneristic result is hardly justifiable on functional grounds. In this case, the introduction of natural light has distorted the building in an unprecedented, almost a grotesque way.

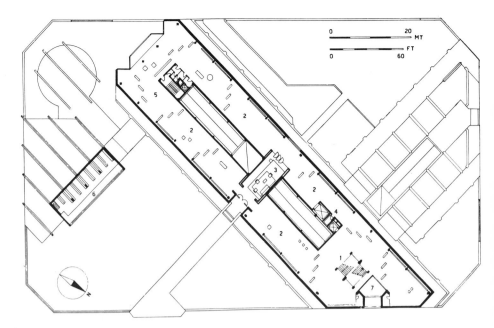

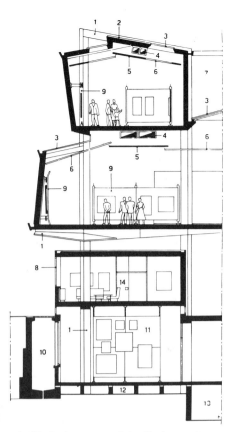

Pl. 122 Carlo Bassi and Geoffredo Boschetti, The Gallery of Modern Art, Turin, semi-cross-section through permanent exhibition building and second floor plan.

Pl. 123 Carlo Bassi and Geoffredo Boschetti, The Gallery of Modern Art, Turin. An exhibition hall on the second floor.
Special display panels of wood with iron support were built for the pictures which are hung on metal wires, so that they seem to float uncomfortably in the air. The rest of the collection is attached to temporary screens. Hardly any picture is displayed against a "conventional" straight wall.

designers. In 1977 Walter Kuhn designed special installation frames and partitions to subdivide the universal space of the Neue Nationalgalerie. Small partitions divide the loft space into small cubicles. This new arrangement perhaps makes it easier to display art, but the unique qualities of the large flowing space have disappeared.

The exterior of Philip Johnson's Museum of the Munson-Proctor-Williams Institute at Utica, New York (1957–60) clearly derives from Mies: notably the cube form and the external structural supports (Pl. 139). However, the transformation of the glass screen wall into a solid curtain at the upper level and the retention of the glass curtain wall at the ground level depart from Mies's concept (Pl. 140). The blocked, self-contained upper floor and the open lower floor seem in fact to be an inverted version of the Neue Nationalgalerie, as the interior dramatically illustrates. Instead of Mies's free uninterrupted space, Johnson designed long, narrow galleries, artificially lit (Pls. 141, 142), and a large top-lit, almost empty, two-level court (Pl. 143)[117].

The 7.5 meter high tube space of Sainsbury Center's "well serviced shed" is divided by the most ordinary partitions (Pls. 144, 145). Leo Krier criticized the appropriateness of large span sheds for virtually any situation as a false myth. "Foster is forcing us to eat soup with a fork and with a very well designed fork at that," he commented[118].

Peter Cook's criticism is that "...we have to be reminded iconographically of the joy of technology." He has serious doubts whether this technological shed can be flexible, whether the apparatus can be reinterpreted and moved. "One has the suspicion that this building remains more of a monumental than a dynamic shed." Cook believes that Sainsbury Center for the Visual Arts "...is not yet the ultimate cool tube. But it comes tantalizingly close to being so."[119]

Piano and Rogers's design for the Centre Pompidou (1971–77) is a most appropriate symbol of the machine age, a monument to transition (Pls. 188–194). Reyner Banham interprets the Centre Pompidou as a facility ("building is not the word for it"), based on Futurist ideas of the impermanence of technology. He evaluates this Centre as the apotheosis of the Archigram and the megastructure idea. According to Banham, "...impermanence, in the sense of adaptability, applies to everything except the most massive members of the structure."[120] The external multi-colored pipes, the transparent walls, the escalators and elevators leave the gallery space completely free. The span between facades is 45 meters; beyond this free span the structure is extended to 60 meters to include the walkways and service area. The color code of the external service systems (red for the transportation system, blue for the air-conditioning system, yellow for the electrical system and green for the water system), were not continued inside the galleries due to the objections of the museum director. He believed that it would distract the visitors' attention from the works of art. As a result the color code lost, to some extent, its functional justification. It is quite surprising to learn that the special installation design with the small partitions and false ceiling artificially create a space which closely resembles that which the museum of modern art in Paris had in its former building. It is the same kind of white, clean and artificial space which Brian O'Doherty described in his essay on the gallery space[121].

An interesting final indication of the importance of the nineteenth century exhibition hall tradition in the creation of flexible museum space is that the last buildings of Le Corbusier (the Centre Le Corbusier in Zurich; 1964—68)[122] and Mies van der Rohe (the Neue Nationalgalerie in Berlin; 1962—68), as well as Piano and Rogers's Centre Pompidou (1972—77) and Foster Associates' Sainsbury Center in Norwich (1974—77), are all pre-fabricated metal structures with steel substituted for the iron of the Crystal Palace (Pl. 146). These structures are supported from the outside and all four create largely free interior space. Although they vary in style and in scale, they share an emphasis on versatility. They are manifestly the modern heirs to Paxton's great glass hall.

Pl. 126 The National Gallery, Washsington, 1937–1941, the attic of the skylit galleries.
The traditional attic or light mixing chamber dictates a low building with one or two stories for
display. The other functions of the museum are confined to the basement.
Pl. 127 The Frick Collection, New York, 1935, control board for all year air-conditioning.
Complete air-conditioning with winter heating, summer cooling year round.

Chapter IV.
The formal aspect of museum design

To our discussion of the social role of the modern museum and the functional requirements its structure ought to fulfill must now be added a consideration of its formal design. How is form to be related to function in the modern museum?

1. Form versus function.

The dominant traditional view of museum form always saw it as expressing certain values. Historical styles borrowed from other kinds of institutions — the Classical temple, Renaissance palace, or Medieval church — long remained the fixed models for museum design. The vast majority of museum buildings constructed early in the twentieth century took the form of Neo-classical temples (Pl. 147). In Ada Louise Huxtable's words, the first museum explosion "took place just before, at, and after the turn of the century, stamping every major city with the classical culture symbol of the great colonnaded monument that served art, science and the general public with consummate architectural cool."[1]

As late as the turn of the century few museums were being built in contemporary style (at that time Art Nouveau). A notable exception is van de Velde's Folkwang Museum in Hagen, 1902. C. Harrison Townsend's museums — the Whitechapel Art Gallery, 1897—1901, and the Horniman Museum, 1900—01 — although vaguely historical, also approach Art Nouveau style[2] (Pls. 148, 149).

Only in the mid-1930's did the trend shift, as museum planners began to adopt a building style drawn from other branches of architecture. e.g. the Gemeente Museum, 1935, and the Rijksmuseum Kröller-Müller, 1938 (Pls. 150, 151, 152). In 1939 the Museum of Modern Art in New York was built in the most advanced style of its time — the International Style (Pl. 15). From then on, new expressive museum forms were created, as museums were built to answer specific needs. The structures reflected the particular character, place, and function of the museum. And to achieve these ends, new materials and construction methods were employed.

Pl. 128 Paxton with Fox and Henderson, Crystal Palace, London, 1951.

a. Two main approaches.

Two main approaches to museum design can be recognized. The first sees the museum as the ultimate display object. Thus, designing a museum challenges the architect to express his own originality as form-giver. The museum in itself becomes an impressive, although not necessarily monumental, work of art. The opposing attitude views the museum building strictly as a functional frame, neutral in itself. Such an architectural frame offers no competition to the exhibited objects.

At the International Congress of Art Museums held in Madrid in 1934, this question was raised:

> L'architecture doit-il décorer le musée? Doit-il se concevoir comme une oeuvre d'art indépendent de celle qu'il renferme ou bien comme une simple 'machine' à exposer des objets? Jusqu'à la fin du XIXe siècle, on l'a dit, la première conception l'a emporté. Quelque théoriciens sont aujourd'hui partisans de la seconde.[3]

If at the Madrid conference the "simple 'machine' à exposer des objets" was not more than an idea put forward by a few theoreticians, a few years later it became an actual design trend. The 1939 MOMA building provided a space which was both flexible and neutral (Pl. 15). Three years later Mies designed his unbuilt project for the Museum of a Small City (Pl. 137); and later his ideas on flexible museum space were partially realized in extensions to the Museum of Fine Arts, Houston (Pl. 87) and at the Neue Nationalgalerie, Berlin (Pl. 89).

Once the demand for an expressive form disappears, the result may be no form at all. The extension to the Stedelijk Museum in Amsterdam (1954) can serve as an early example of a well-lit warehouse (Pl. 155). In contrast to the stately Rijksmuseum and the Concertgebouw buildings nearby, the new wing of the Stedelijk is flexible but "formless."

The stress is strictly on functionality. The two story building is entirely side lit. Venetian blinds modulate the intensity of light while direct daylight is shut out. Additional illumination is provided by fluorescent lamps located parallel to the windows and by light reflection projectors mounted on metal columns. Although originally intended to house temporary exhibitions, the extension was readily adapted to display mainly the permanent collection. The photograph of one of its exhibition halls with the *Guernica* would seem to manifest its versatility[4]. At the same time, however, hardly any attention was given to its exterior or interior appearance, so that the main attribute of the annex is its very formlessness.

Interior design was also debated at the Madrid conference. One approach would eliminate all ornamentation while the second adapts the decor to the character of the collection[5]. While Dorner in his atmosphere rooms at the Landesmuseum, Hanover, tried to adapt the background to reflect the character of different periods, from medieval to contemporary art, other museums in the nineteen-thirties, e.g. Gemeente, Boymans, Kröller-Müller (Pl. 152) eliminated all background decoration and ornament[6]. For example, the Albini renovation of the Palazzo Bianco Museum following the Second World War freed the paintings and sculptures from any

118

Pl. 129 The Ideal Home Exhibition, 1973, Olympia, London.
The structure of the Great Exhibition of 1851 had an immense impact on exhibition halls and fairs throughout the nineteenth and twentieth centuries. The same kind of flowing space can be found in the Grand Palais in Paris and the Olympia in London.
Pl. 130 Larry Madelin in consultation with Frei Otto, The Museum of Modern Art, New York, Frei Otto Exhibition, 1971.
A contemporary criticism of Crystal Palace was that Paxton produced a tentlike structure, not a building. The design for an exhibition of photographs and plans of Frei Otto's work at the MOMA was a tension net recalling a tent.

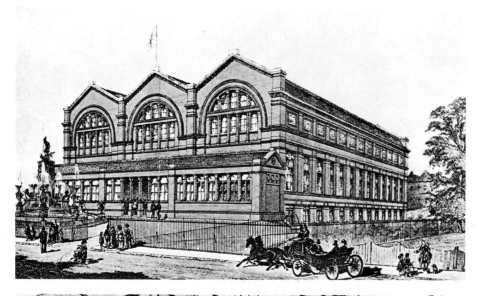

relation to the background. The walls were painted white, and some of the paintings were even displayed entirely without frames. Here the white walls serve as a luminous background[7].

The museums designed by Le Corbusier, from the project of 1931 to the museums of Ahmedabad, Tokyo and Chandigarh, are further examples in which the external form of the museum is fixed by functional rather than formal considerations. Although preplanned expansion and circulation schemes — and not considerations of flexibility — determine the external appearance of Le Corbusier's museums, the starting point for the designs is still the functional aspect; form has only a supplementary role. Le Corbusier's museums are raised cubes, like Mies van der Rohe's Neue Nationalgalerie in Berlin. But whereas with Le Corbusier the box shape is uplifted by piloti, for Mies it is elevated by a more traditional podium. In Le Corbusier's museums the exterior wall is only a temporary facade destined to become an interior surface when another spiral is added and a new external wall (temporary facade) created. In Mies's design the undivided space is enclosed by glass screens, but the columns supporting the cantilevered roof, the 'entablature,' and coffered ceiling echo a long historical tradition of museum design. They create a monumental and noble structure, and not merely a neutral, anonymous, space frame.

According to C. Ray Smith, only in a late phase of designing a museum

> ...an architect comes to a consideration of what the exterior of his project will look like. Traditionally the word "museum" has conjured up an image of monumentality — justly since they are prestige treasure houses that express the pride of communities. Here obviously the architect has a free hand and in the facility of their vision, architects have recently designed museums not only as monuments

and monumental sculptures, but also turning the tables as non-monuments as invisible non buildings. What exhibition designers warn against is turning the tables so completely that a non-monument also becomes non-humble on the interior. That, they feel, is central to the museum as a museum.[8]

Smith quotes the architect Bernardo as saying, "A museum can be monument on the outside but it should be humble on the inside." This "is the only way that the exhibition rather than the building can be the star."

A few years earlier Michael Brawne expressed a different opinion. He found two strongly disparate theories. "According to the first concept the museum itself constitutes a work of art actively contributing to the communication between the viewer and the art objects for which it presents a dramatic setting." The second idea is that the museum is a neutral entity which should "withdraw as much as possible so that nothing will distract the visitor's attention from the exhibits."[9]

Since Brawne believes that the communication between visitors and objects is the most important element in museum design ("it is what distinguishes it from other building types"), he rejects limitless versatility and undifferentiated space,

> since it rests on two profound misconceptions of art and architecture. The first assumes that there is a kind of competition between art and environment, and that unless this environment is completely negated the work on display will be crushed; the second, which is a corollary of the first, suggests that each work has such a degree of independence that it can be shown anywhere, that it is entirely free from its background. Both assumptions are abstract notions unrelated to the actual process of viewing and the total experience of visiting a museum. Neither art nor architecture is anonymous.[10]

A sense of uniqueness is one of the distinguishing characteristics of art and architecture. It is "...not a matter of competition between art and its environment, between picture and architecture, in which one or another aspect has to be negated, but of arriving at a working relationship between the two." Brawne points to the Italian museums as an example. As in a concert performance, he notes,

> museum display, apart from the quality of the objects, is more than a case of correct background or balanced illumination. It is again the totality of the experience which becomes an event in its own right with this totality; architecture, as space manipulation must of necessity assume a positive function... To aim at an environment of nothingness is to abnegate architectural responsibility.[11]

b. Frank Lloyd Wright at the Guggenheim.
Perhaps the most prominent museum building in which form is alleged to overpower function is Frank Lloyd Wright's Guggenheim Museum (Pls. 156—165), originally designed to house the collection of the Museum of Non-Objective Painting. In an article entitled "What Wright Hath Wrought", Lewis Mumford accepted that "...as an external symbol of contemporary abstract art this building has genuine fitness in its severe rationality of form" (Pl. 156), "but architecture is not simple sculpture and this building was meant also to serve a museum." According to Mumford, "If the purpose of the museum is solely to exhibit Wright the interior has magnificent justification for its existence." Mumford felt that in a museum the works of art should impose their needs. "But Wright never has a place for the painter in any of his buildings, and it was perhaps too much to hope that there would be a place for him even in an art museum."[12]

Peter Blake argued that the Guggenheim Museum is almost impossible as a museum

> The Guggenheim Foundation got a fabulous piece of architectural sculpture — the only completed work of uncompromising plasticity and continuity achieved by Wright — and should now make plans to build a place in which to show its paintings.[13]

In fact the Guggenheim's strong sculptural shape has even inspired the work of several artists. Richard Hamilton's many drawings, reliefs, and prints based on the Guggenheim shape were acquired by the museum and when on display, the "Guggenheims within the Guggenheim" remind visitors of the work of art in which they circulate. Also on exhibit is a painting of the Guggenheim by Richard Estes (Pl. 166).

While most critics praise the Guggenheim Museum's formal success, they generally consider it to be functionally inadequate. Yet the Guggenheim has proved to be both workable and functional. It should be clear by now that a powerful form does not necessarily result in an unsuccessful museum. The Guggenheim Museum offers an arresting solution to the circulation problem, clearly reduces museum fatigue[14], and in practice its interior does not overpower the exhibits. Visitors who come to the Museum frequently become familiar with its form and find it easier to direct their

Pls. 133, 134 Bethnal Green Museum, London.
The large space defined by simple structural frames provided freedom of display. As in the Crystal Palace, free-standing screens were used to isolate exhibits or helped to focus visitors' attention on certain objects.

attention to the exhibits. Moreover, visitors have to choose between contemplating the inner space or concentrating on a particular work of art; they cannot experience both views simultaneously. And, finally, the interior walls become irrelevant to a three-dimensional work of art exhibited in the central space unlike the situation in most rectangular galleries.

Mumford, on the one hand, believes that "...in the state Wright left the museum, it was magnificent but unusable and the very worst service James Johnson Sweeney, its director, could have done Wright's reputation would have been to open the museum without making any changes."[15] Vincent Scully, Jr., on the other hand, feels that "...once the design was accepted as a museum, it may be that the authorities would have been well advised to follow Wright's intentions to the letter."[16] Edgar Kaufmann Jr., points out that modifications and misunderstanding in the final execution of building caused many of its defects.

The building has been criticized for being inflexible, for affording exhibition space of unalterable dimensions, for lacking sufficient storage space, for raising difficulties of display against the tilted, backward curving wall, and for seeming to fix a set level of light intensity. In other words, the museum, however beautiful, was attacked for being unworkable.

Yet the Guggenheim was not originally intended to house changing exhibitions or to cater to a variety of tastes. As its original name, the Solomon Guggenheim Museum of Non-Objective Painting, implies, the collection was to be of limited range focussing on a particular movement of modern art, abstract art. Wright had a detailed list of the objects in the collection and made his design with this limitation in mind. The requirements changed after the death of Solomon Guggenheim in 1949 and the departure of the directress, Baroness Hilla Rebay, in 1952[17]. The building then had to serve temporary exhibitions of modern and contemporary art instead of a permanent collection.

To adapt the Museum to its changed purpose, Wright in fact proposed to construct an apartment and office building next door in which the lower floors would provide additional storage space, offices, and possibly a gallery in more conventional, rectangular rooms[18]. But in the end only a small annex was built for storage and a conservation department.

Although the dimensions of the display space are fixed, several exhibitions can be shown simultaneously. Should a visitor wish to see only one of the displays he can take the elevator to the appropriate level, follow the ramp down or return by elevator or the nearby staircase. By reversing the flow of the ramp near the elevator shaft and staircase, Wright made the spiral more dramatic. As Laundis Gores, the Connecticut architect, observed, "...a lesser man would have made the spiral a continuous, uninterrupted corkscrew. Such a scheme would have been boring as well as confusing, for it would lack points of reference that would give a visitor a chance to orient himself."[19]

The building forces the exhibition designer and curator to arrange the display according to vertical as well as horizontal considerations, since the visitor can observe a large portion of the spiral at any one time (Pl. 164). Difficult problems are also raised by the curved walls of the expanding spiral. Wright had intended to hang the paintings against the highly sloping walls. Indeed the Guggenheim was already famous for the unorthodox display methods used at its former premises — there the paintings were hung extremely low, much closer to the floor than to the ceiling, and later they were even exhibited without frames. Nonetheless, Wright's intentions were unacceptable to the director. Sweeney used projecting rods behind the paintings to locate them further away from the ribbon window and bring them closer to the viewer. The display angle did not follow the five degree backward slope of the curved wall, but was set perpendicular to the earth. As a result, the frameless picture seemed to float freely and the intensively lit wall became the frame for the paintings. Sweeney's successor as museum director (1961), Thomas M. Messer, also hung the paintings perpendicularly, but preferred to place them closer to the wall, a sort of compromise between Wright's intention and the display method used by Sweeney (Pls. 162, 163).

At the same time the Museum does lack sufficient changes of light and space. Originally light was to be reflected from the slab windows to supplement the general top lighting. Lights from the top of the temporary screens and concrete partitions could help focus visitor attention on certain aspects or specific works of art. As can be learned from Wright's drawings, he intended to use movable partitions for the smaller works of art, mainly on the upper part of the ramp, and circular seats were

Pl. 135 Royal Scottish Museum, Edinburgh, 1861–1888, opened 1866. Photographed after the recent modernization of the museum by the Department of the Environment with Stephen Buzas and Alan Irvine.
Another example where the space concept of the Crystal Palace has been applied to museums. The space of the central high nave is very impressive, but the side galleries are too narrow to provide flexibility.
Pl. 136 Mies van der Rohe, Row House with Interior Court, 1931. Pencil and cut-out reproductions (Wilhelm Lehmbruck Standing Figure 1910 and a painting) on illus. board. 30 × 40". (Collection, the Museum of Modern Art, New York).
The display of art preoccupied Mies throughout his career as can be seen in his photomontages and drawings for private houses as well as public halls.
Pl. 137 Mies van der Rohe, a project for a Museum for a Small City, 1942. Idea for an exhibition of Picasso's Guernica *(Collection, the Museum of Modern Art, New York).*
Mies's design offered a free uninterrupted interior in which the works of art define the space.
Pl. 138 Mies van der Rohe, Crown Hall, Illinois, Institute of Technology, Chicago, 1950–1956. Movable partitions define the flowing space.

to be placed in different part of the spirals. Had these means been adopted, they would have prevented the present monotony of illumination.

The lighting system was changed by the director, James Johnson Sweeney, with the help of the engineer, Alfred Binder. They applied a system of back illumination that diffuses the natural light from the narrow ribbon windows and supplements it with fluorescent light. In addition strong front lighting from the ramp ceiling is focussed directly on the pictures. To eliminate shadows Sweeney markedly increased the light intensity, but in doing so was criticized for creating a glare. Later the illumination level was reduced but kept uniform.

Wright and Sweeney also disagreed as to the color of the interior. The architect intended to have it painted in buff white, but the director preferred the whitewash of International Style artist studios and galleries[21]. The Trustees' compromise was to paint the structural parts in buff white (the same color used for the exterior), and to leave the exhibition area to the discretion of the director. In each spiral the white paint used for the walls changes to a warmer hue. The director probably wanted conditions similar to those the Museum had enjoyed in its former building. When Sweeney oversaw the reconditioning of the Museum's former quarters, a six-story mansion on the future site of Wright's building, the draperies were taken down and the walls painted pristine white; the large golden picture frames were removed[22]. A large heavy frame serves as a transitional area between the painting and its background, which helps to disassociate it from its environment. Once the background is neutral there is no need for the frame[23]. The system of front lighting, masked by long straight gallery shades, is very similar to what had been used at the Museum of Non-Objective Painting[24]. It is, moreover, insensitive to the round shape of the building, straight tubes having been used instead of round or curved fluorescent lights, allegedly due to the latter's high cost.

The exterior color and texture of the Guggenheim have also been criticized.

Mumford objected to the smooth concrete exterior since cracks were found to show from the beginning. In addition, he claimed that such a surface lacks character. In fact, the appearance of the exterior was one of the most important sacrifices imposed on Wright for lack of funds. He sought a richer texture and considered adopting a white marble surface or alternatively a marble dust covering which would be cheaper and easier to apply. In the end Wright decided, however, to use color, on the assumption that the execution would be satisfactory, which indeed it was not; the result is a very crude exterior. The latex paint shows every possible disadvantage. According to one explanation, Wright accepted the results only because he could not see details in his old age and failed to realize how unsatisfactory the execution actually was.

A bigger sacrifice, perhaps, was the interior dome designed with plastic tubes, disallowed because of fire regulations. Instead of the inner dome, Wright added a pattern of glazing bars to the executed dome. Early designs called for dividing the dome into circles, similar to the pattern at the Johnson Wax Building. According to Peter Blake, this concept also had to be abandoned due to its cost[25]. Either of these designs, it appears, would have heightened the unity of the central space. Even so, the main space is quite successful in my view and substantially corresponds to what Wright had in mind. It is cetainly one of the most impressive spaces of the twentieth century.

The last argument against the Guggenheim to be discussed here is that Wright "...turned his back on that open landscape and the varied natural light that were his for the asking."[26] As a matter of fact, Wright did design a large window at the

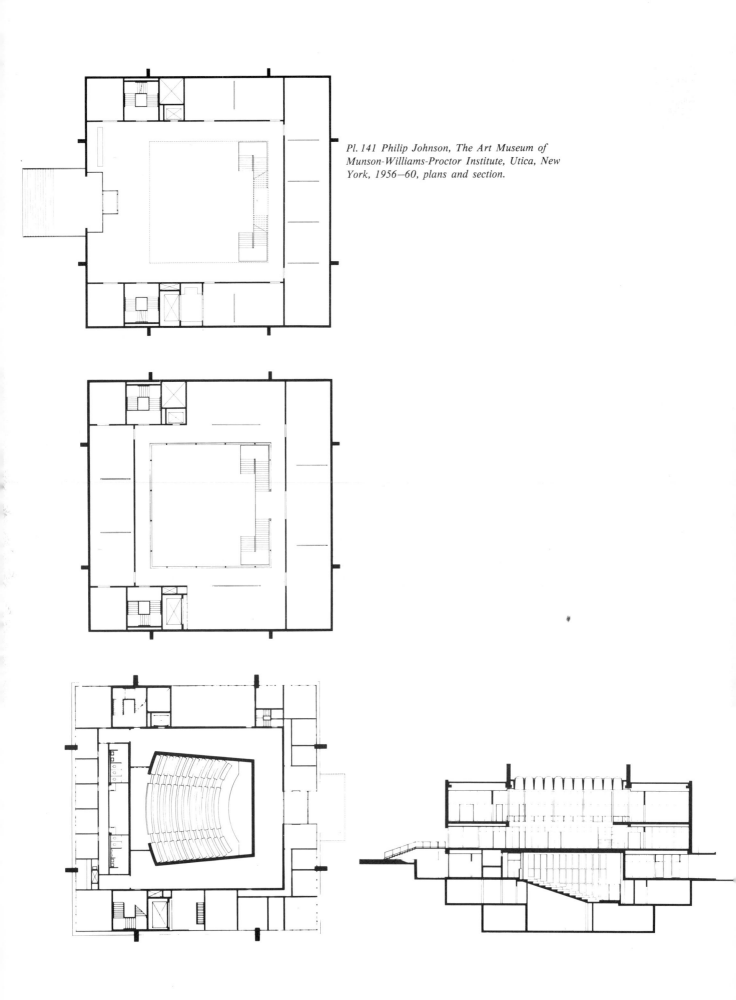

Pl. 141 Philip Johnson, The Art Museum of Munson-Williams-Proctor Institute, Utica, New York, 1956—60, plans and section.

Pl. 142 Philip Johnson, The Art Museum of Munson-Williams-Proctor Institute, Utica, New York, 1956–1960.
Instead of Mies's free uninterrupted space, Johnson designed long narrow galleries artificially lit and a large, toplit, almost empty, two-level court.

ground level which opens the main space to Fifth Avenue and Central Park (Pl. 158). As such, the Museum deviates from other monumental, single-space buildings by Wright, such as the Larkin Building (1904), Unity Church (1906), or the S.C. Johnson and Son Administration building (1936—39), where skylight and clerestory windows are the only sources of natural light and the outside world cannot be seen from the inside.

Other museums in which form seems to take precedence over function are the Shrine of the Book by Kiesler and Bartos with its white dome "floating" on a water-pool and set against a non-functional black wall (Pl. 11), and the Hayward Gallery. The *Architect's Journal* expressed reservations as to the latter's fortress-like character and serene and inflexible architecture. The Hayward Gallery

> ...follows the architectural style previously adopted for Queen Elizabeth Hall and the Purcell Room... in the case of the concert halls this architectural vocabulary has resulted in a relatively simple block, but for the Hayward Gallery, which lacks any large central element to hold the composition together, the result is a confusing arrangement of facades all heavily molded and overlaid with a bewildering arrangement of ducts and terraces. When seen from a distance these terraces, staircases and ventilators pile up in a disorderly rather than a picturesque confusion.[27] (Pls. 167, 168, 169).

One of the project's architects, Norman Engleback, justified the Gallery's strong expressive character on the grounds of its particular location "...in the context of this important reach of the river against Waterloo Bridge and in the foreground of the more dominant Shell office buildings, this was the power and handling necessary to achieve a significant contribution to the whole..."[28] Intended for sculpture display, the "trays" add perhaps to the general form of the building, but they are rarely used due to strong winds.

An extreme example of formal emphasis is the Denver Art Museum, designed by James Sudler Associates and Gio Ponti (1972). Although no openings were required by the Museum's director, windows of various sizes and shapes were introduced. In the upper part of the building the openings were left unglazed and grey tiles used to create intriguing patterns where there are no decorative windows. The free standing, self-contained museum seems to suggest a medieval structure[29].

c. The counterattack.

Another observation on the formal and functional trends in museum design was made by the architectural critic, Ada Louise Huxtable. In her highly polemical review of the 1968 MOMA exhibition, "Architecture of Museums," she wrote that "...all the museums included in the show" (e.g. Whitney, Oakland, Guggenheim, Israel Museum, Neue Nationalgalerie Berlin, Everson) "are also architecture. It is quite a well known fact," she added, "that most museum directors do not want architecture although the examples shown indicate that a good number of them get it." According to Huxtable, "There is a perpetual tug of war between directors and architects with the director asking for a faceless and flexible space with all the specific character of a factory and the architect bent on producing an *objet d'art* that shoves the other art works into the wings."[30]

Views expressed by museum staff and other experts lend support to Huxtable's observation. They have observed:

> Monumental museums have had their day. The modern solution is a framework costing as little as possible with maximum flexibility of space arrangements. This framework must offer the facilities (e.g. electricity, stereo systems, gas, fire) necessary for artists and other collaborators to implement all their projects. How many projects still cannot be organized today because of inadequate power supplies? Activities should also spill over outside the museum. This is purely a matter of organization. The erection of a new museum calls for a detailed program of action rather than specialized architecture. If we hope to fire the interest of our visitors and turn shepherd girls into princesses we have no need for a monument in honour of the architect, the collection and the government which has dipped into its pocket.[31]

But even if museum directors may in many cases aim at a neutral flexible space, often it is the architect himself who thinks in these terms and for whom such a space constitutes both a functional and formal ideal. Mies's Neue Nationalgalerie in Berlin and Barnes's Walker Art Center in Minneapolis are cases in point: flexible spaces which reflect the architect's convictions. In building the Walker Art Center (1971), Barnes was trying to achieve

> ...architecture that does not compete with art — to put the priorities in the right order. We want the visitor to remember painting in space, sculpture against sky and a sense of continuous flow. It is flow more than form that has concerned us.

Pl. 143 Philip Johnson, The Art Museum of Munson-Williams-Proctor Institute, Utica, New York, 1956—1960, central court. Johnson does not see the central court as a sculpture court. Intended mainly for architectural effect, it serves as an orientation device, allows the visitors to "breathe' and provides Utica with public space for communal activities, "since the cathedrals were gone."

131

Pls. 144, 145 Foster Associates, Sainsbury Center for the Visual Arts, University of East Anglia, Norwich, 1974–1977.
Pl. 146 Le Corbusier, Centre Le Corbusier, Zurich, 1963–1967.

The sequence of space must be seductive. There must be a subtle sense of going somewhere, like a river. At the same time the architecture must be relatively uneventful and anonymous.[32] (Pl. 77)

The floors, walls, and ceiling of the Center were painted white to provide a light-reflecting, but essentially neutral environment for exhibiting contemporary art. In Barnes's opinion, "A museum is not a temple to donors, or a monument to the architect, or a security vault — in short, it is not a thing unto itself. It is part of the fabric of daily life, sharing urban benefits and problems with its neighbors."

Here Barnes may have been referring indirectly to the Guggenheim which was criticized for being a monument to the architect, serving "as a cenotaph for himself as a creative individual,"[33] or, in Mumford's ironic phrasing, "...the interior says Ego, an ego far deeper than the pool in which Narcissus too long gazed."[34]

Yet Barnes did not hesitate to follow the Guggenheim's circulation plan. He termed the spiral solution "the generating idea behind the design." It "provides sequential flow from the lobby to the roof whether going up or down. At the same time direct access to individual galleries is possible by using the elevator or core stairs. The circulation system is the armature of the building," (Pl. 77). Yet the very same "sense of continuous flow" is what Wright had in mind. His spiral provided this sense of "going somewhere" which Barnes sought. The main difference stems from Barnes's demand that "the architecture must be uneventful and anonymous."

2. Synthesizing flexible space and expressive form.

Only in the last few years can one observe in several museums a synthesis of flexible space with expressive form.

133

Pl. 147 Horace Trumbauer, C.L. Borie and C.C. Zantzinger, The Philadelphia Museum of Art, 1919—1928.
The vast majority of museum buildings in the early part of the twentieth century were in the form of Neo-calssical temples.

a. The Whitney, a square Guggenheim.

The Whitney Museum continues the MOMA functional tradition of flexible space and display, developing it to answer the most recent demands. Like the Museum of Modern Art, it provides contact with the street by opening the lobby and lower sculpture gallery through a glass curtain wall (Pl. 18). The sculpture court alongside Madison Avenue as well as the canopy also relate the museum to the street (Pls. 170, 171, 172). Breuer and Hamilton provided two kinds of spaces: smaller, more intimate rooms for the permanent exhibitions on the side facing 75th Street and large open spaces for temporary shows next to them, on the three gallery floors. Unlike MOMA the Whitney offers galleries of different sizes and heights: a small room on ground level and three upper display floors which grow in height and length as the museum rises. The length increases from 102 feet on the second floor, to 108 on the third, to 118 on the fourth level. The second and third floors are 12 feet 9 inches high, while the fourth floor's clear height is 17 feet 6 inches (Pl. 176). Without covering the sculpture court with shadows, the cantilevered upper floors afford maximum gallery space and give the museum its unique silhouette (Pl. 175).

Large floor-to-ceiling panels subdivide the tall galleries. The partition system is related to the suspended ceiling grid of precast, lightweight, concrete coffers. These concrete blocks conceal pipes and ducts, air grills, and sprayed acoustical material, as well as the indirect low level general illumination. The grid provides a two foot module which coordinates the panel with the lighting fixture. Lighter and less sculptural than the functional ceiling at Yale Art Gallery, the Whitney's ceiling grid is therefore less distracting. In contrast to Kahn's design, the ceiling grid is not part of the structural frame; it is suspended from the structure above, so as to float free of the permanent enclosing walls. To provide a large uninterrupted flexible space, the elevators and stairwell are located at the side of the building as in the Museum of Modern Art instead of in a central utility core which would cut the space into two separate halves as at Yale (Pl. 110).

The architects sought a neutral, but not a sterile background, and preferred to subordinate the gallery space to the paintings and sculptures on display.

In presenting the project in 1963, Breuer commented

> It seems that large open gallery spaces with interchangeable partitions have to be watched, otherwise the general impression will be too clinical, too remote from the role of art in our society, or in our building, in our spaces not necessarily specialized to showing art. To avoid this danger — the danger of *l'art pour l'art* museum-art — we suggest for the galleries rather unsophisticated close to earth materials; roughly textured concrete ceilings, split-slate floors, walls covered probably with canvas and painted flat. Furthermore, the design includes a number of smaller, non-interchangeable rooms of definite decoration and furnishings. Painting and sculpture can be shown in those in surroundings similar to a home or a place of assembly or an office or a public building, theater, restaurant, school.[35]

But a few years after the Museum's opening, the wood-panelled walls of the smaller, non-interchangeable rooms, which gave an air of definite decoration and furnishing, were covered with another (removable) layer of white plaster to provide a more neutral background. These smaller spaces enclosed by permanent partitions are now used for temporary exhibitions as well[36].

Externally, however, the Whitney is closer to the Guggenheim than to the Museum of Modern Art[37]. Like the latter it has direct contact with the street, but it also has an expressive self-contained sculptural form[38]. When the architect pondered how a museum should look, and more particularly a museum in Manhattan, his answer was,

> It should not look like a business or office building, nor should it look like a place of light entertainment. Its form and its material should have identity and weight in the neighborhood of 50 story skyscrapers, of mile long bridges, in the midst of the dynamic jungle of our colorful city. It should be an independent and self-reliant unit, exposed to history and at the same time it should have visual connection with the street, as deems the housing for twentieth century art. It should transform the vitality of the street into the sincerity and profundity of art.[39]

The new building did to the Whitney Museum of American Art more than all the years of activity in its two former buildings: it focussed national and international attention on the Museum and helped to create a new image. "It was intended to be a landmark," wrote John Morris Dixon, reviewing the building for the *Architectural Forum*. "After 35 years on the side streets of New York, the Whitney Museum wanted its third home to be in the spirit, if not the form of Wright's defiant Guggenheim."[40] As a matter of fact, it was called by some critics a square Guggenheim. Curiously enough, at one stage in the planning of the Guggenheim, Wright did con-

Pl. 148 C. Harrison Townsend, Whitechapel Art Gallery, London, 1897—1901.
Several art exhibitions in the area preceded the building. The museum's facade fronts the sidewalk of the main street as an ordinary building.

Pl. 149 C. Harrison Townsend, Horniman Museum, London, 1901.
The building is close in spirit to the contemporary style, Art Nouveau, although the high tower pilasters and ornamental capitals are vaguely historical.

Pl. 150 Hendrik Petrus Berlage, Gemeentemuseum, The Hague, 1935.

Pl. 151 Henry van de Velde, Rijksmuseum Kröller-Müller, Otterlo, 1938.

sider a hexagon composed of normal flat floors with a ramp to connect the separate levels[41].

But the similarity between the Whitney and the Guggenheim is more than a superficial external resemblance to an upside-down ziggurat. They share the approach to the museum as an expressive monument. Like the Guggenheim, the Whitney is set apart from the surrounding buildings, in this case not only by its striking shape but also by the two concrete walls blocking it from the adjoining properties on Madison Avenue and 75th Street.

Breuer and Smith chose a noble material, a dark, warm-toned grey granite as the facing material for the surfaces open to the public and visible from the street. It was polished "...to give an ancient material a contemporary dimension."[42] (Wright, it will be remembered, also considered marble or marble dust for the exterior of the Guggenheim.) The Whitney's service departments, however, are situated above the fourth floor galleries in an unfaced concrete superstructure which can hardly be seen from the street since it recedes as it rises above the mass of the museum in ziggurat fashion. Furthermore, the moat or level differences between the sidewalk and the structure can be found at both the Whitney and the Guggenheim.

In other words, the Whitney combines the flexibility and contact with the street of the Museum of Modern Art with the expressive form of another museum in Manhattan, the Guggenheim. In addition, the architects tried to create a neutral but not clinical interior which could provide a sympathetic background to the works of art it serves.

Breuer and Smith also sought to synthesize expressive form with flexible (but not clinical) space in the new wing for the Cleveland Museum of Art, 1967–71 (Pls. 97, 98). The wall planes project outward or recede "...as called for by differences in the spaces which they enclose."[43] Again, the 'old and noble material, granite' was used to face the exterior, but in a new way by which granite is laid in alternating color bands.

The clear ceiling height of the Cleveland exhibition galleries was raised from the 12'9" which characterizes the first three floors at the Whitney to 15 feet. In addition, the architects further refined the detailing of the ceiling and partitions: the smaller coffers are no longer prefabricated cast concrete but tectum, a wood fiber-based material. As in the Whitney the units are modular and tracked for the installation of partitions or lighting (Pl. 99). Power outlets are provided in the granite floor at eight feet intervals as well as overhead.

b. Museums as useful sculpture.

A highly successful sculpture form is what distinguishes I.M. Pei's synthesis of expressive form and flexible space. The Everson Museum of Art, Syracuse, can stand against the most advanced contemporary minimalist sculpture as a pure formal composition. Although it appears as a monumental sculpture, the museum is a small building, 130 feet by 140 feet above ground. It stands free next to a plaza and a pool (Pl. 177). Located at the time of its construction in the middle of nowhere, it now serves as a focal point for Syracuse's urban renewal. The nearby municipal steam plant was discreetly concealed by means of a rough concrete wall and trees (Pl. 179), just as Breuer installed concrete walls to separate the Whitney from its neighbors.

The Syracuse museum's external walls as well as the interior walls of the central sculpture court are bush-hammered in a diagonal pattern exposing a red granite aggregate, while the margins are left unexposed (Pl. 183). This diagonal pattern is repeated in the plaza pavement. Some smaller sections (some floors and external 'benches') are rose-colored, consisting of ground terrazzo containing the red granite aggregate. This texture also helps to prevent the mass from becoming too monumental.

In this case the architect and the museum director preferred the flexibility of different sizes of space, from small intimate gallery to the large sculpture court, to one large exhibition space which can be subdivided[44]. Instead of a single box the architect designed a more complicated geometric organization by clustering four cantilevered boxes around the two-level central sculpture court. Although the plan is extremely simple (Pl. 178), the building offers varied and complex views and spatial relationships. Glimpses of the outside are offered by two floor-to-ceiling window strips at two corners. The bridges connecting the galleries, the semicircular balcony, and the spiral stairs provide stimulating views of the exhibits and the spaces. (Pls. 177–183).

The Everson Museum can be considered as a "dress rehearsal" for the monumental undertaking of the National Gallery East Wing. There the rectangular shapes were replaced by triangles as the basic form. The inner court in Washington shares many features with that in Syracuse, such as the multiplicity of levels connected by bridges, staircases, and balconies. The larger scale obviates some of the limitations of Syracuse's small central court, but it also creates new problems. Rather than serve as a site for works of art drawn from the permanent collection, the Washington court is so monumental that "public scale" works had to be especially commissioned for the site.

I.M. Pei's solution for the trapezoidal site of the East Wing was to divide the area diagonally, thereby creating two triangles: one large isosceles triangle for exhibitions and another long right triangle for the research center (Pls. 84, 85, 184—187). The triangle is not only the basic form in the ground plan, it also governs many other architectural details.

The building creates an exciting spatial experience, with the central hall full of action and movement. This atrium serves as a focal point for orientation and circulation. Its triangular roof ties together the two triangles of the gallery and research center. But a large proportion of the building's space is wasted, and the exhibition space is limited: small galleries in the towers and one large underground area.

Another significant attempt to reach a balanced synthesis is the Centre Pompidou (Pls. 188—194). The emphasis in Paris was to create a "machine esthetics" frame for a flexible, versatile space. Centre Pompidou is a steel and glass structure designed 120 years after the Crystal Palace without the Neo-classical spirit of the frame for the 'universal space' of the Neue Nationalgalerie in Berlin.

Washington's answer to Piano and Rogers's 'Futuristic well-serviced shed' was a monumental temple. Tennessee marble frames the exhibition space instead of the red, green, yellow, and the blue external service system. Instead of providing a neutral flexible container, I.M. Pei emphasized the unique spatial experience. Some critics saw the difference between these two museums as renewed arguments in the debate between elitist and populist approaches.

In the final analysis the attention given to the formal aspect of museum design need not undermine its functional efficiency. The needs and preferences of the museum staff can be combined with those of the architect to achieve a functional museum with an expressive form.

Pl. 154 W.G. Quist, Rijksmuseum Kröller-Müller, Otterlo, New Wing, 1969–1978.

Pl. 155 Architectural Department, Municipality of Amsterdam (exterior) and F.H. Eschavzier (interior). Stedelijk Museum, Amsterdam, 1954. An example of a flexible, "formless" structure, a well lit warehouse.

Chapter V.
Fulfillment and Challenge

Pl. 156 Frank Lloyd Wright, Solomon R. Guggenheim Museum, New York, 1943—59. "Eternal symbol of contemporary abstract art" (Mumford). The museum was originally called the Solomon R. Guggenheim Collection of Non-Objective Painting.

Before examining the fulfillment of the modern museum concept, it is worth recalling the criteria we proposed at the outset of our discussion: (1) multiplicity of function; (2) expansion and diversification of exhibited material; (3) a new approach to light; (4) conservation; (5) flexibility; and (6) expressive form.

1. Fulfillment.

One or more of these characteristics can be found in institutions founded as early as the turn of the century, but only in the late 1930's does one find a structure which epitomizes in all respects the modern museum.

a. New functions for an old institution.
Several art exhibitions in the vicinity preceded the actual construction of the Whitechapel Art Gallery in London, designed by C. Harrison Townsend (1897—1901)[1]. Lacking a permanent collection and intended for temporary exhibitions (the space was also used for concerts and meetings), the Gallery was built on purpose in a lower-income area to fulfill an important educational role.

Another element in the museum's new educational responsibility, separate collections for display and study, can be found in the Boston Museum of Fine Arts, 1909. Yet only at the end of the 1930's does one find a museum (MOMA) which fully demonstrates the multiplicity of museum functions. Undertaking an active education program, the Museum of Modern Art, New York, started not with a permanent collection but with temporary exhibitions. Its precedents were many: the Armory Show of 1913, for example, was organized by a group of artists concerned by the difficulties of exhibiting contemporary works of art[2]. In addition, the Museum of Modern Art of the Société Anonyme, founded in 1920, arranged displays to be shown mainly in other museums. Significantly, some of the pictures of the Société Anonyme were loaned to the Museum of Modern Art in 1929. Another precedent is A.E. Gallatin's Gallery of Living Art at New York University, which was, at the date of its foundation, the only public gallery entirely devoted to new trends in painting. It was opened to the public on 12 December, 1927, two years before the Museum of Modern Art settled in its first home. Neither collection, however, ended up at the Museum of Modern Art[3].

Another source for MOMA's emphasis on temporary exhibitions was the commercial gallery, notably Alfred Stieglitz's Photo-Secession, or 291 Gallery which

145

introduced major European artists and art movements. MOMA's sources, therefore, were not royal, noble, or church treasure rooms, but exhibition halls and commercial galleries. Its showroom windows were close in spirit to the shop of the Parisian merchant, Gersaint, as depicted by Watteau[4]. Besides collecting, presenting, and studying works of art, MOMA organized travelling exhibitions, lectures, and concerts; screened films; and sold and distributed museum publications and reproductions long before such activities became a commonplace of modern museum management.

b. Boundaries are made to be enlarged.

The second criterion of the modern museum, it will be remembered, is the diversification of exhibited material. African sculpture, for example, had been exhibited as art, and not as ethnological material, as early as 1912 at the Folkwang Museum, Essen. In 1926 the Munich Museum featuring such objects was reorganized on an art historical-esthetic basis. But it was only in 1935 that the Museum of Modern Art first organized an exhibition of African-Negro Art. Not until the 1970's, however, with the Museum of Primitive Art in New York (founded in in 1954) did such works become a part of the Metropolitan.

MOMA was also an important pioneer in other fields. In 1932 the first museum department of architecture was founded there and in 1933 a section concerned with industrial design was also added. In the same year MOMA presented the first one-man photography exhibition in a museum and seven years later became the first to open a department of photography. In 1935 the museum also inaugurated a film archive. In other words, even before its permanent home was designed, the MOMA displayed the first two characteristics of the modern museum.

c. *Lighting, conservation, and flexible display.*

By adopting a flexible lighting system (glass screen walls artificially supplemented), it became possible to construct for MOMA a multi-story building, thereby fulfilling the third criterion.

The fourth element of the definition suggested here is conservation. The Boston Museum of Fine Arts made the first step towards climate control in 1909, regulating the humidity in order to overcome the dryness caused by winter heating. Although the Frick Collection, opened to the public in 1935, was the first museum to have complete climate control, MOMA's 1939 building was not merely air-conditioned. For the first time planners also allocated large spaces for workshops, laboratories, conservation, and administration offices on the upper floors as well as in the basement.

The Grand Palais, designed by Deglane, Lovet, and Thomas, and built between 1897 and 1900 for the Great Exhibition of 1900, took advantage of flexible exhibition space. In replacing the Palais de l'Industrie (1855), it carried on the nineteenth century exhibition tradition which originated in the Crystal Palace. But as in its predecessor, the external stone facade of the exhibition building masks the immense open spaces of the interior, creating a conventional architectural frame. MOMA satisfied the fifth criterion by applying flexible office space techniques and using temporary partitions to alter display spaces as needed.

d. *The origins of expressive form.*

The Whitechapel Gallery mentioned earlier also suits the suggested formal criterion. Although the Richardsonian arch and the small towers at the top are somewhat historical, the turn-of-the-century building as a whole is closer in spirit to the contemporary style, Art Nouveau. Its facade fronts the sidewalk of the main street just as an ordinary building would (Pl. 148), but perhaps its most modern feature is its simple and functional, loft-like interior. Yet this gallery was not an influential source for future museum design; it remained no more than a pointer to what was still to come. Townsend also designed the Horniman Museum (1900–01) close to the Art Nouveau style, although the high tower, pilasters, and ornamental capitals are similarly historical (Pl. 149).

An early continental approach to modernity is demonstrated by van de Velde's Folkwang Museum in Hagen, 1900–02. "Modern" as far as its external and internal form is concerned, it is nonetheless a traditional museum from all other points of view.

But besides the few Art Nouveau museums designed around the turn of the century, one can rarely find museums built in a non-historical style until the mid-thirties. The steps eliminated at the Brooklyn Museum of Art and the entrance relocated to

Pl. 157 Frank Llyod Wright, Solomon R. Guggenheim Museum, New York, 1943–59, as seen from the sidewalk.

Pl. 158 Frank Lloyd Wright, Solomon R. Guggenheim Museum, New York, 1943–59.
Wright designed a large window at the ground level which opens the large main space to Fifth Avenue
and Central Park. As such the Museum deviates from other monumental, single space buildings by
Wright.
Pl. 159 Frank Lloyd Wright, Solomon R. Guggenheim Museum, New York, 1943–59.
The visitor can see most of the paintings on display at once. As a result critics feel that the element of
surprise is eliminated. But this does allow the visitor to have an overall view and gives him an idea of
how much he has already seen, and how much is left to be studied.

the ground floor in the mid-1930's was a sign that the monumental, classical order was losing ground (Pls. 26, 27). But Berlage's Gemeentemuseum, a modern-style museum opened in the same year in the Hague, can hardly be considered a major architectural statement of modernity; it is no more advanced than the buildings designed by Frank Lloyd Wright a quarter of a century earlier (Pl. 150). Moreover, like the traditional museum the Gemeentemuseum was based mainly on skylighting, lending another familiar element to its non-historical, though hardly radical modernism. Van de Velde in the Rijksmuseum Kröller-Müller (1938) also rejected historical styles in his design (Pl. 151). But only in 1939 was a museum building designed in the most advanced contemporary architectural style available, the International Style. Appropriately enough, that structure was for the Museum of Modern Art, the museum which had organized the pioneer American exhibition of this architectural movement in 1932 (Pl. 15).

In the architectural competition to build the Smithsonian Gallery of Art in 1939, modern designs took all the prizes, in clear opposition to the Neo-classical National Gallery in Washington, then under construction. Eliel and Eero Saarinen Associates with J. Robert and F. Swanson won the first prize, but the MOMA architects also participated in this competition: Goodwin prepared a project with Louis C. Jaeger and Albert Frey Associates and won one of the eight third prizes, as did Stone, who submitted a separate design[5].

The two main tendencies of museum design — one striving to achieve an expressive building form, the other seeking an anonymous functional frame — parallel the distinction between temple and showroom. Generally, the art temple is a museum with an expressive form, whereas the showroom is found within a more-or-less anonymous space. Currently one observes in both cases movement towards synthesis. On the one hand, the temple and showroom types have come much closer to each other in recent years, and on the other hand, there are now functional museums with strong expressive forms, such as the Whitney Museum of American Art, Centre Pompidou, and the East Wing of the National Gallery, Washington.

At the Whitney the architects achieved a synthesis of elements present in the Museum of Modern Art and the Guggenheim: the sunken sculpture court and the glass screen wall echo MOMA's opening to the street, while the flanking walls, the "moat," and the strong sculptural form of the building, recall the separation of the Guggenheim Museum — "the temple in the park" — from the rest of Fifth Avenue. This emphasis on form was combined with an elaboration and development of flexible space and display as applied at the Museum of Modern Art.

2. Challenge.

Parallel to the fulfillment of the new museum concept, however, there arose a new challenge to the museum's viability as an institution. Early in the century the Futurists and Dadaists threw down the gauntlet. The initial manifesto of Futurism, first published in Le Figaro on 20 February, 1909, and signed by Marinetti, called for the destruction of the museum. Marinetti compared museums with cemeteries:

> ...truly identical with their sinister jostling of bodies that know one another not. Public dormitories where one sleeps forever side by side with detested or unknown beings. Mutual ferocity of painters and sculptors slaying one another with blows of lines and color in a single museum. Let one pay a visit there each year as one visits one's dead once a year... That we can allow! ... deposit flowers even once a year at the feet of the Giaconda if you will! ... but to walk daily in the museums with our sorrows, our fragile courage and our anxiety, that it is inadmissable!... Would you, then, poison yourselves? Do you want to decay?[6]

More than sixty years later, Peter Plagens, reviewing the opening of a new museum at Berkeley for *Artforum,* felt that this museum is "...basically another dinosaur, maybe the newest born, but surely close to the last of a breed of inherently cumbersome, class-oriented, and anachronistic institutions."[7]

Jean Dubuffet also rejects the museum as an institution. "Je voudrais voir les productions d'art apparaître dans la cité, dans les lieux les plus vivants de la cité, et non pas confinées dans les sinistres musées." He rejects the

> "...morgues d'embarrassement, ces citadelles de la culture mandarine, qui sont les musées... Leur nom déjà, avec sa référence a l'imbécile notion greco-latine des muses, dit assez quel vent le pousse. Je suis fort persuade de laction stérilisante des pompes culturelles."[8]

But then is there really an alternative? When Dubuffet had to decide what to do with his own collection he could find no better solution than to present and exhibit

Pls. 160, 161 Frank Lloyd Wright, Solomon R. Guggenheim Museum, New York, 1943—59, interior.

Pls. 162, 163 Frank Lloyd Wright, Solomon R. Guggenheim, New York, 1943–59, problems of display.
Wright had intended to hang the paintings against the highly sloping walls. Sweeney, the former museum director, used projecting rods behind the paintings to locate them further away from the ribbon window and bring them closer to the viewer. Messer, the present director of the museum, prefers to hang the paintings closer to the wall, but perpendicularly as a sort of compromise between Wright's intention and the display method used by Sweeney.

his art for public benefit and, therefore, he finally gave it to the Musée des Arts Décoratifs:

> dans l'état actuel des choses, et quoi que j'y veille, il n'existe pas dans la cité vivante de place pour la production d'art et les esprits sont si parfaitement endoctrinés que des productions d'art présentées ailleurs que dans un musée n'ont pas la moindre chance quoi je me suis — sur le dard-décidé à les accrocher quand même finalement dans un musée.[9]

a. The search for alternatives.

Marcel Duchamp's alternative to the museum was "The Box in the Valise," on which he worked from 1936 to 1941. It includes color reproductions and miniature replicas of his major works. About 300 copies of this box were made over the years. In an interview with James Johnson Sweeney, Duchamp explained that the

> aim was to reproduce the paintings and the objects I liked and collect them in a space as small as possible. I did not know how to go about it. I first thought of a book [Malraux's alternative], but did not like the idea. Then it occurred to me that it could be a box in which all my works would be collected and mounted like in a small museum, a portable museum, so to speak.[10]

Another attempt to create a feasible alternative to the modern museum was Mathias Goeritz's El Eco Experimental Museum, Mexico City (1952—53) (Pls. 195, 196). This museum was an empty space in which artists were invited to perform or contribute works or art. The only pre-existing works of art were the space itself and the open court with a proto-minimal environmental sculpture. El Eco was the first realization of Goeritz's anti-functional and anti-rational attitude towards modern architecture as expressed in his "Manifesto of Emotional Architecture." Goeritz also opposed the notion of the respected traditional museum with its collection of masterpieces. His museum emphasized the experimental and the momentary. Instead of flexible space with clean, straight lines, he designed an expressive space in which ninety degree angles were almost completely absent. The corridor leading into an open court narrowed almost to a point suggesting the architectural spaces in Fritz Lang's film, "Dr. Caligari." But the life of the El Eco Experimental Museum was almost as short as that of an exhibition. Due to the sudden death of the patron, the building was used soon after its completion for other purposes[11].

At the time of his "store" in the early 1960's, the pop artist Claes Oldenburg gave his opinion: "I am for an art that is political — erotical (sic) — mystical, that does something other than sit on its ass in a museum. I am for an art that grows up not knowing it is an art at all, an art given the chance of having a starting point of zero."[12] About a decade later, he made his own version of a museum, the Mouse Museum, which was exhibited in Kassel's fifth Documenta (1972)[13]. Designed in the shape of a geometric mouse with a bilingual museum guide, ground plan, stamp, and so forth, the museum contained "...salvaged objects more or less altered from inside and outside the studio." His comment on the Mouse Museum recalls Duchamp's explanation of his "Box in a Valise." "What I contributed," said Oldenburg, "was certainly historical. It was a perspective on my activities for the past ten or fifteen years represented by miniatures; it was like a history of my work." Oldenburg clearly reacted to the overly scholarly approach of the Documenta prospectus by claiming that his catalogue ...reaches toward the same kind of inclusive scholarship by listing each item in two languages."[14] The geometric mouse was included in his earlier "System of iconography — plug, mouse, good humor, lipstick, switches," 1970[15].

A revised version of the Mouse Museum was constructed in 1976—77 by the Museum of Contemporary Art in Chicago for a tour of several American museums (Pl. 197). This time the emphasis was no longer on the interior space. Since the exterior form was the same as the interior, the Mouse Museum shape could be perceived from without as well as from within. It became architecture as well as sculpture. The Ray Gun Wing was designed as an extension to the geometric Mouse Museum[15].

Another variation on this theme of museum alternatives is the Herbert Distel Museum of Drawers. It took the Swiss artist Herbert Distel seven years (1970—1977) to complete his project which includes 500 small rooms ($2^1/_2$" wide, $1^7/_8$" deep and $1^{11}/_{16}$" high) (Pls. 198, 199). He acted as museum curator and asked five hundred and one contemporary artists to contribute a work. Peter Killer pointed out that the artist "...was at liberty to build up his collection as he wished and did not need to consider commissions or financial limits."[17] There is no classification and the works were arranged in the order in which they were received. It was relatively easy to transport the miniature collection, and it has been on display in Documenta 5

164 Frank Lloyd Wright, The Solomon R. Guggenheim Museum, New York, 1943—59, interior.
The building forces the exhibition designer and curator to arrange the display according to vertical as well as horizontal considerations, since the visitor can observe a large portion of the spiral at any one time.

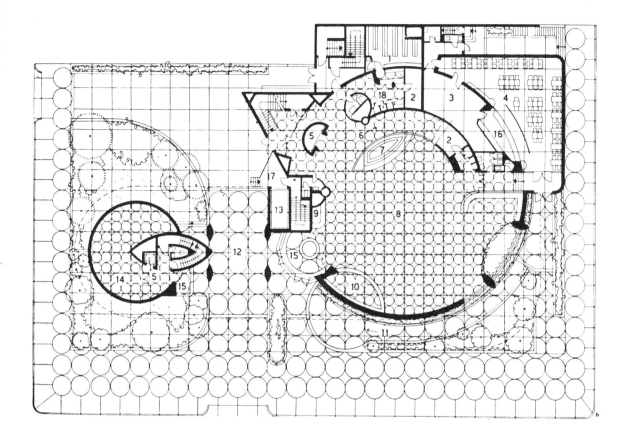

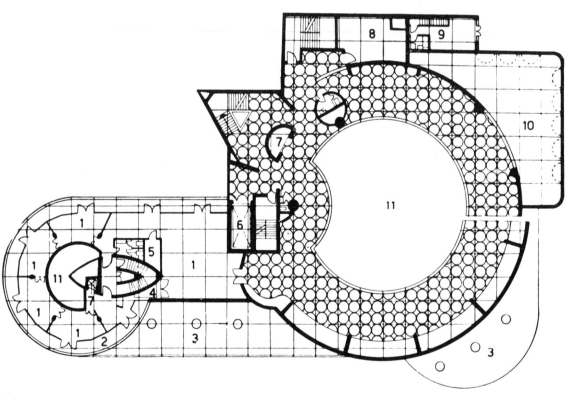

Pl. 165 Frank Lloyd Wright, Solomon R. Guggenheim Museum, New York, 43–59, plans.

Pl. 166 Richard Hamilton and Richard Estes. Guggenheim Museum on display at the Solomon R. Guggenheim Museum, 1980.
The Guggenheims within the Guggenheim serve as reminders for the visitors of the sculpture in which they move around.
Pl. 167 Greater London Council, Hayward Gallery, London, 1968.
A temporary exhibitions pavilion as one component in a cultural center which includes concert halls, National Film Theatre, and the new National Theatre. It is a parallel development to the multi-function museum with everything under one roof.

*Pl. 168 Greater London Council, Hayward Gallery, London, 1968.
The "trays" intended for sculpture display add, perhaps, to the general
form of the building, but because of the strong winds they are rarely used.
Pl. 169 Greater London Council, Hayward Gallery, London, 1968.
Form seems to dominate, not function.*

*Pl. 170 Marcel Breuer and Hamilton Smith,
Whitney Museum of American Art, New York,
1963—66.
An example of a synthesis of a flexible space with
expressive form. The Whitney combines the
versatility and contact with the street of the
MOMA with the expressieve form of another
museum in Manhattan, the Guggenheim.*

(1972) and since 1976 in different museums in Europe. But even this effort to preserve culture outside the realm of museums ended up in a museum. Upon completion it was given to the Kunsthaus in Zurich. Ed Kienholz's contribution to the smallest museum of modern art was the metal slab base which raised the revolutionary museum on a traditional pedestal...

b. Against art and artists.

The museum has also been criticized by others for dictating a certain kind of artistic production. Like the commercial gallery it encourages artists to create objects which can be exhibited and purchased and also forces artists to conform to the limited size the gallery or the museum can provide.

Michael Kustow, former director of the Institute of Contemporary Art in London, believes that artists need free channels of distribution for their work. He assumes that, "If the museum can demonstrate an alternative way to communicate artistic experience, the art itself may change — it is bursting the museums at the seams already." He expects more social awareness from the museum as well as from artists whose consciousness "...has been moulded by an image of the only available channels of distribution." He believes that "Shows of 'pure art' may well gain in intensity and meaning if they are presented as part of continuous coherent programs of polemical exhibitions..."[18]

The present state of the museum has been challenged by artists like Christo, Michael Heizer, Richard Long, Robert Smithson, and other conceptual and minimal artists. Neither the earthworks of Michael Heizer in the desert of Nevada, such as "Double Negative" 1110 × 42 × 30 feet, Virgin River, 1969; Robert Smithson's "Spiral Jetty" of 1970 in Great Salt Lake, Utah, a strip which measured 1500 feet wound into a spiral about 15 feet wide[19]; nor "Christo's Wrapped Coast," one million square feet, Little Bay, Australia (1969); nor the 24-mile long Running Fence in California (1972—76) can be exhibited in a museum. Ironically, only Christo's photomontage of the Museum of Modern Art in New York could be exhibited there (1968) (Pl. 200)[20]. But in the same year he managed to persuade the more adventurous Kunsthalle in Bern to allow him to pack it with plastic wrapping, so that the museum did not serve as a frame for works of art; it itself became the exhibit[21]. Richard Long's concentric circles of pebbles could not be purchased or even stocked in a museum since they were intended to be thrown back into the sea after the exhibition[22]. Nothing is left besides photographs or tapes after a George and Gilbert exhibition since they display themselves as a "living sculpture."

c. For the museum.

But these trends are by no means universally accepted. A critical observation on museums which exhibit minimal art, conceptual art, or "earthworks," is Hilton Kramer's review in *The New York Times* of two such exhibitions in 1971: the Guggenheim International Exhibition and Earth, Air, Fire, Water, an Elements of Art exhibition at the Museum of Fine Arts in Boston. Kramer believes that "...the resistance to museum presentation makes it all the more attractive to organizers of museum exhibitions." According to this critic, "If there is a trend toward the dismantling of the artistic enterprise and casting contempt on the integrity of the museum, no with-it museum director wants to be left out of the game."[23]

The museums may very well need the new art, even if this art is critical of it, but more often than not the radical artists also require the museum space to present their ideas and works or records of them. The Artist Placement Group presentation at the Hayward Gallery is one example. This group sought to involve artists in industry in a new way.

> They reject the idea of artists as a designer of end-products; they reject the idea of the artist approaching industry to get materials, equipment or technical expertise for his own projects; and they condemn the role of the artist as a decorator of boardrooms or factories. Instead they propose to big firms and concerns that they would engage an artist as a 'new kind of professional person.' He would be paid a salary and have free access to all part of the firm. He would be free from profit motive, ideally an independent person who sees and tests the possibilities for more creative work.[24]

Their presentation included records of the artists who had already worked with firms and a conference area called "the Sculpture." Yet where did this presentation take place? The poster of the exhibitions read: "The Hayward Gallery... For Sale," (in bold red letters) "Property to be inspected: December 2nd — 23rd, 1971." As the last line clarified, they needed this unwanted institute to present their ideas: "Hayward Gallery made available by the Arts Council of Great Britain" (Pl. 201).

Radical opinion has suggested that the museum should operate far more in the community, but the most striking attempt to do so, the attempt by a group at the Kunsthaus in Hamburg to function in housing projects rather than in the museum, was an admitted failure. After a comparatively short time the group was back under the protective umbrella of the institution[25].

In contrast to avant-garde criticism of the museum and the tendency to exhibit art outside an institutional framework, one also finds an unexpected trend towards "installation shows" and "process art" which require a museum setting and could not even be conceived outside its walls. Out of the five works included in Robert Morris's Installation Show at the Whitney Museum in 1970, the largest was a 95 × 12 × 7 foot configuration of huge concrete shapes and timbers, composed for and during the exhibition. The artist planned to allow the public to visit the exhibition from the first day, so as to stress the installation process and avoid having the pieces perceived as fixed forms and, indeed, as objects. Although for reasons of security the opening had to be postponed, the process was recorded through films, photographs, and tapes[26].

The museum has also found ways to accommodate the new pressures. Artists are increasingly given an important part in selecting and organizing their own exhibitions. The former director of the Tate Gallery, Norman Reid, for example, thanked Paolozzi "...for his major role in devising the show itself and for designing and making the image section which forms the central part of this book. The curator of the Musée des Art Decoratifs has a similar view, "Je ne juge pas, j'informe."[27]

The openness of the museum is perhaps its saving grace. According to Michael Kustow,

> ...even the most sophisticated and well-equipped museum may now find itself too rigid, too well organized and structured to keep up with the latest authentic developments from the artists... in museums where both memory and current activity are combined, it seems essential to think things out in such a way that the habits of conservation and security associated with highly priced treasures of the past are not allowed to infect the open space of the present in an inhibiting way. Politeness, good taste and 'quality,' however essential, can become traps in themselves: we should not banish provocation, doubt, even disorder from our museums. They are still in many respects one of the last melting-pots and unconditional spaces in our societies.[28]

3. In conclusion

The museum of today is no longer the same institution attacked by the Futurists. The concept of the museum has changed. Ceasing to be a cemetery of 'dead art,' the museum has become a center of activity, providing a broad program of education through special departments, junior wings, lectures, publications, and exhibitions. The museum tries to exhibit not only the established artist after his death (still the anachronistic policy of the Louvre), but also to present the most recent trends of artistic creativity. The "showroom" museum has moved closer to daily life. Moreover, conservation, always a major function of the museum, has become even more crucial as pollution too has gone modern and our scientific knowledge of how objects deteriorate has improved. The name of the institution remains the same, but its content and meaning have been altered.

However much the modern museum may have changed already, its future survival depends on its adaptability. To meet the challenges posed by contemporary artists, the modern museum has to undergo changes of form and content. To bridge the gap between life and art, it has become more like a showroom than a temple. The activities of the modern museum have been diversified and exhibited material extended to include anti-institutional displays. All the other features which we attributed to the showroom (e.g. the storefront, the central location, flexible galleries, and additional activities such as movies, concerts, museum shop) are attempts to adjust. To judge from the variety and scope of these changes and the creative energy they have unleashed, the museum will continue to be a vital institution for many years to come.

Pl. 171 Marcel Breuer and Hamilton Smith, Whitney Museum of American Art, New York, 1963.
A. The canopy.
B. The bridge and the sunken sculpture court seen from the sidewalk.
The sculpture court along Madison Avenue and the canopy were designed to relate the Museum to the street.
Pl. 172 Marcel Breuer and Hamilton Smith, Whitney Museum of American Art, New York, 1963, sculpture court seen from the inside.

Pls. 173, 174 Marcel Breuer and Hamilton Smith, Whitney Museum of American Art, New York, 1963—66. The large window facing Madison Avenue.
A. Outside view.
B. Inside view.
Pl. 175 Marcel Breuer and Hamilton Smith, Whitney Museum of American Art, New York, 1963—66, section.
In order to incorporate the lower sculpture court and provide large flexible galleries, the upper floors had to be cantilevered in a dramatic fashion. The upper floors afford maximum gallery space without covering the sculpture court with shadows and give the Museum its unique silhouette.
Pl. 176 Marcel Breuer and Hamilton Smith, Whitney Museum of American Art, New York, 1963—66, floor plans.
Two kinds of space were provided by the architects, smaller and more intimate rooms for the permanent exhibition on the side facing 75th Street and next to it on the three gallery floors large open space for temporary exhibitions. But, within a few years after the Museum opened, the smaller spaces enclosed by permanent partitions were being used for temporary exhibitions as well.
The elevators and stairs are located at the side of the building to provide a large uninterrupted flexible space (like MOMA). They do not cut the space into two separate halves by placing the utility core in the center of the building as Kahn did at Yale (see Pl. 112).

160

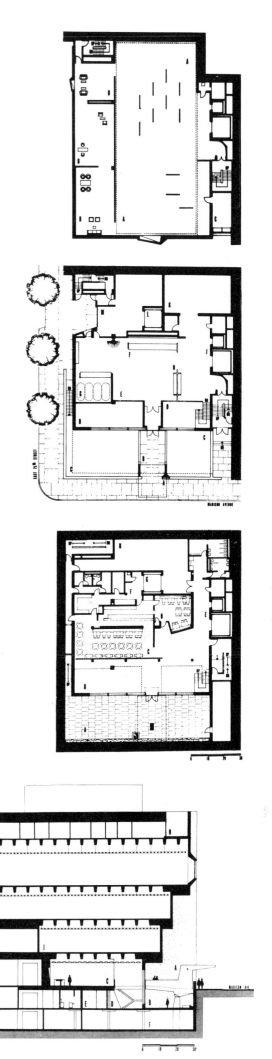

161

Pl. 177 I.M. Pei, Everson Museum of Art, Syracuse, New York, 1961–69.
A successful synthesis of expressive form and flexible space, the Museum can stand against the most
advanced contemporary minimalist sculpture as a pure formal composition. It now serves as a focal
point for Syracuse's urban renewal.

Pl. 178 I.M. Pei, Everson Museum of Art, Syracuse, New York, 1961–69, plans and section.
The architect and museum director preferred the flexibility of spaces of different sizes — from small
intimate gallery to the large sculpture court — to one large exhibition space which can be subdividied.

SECOND LEVEL

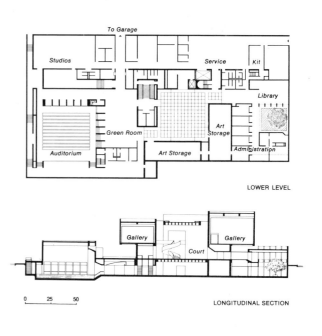

LOWER LEVEL

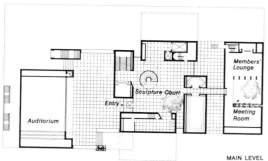

MAIN LEVEL

LONGITUDINAL SECTION

Pl. 179 I.M. Pei, Everson Museum of Art, Syracuse, New York, 1961–69.
The nearby municipal steam plant was discreetly concealed by a rough concrete fence and trees, just as Breuer installed concrete walls to separate the Whitney from its neighbors, (Pl. 49).
Pl. 180 I.M. Pei, Everson Museum of Art, Syracuse, New York, 1961–69, a two-level sculpture court.
The bridges connecting the galleries, the semicircular balconies (Pl. 182), the spiral stairs (Pl. 179), provide stimulating views of the exhibits and the spaces.

Pl. 181 I.M. Pei, Everson Museum of Art, Syracuse, New York, 1961—69.
A concrete spiral staircase leads up to the four galleries that surround the sculpture court.
Pl. 182 I.M. Pei, Everson Museum of Art, Syracuse, New York, 1961—69.
Upper floor bridge, spiral staircase, and semicircular balcony.
Pl. 183 I.M. Pei, Everson Museum of Art, Syracuse, New York, 1961—69.
The concrete walls are bush-hammered in a diagonal pattern exposing a red granite aggregate, while the margins are left unexposed. The texture helps to prevent the mass from becoming too monumental.

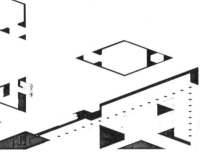

85 I.M. Pei, The National Gallery East
g, Washington, D.C., designed 1967–1971,
oleted 1978, plan level 3.

LEVEL 3

Pl. 184 I.M. Pei, The National Gallery East Wing, Washington, D.C., designed 1967–1971,
completed 1978, (photograph: Ezra Stoller, ESTO).
Everson Museum of Art can be considered a "dress rehearsal" for the monumental scale of the
National Gallery East Wing. There the rectangular shapes were replaced by triangles as the basic
form.

Pls. 186, 187 I.M. Pei, The National Gallery East Wing, Washington, D.C., designed 1967–1971,
completed 1978.
The inner court in Washington shows many features in common with the Syracuse court (Pls. 178,
179, 182), such as the multiplicity of levels connected by bridges, staircases and balconies.
The building creates an exciting spatial experience, with the central hall full of action and movement.

Pl. 188 Piano and Rogers, (architects); Ove Arup and Partners, (engineers), Centre national d'art et de culture George Pompidou, Paris, 1971—1977.
The form was determined by the desire to provide flexible space. One of the main advantages of the Piano-Rogers project was that it left almost half of the allocated building site for the plaza.

Pl. 189 Piano and Rogers, (architects); Ove Arup and Partners, (engineers), Centre national d'art et de culture George Pompidou, Paris, 1971—1977.
The most appropriate symbol for the machine age, a monument to transition. According to Reyner Banham, "...impermanence, in the sense of adaptability, applies to everything except the most massive members of the structure."

Pl. 190 Piano and Rogers, (architects); Ove Arup and Partners, (engineers), Centre national d'art et de culture George Pompidou, Paris, 1971—1977. East facade, Rue du Renard, with all the services exposed. The color coding is blue for air-conditioning, green for water, red for transportation and yellow for electricity.

*Pls. 191, 192 Piano and Rogers, (architects);
Ove Arup and Partners, (engineers), Centre
national d'art et de culture George Pompidou,
Paris, 1971—77.*

*The transparent perspex external escalators
provide magnificent views of Paris. This dynamic
solution for the circulation exposes the endless
flow of visitors to the center (6,000,000 in the
first year), and allows maximum flexibility in the
exhibition galleries (1,000,000 visited the
N.Y.—Paris show).*

*Pls. 193, 194 Piano and Rogers, (architects);
Ove Arup and Partners, (engineers), Centre
national d'art et de culture George Pompidou,
Paris, 1971—77.*

*The ultimate flexible frame. A steel and glass
structure designed 120 years after the Crystal
Palace without the Neo-classical spirit of Mies's
Neue Nationalgalerie, Berlin (Pl. 8).*

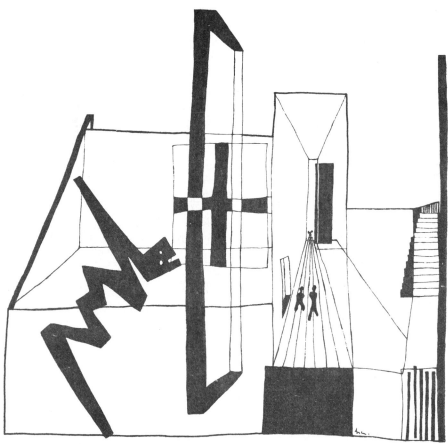

Pl. 195 Mathias Goeritz, El Eco Experimental
Museum, Mexico City, 1952–53.
Goeritz opposed the notion of the respected
traditional museum with its collection of
masterpieces. His museum emphasized the
experimental and the momentary. Instead of
flexible space with clear, straight lines, he
designed an expressive space in which
ninety degree angles were almost completely
absent.
Pl. 196 Mathias Goeritz, El Eco Experimental
Museum, Mexico City, 1952–53.
The museum was an empty space in which artists
were invited to perform or contribute works of
art. The only pre-existing works of art were the
space itself and the open court with a
protominimal environmental sculpture.

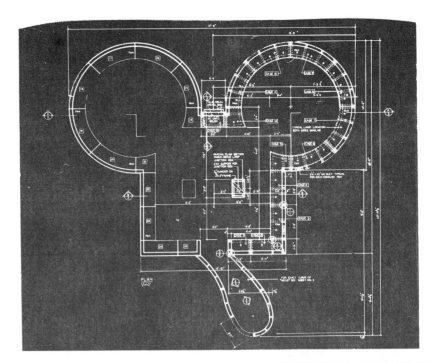

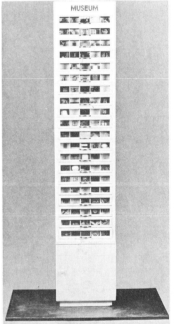

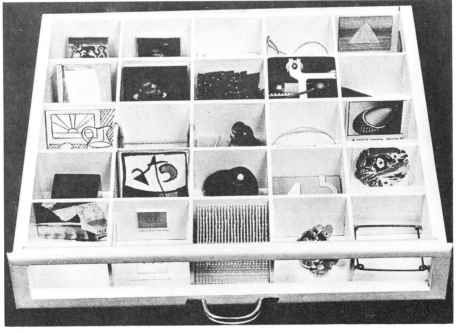

Pl. 197 Claes Oldenburg, The Mouse Museum 1972, revised version 1976—77.
Pl. 198 Herbert Distel, Museum of Drawers, Kunsthaus, Zurich, 1970—77.
The Swiss artist Herbert Distel acted as museum curator and asked five hundred and one contemporary artists to contribute a work. There is no classification and the works were arranged in the order in which they were received.
Pl. 199 Herbert Distel, Museum of Drawers, Kunsthaus, Zurich, 1970—77.
The Museum of Drawers includes 500 small rooms ($2^1/_2$" wide, $1^3/_8$" deep and $1^{11}/_{16}$" high). Kienholz's contribution to the smallest museum of modern art was the metal slab base which raised the revolutionary museum on a traditional pedestal...

171

pl. 201 Poster of the Artists Placement Group exhibition inn$_7$0 at the Hayward Gallery, 1971.
The unwanted institution was needed for the presentation of the Artists Placement Group's ideas.
Michael Kustow believes that "...we should not banish provocation, doubt, even distortion from our
museums. They are still in many respects one of the last melting-pots and unconditional spaces in our
societies."

pl. 200 Christo, The Museum of Modern Art
Packed, photomontage, 1967.
Ironically, only Christo's photomontages of the
MOMA could be exhibited there. But, in the
same year he managed to persuade the more
adventurous Kunsthalle in Bern to allow him to
pack it with plastic wrapping, so that the
museum did not serve as a frame for works of art,
but became in itself the exhibit.

Appendix

Sculpture Gardens.

Although contemporary museums offer large, high-ceilinged exhibition space, for the display of three dimensional art works there seems to be no alternative to an outdoor architectural setting. Indeed outdoor sculpture displays have a long tradition. They may either open to the street, as in the Loggia dei Lanzi in Florence (indeed,the entire Piazza della Signoria can be regarded as an open-air museum), or be enclosed in a walled-in garden such as the Cortile del Belvedere in the Vatican (Pl. 48). Hammarskjöld Plaza on Second Avenue at 47th Street, New York, is an example of sculpture display in the middle of an urban cityscape, almost part of the street. There is, as well, Philip Johnson's Museum of Modern Art sculpture garden which, as was demonstrated in Chapter II[1], relates to the Cortile del Belvedere[2] (Pls. 46, 47, 48). Italian piazzas, Japanese shoin gardens, English landscape gardens, Moslem and Chinese canals offer other possible sources for the design of the garden[3].

Even the Whitney's sculpture court (1966), which is open to the sidewalk to allow the passers-by to see the works on display, is an enclosed court. When the museum visitor leaves the glazed sculpture gallery on the lower floor (below street level) to examine more closely the sculpture in the courtyard, he realizes that he is surrounded by high concrete walls (Pls. 171, 172).

Sculpture can also be displayed in a park without an architectural setting, such as the open-air exhibitions in the Battersea and Holland Parks since 1948[4] and the Rijksmuseum Kröller-Müller sculpture garden. The first phase of the latter garden was opened to the public in 1961 and the second in 1966; both designed by Professor J. Bijhouwer. Only part of the garden was laid out, while the rest was left in its natural state, as far as possible. The spacious display and the trees help to divide the area, creating intimate corners and thereby eliminating possible clashes between the different styles (Pl. 202).

The architectural setting of Noguchi's Billy Rose Art Garden, which is part of the Israel Museum, Jerusalem (1965), includes large terraces made of rough local stone, semi-circular basaltwalls, and elegant formal areas with reinforced concrete walls in different geometrical shapes; some of the surfaces are covered with polished stone. These walls subdivide the space and help emphasize certain works which provide a background for smaller objects (for fragile and more diminutive works of art there are two small pavilions). The display of Henry Moore's polished reclining figure next to the exposed rough rocks which Noguchi left intact suggests the latter's sculptures which often juxtapose polished and rough textures. Although Noguchi's work may

Pl. 202 Bijhouwer, Rijksmuseum Kröller-Müller, Sculpture Garden, first phase 1961; second part opened in 1966.
The spacious display and the trees help to divide the space and avoid possible clashes between the different styles.

pls. 203, 204 Gerrit Rietveld, Rietveld Pavilion, Rijksmuseum Kröller-Müller, sculpture park (1955 in Arnheim, reconstructed at Otterlo in 1965).

The pavilion was built in 1955 for the Third International Exhibition of Sculpture in the open air, Sonsbeek Park, Arnheim, and was reconstructed in 1965 as a tribute to Rietvelt in the garden of the Rijksmuseum Kröller-Müller, Otterlo.

The sculpture and architectural form complement each other. A very effective means of emphasizing the display and subdividing the space, the pavilion does not shelter either the visitor or the works of art in bad weather.

Pls. 205, 206, 207 Isamu Noguchi, The Billy Rose Sculpture Garden, Israel Museum, Jerusalem, 1965.
There seems to be no alternative to the display of three dimensional works of art in an outdoor setting.

stem, to a large extent, from the Japanese garden, in this case he also assimilated a Mediterranean tradition. Here the practice of making terraces to avoid erosion in a mountainous terrain (Pls. 205, 206, 207) was adopted in order to create sufficient space on a confined sloping site[5].

Artificial concrete terraces can be found in Roche-Dinkeloo's Oakland Museum of Art, 1970, which, however, is more a park with a few sculptures on display than a sculpture garden (Pls. 24, 25).

Open balconies are likewise used by museums for sculpture exhibits, as in the Hayward Gallery (Pl. 168) and the Walker Art Center, Minneapolis.

Sculpture is also displayed in the open Rietveld Pavilion. Built in 1955 for the Third International Exhibition of Sculpture in the open air Sonnsbeek Park (Arnheim), it was reconstructed in 1965 as a tribute to Rietveld in the garden of the Rijksmuseum Kröller-Müller, Otterlo. It is more a frame for sculpture display than a shelter (Pls. 203, 204). Some walls are made of brick or glazed, while others are left open; some parts of the pavilion are covered by a roof while others are not; some sections are high, others low. In this way the sculpture and architectural frame complement each other. Although the arrangement effectively emphasizes the display and subdivides the space, in bad weather it does not provide sufficient shelter for either the visitor or the works of art.

The latest addition to the Rijksmuseum Kröller-Müller, designed by van de Velde (1942—53), includes a gallery for sculpture display. Unlike all the other rooms which are walled up, the sculpture gallery has, in addition to the glazed roof, large windows which open it to the park (Pl. 153).

Another solution for open, yet sheltered display of sculpture is the Wilhelm Lehmbruck Museum in Duisberg, Germany. Designed by the sculptor's son, Manfred, and built between 1959 and 1964, it is, in the words of Ludwig Glaeser, "...less an actual building than a sculpture garden with a roof floating over it."[6] The building for the permanent collection of Wilhelm Lehmbruck sculptures has external concrete walls and an inner glass curtain wall suspended from the roof which opens it to the patio. Light filters in around the edges of the walls, from the central patio, as well as through additional openings in the roof. The structure provides an all-year-round exhibition space for sculpture which is not totally enclosed by museum walls. This comes very close to the Neue Nationalgalerie in Berlin in which the exhibition space is enclosed by glass screens and a 'floating roof' (Pl. 8). Although the latter space is highly suitable for sculpture display, Mies designed in addition a special walled sculpture court on the edge of the podium, next to the glazed wall of the ground level gallery. Mies's design is actually close in spirit to that achieved by his most famous disciple: Philip Johnson's Sculpture Court at the Museum of Modern Art.

Notes

CHAPTER I. THE CONCEPT OF THE MUSEUM.

1. In discussing the different terms for museums used in different periods, Alma S. Wittlin has demonstrated that one term allows more than one interpretation and on many occasions several terms have had identical meanings. Alma S. Wittlin, *The Museum, Its History and its Tasks in Education*, London, 1949, pp. 1—6.

2. *Ibid.*, p. 7. Note No. 6.

3. Michael Brawne, *The New Museum*, London, 1965.
   Brawne does not believe that development trends are international. He groups the museums by countries and regions and states that, "surprisingly enough, despite the publication of display in UNESCO *Museum* — a quarterly with an international circulation and frequent conferences arranged by International Council of Museums — ideas do not seem to cross frontiers easily. A very considerable time lag is involved." (p.29).

4. *Ibid.*, p. 30.

5. *Ibid.*, p. 74.

6. *Ibid.*, pp. 99—102.

7. *Ibid.*, p. 94.

8. "Endless Cave in Jerusalem," *Time*, Vol. 85, No. 18, April 30, 1965, pp. 58—60. See also Karl Katz, P.P. Kahane, Magen Broshi, *From the Beginning*, London, 1968, pp. 25—29, 135—147. Frederick J. Kiesler and Armand P. Bartos, "The Shrine of the Book," *Ariel*, No. 10, Spring 1965, pp. 11—12. "...the double parabolic dome, ribbed as if by the hand of some giant potter..."

9. Lewis Mumford, *The Culture of Cities*, London, 1938, p. 113.
   See also J. Mordaunt Crook, *The British Museum*, London, 1972.
   The British Museum was the first public, secular and national museum in the world.

10. Crook, *The British Museum*, p. 50.

11. Museum attendance rose from 2,051,141 in 1969 to 3,081,141 in 1979.

12. Wittlin, *The Museum*, pp. 130—132.

13. National Gallery, Washington 1976, Annual Report (1979),p. 23.

14. José Ortega y Gasset, *The Dehumanization of Art and Other Essays on Art, Culture and Literature*, Princeton, 1968, p. 5.
    The title of the essay, "The Dehumanization of Art," reflects his assumption that modern art is "Artistic Art." If the new art is not accessible to every man this implies that its impulses are not of a generally human kind ("It is art not for men in general but for a special class of men who may not be better but who evidently are different." p. 8).

15. *Ibid.*, p. 6.

16. *Ibid.*, p. 12.

17. In his conclusion Ortega y Gasset is aware that there can be no turning back, but that one must suggest another way for art so as not to divide society into the masses on one side and the artistic élite on the other. Such art will be accessible to all, but it will not return to the old "beaten and worn out paths." *Ibid.*, p. 54.

18. Clement Greenberg, "Avant-garde and Kitsch," *Art and Culture*, Critical Essays, Boston, 1968,

19. *Ibid.*, p. 9.

20. *Ibid.*, p. 18.

21. *Ibid.*, p. 8.

22. Thomas P.F. Hoving, "Advanced Crisis or Coming of Age?" *Artnews*, Vol. 71, No. 7, November 1972, pp. 34—35.

23. Viscount Eccles, "Reflection on the Future of Museums," *Museums Journal*, Vol. 71, No. 3, December 1971, p. 117.

24. *Ibid.*, pp. 117—119.

25. See Crook, *The British Museum*, p. 54.

26. Eccles, "Reflection on the Future of Museums," p. 117.

27. The Birmingham Council was influenced by the public library movement. In 1968 the Council levied a penny rate to establish a central reference library with reading and news rooms, as well as a museum and gallery of art for district lending libraries.
At the opening of the Birmingham Free Reference Library in 1866, the preacher George Dawson stressed that, "We are a corporation who have undertaken the highest duty that is possible for us; we have made provisions for our people, for all our people..."
Robert William Dale, another non-conformist Birmingham minister, wrote in *The Laws of Christ for Common Life* (1884), "I sometimes think that municipalities can do more for these people than Parliament. They can give to the poor the enjoyment of pleasant parks and gardens and the intellectual cultivation and refinement of public libraries and galleries of art. They can reduce the inequalities of human conditions."
See Asa Briggs, *Victorian Cities*, Harmondsworth, 1971, pp. 196—214.
See also Michael Brawne, *Libraries, Architecture and Equipment*, London, 1970, p. 20.
"During the 19th century libraries were also frequently seen as philanthropic institutions which, like museums, were part of an attempt to make possible the "Improvement" through education of the less privileged; they therefore appeared in Utopian proposals put forward at the beginning of the century and occupied a central place in these."

28. For visitors surveys, see
Kenneth Hudson, *Museums for the 1980's,* a Survey of World Trends, London, 1977, p. 77 and pp. 132—148.

29. Meyer Schapiro, "Democratize the Board of Trustees, Part of an Inquiry, The Metropolitan Museum, 1870—1970—2001," *Artnews*, Vol. 68, January 1970, p. 29.

30. Geraldine Norman, "America's Art Behind Closing Doors," *The Times* Saturday Review, London, December 19, 1972, p. 7.

31. The patronage of A. Conger Goodyear, Nelson Rockefeller, and Mrs. John D. Rockefeller III, Presidents of the Board, was instrumental in commissioning the architects of the main museum building (1939) and extensions (1951 and 1962—64). (Stone designed a private house for Goodyear (1938) and he was the principal designer under Raymond Hood and Wallace K. Harrison of the Rockefeller Center Radio City Music Hall. The Rockefellers have also been long time patrons of Philip Johnson — Rockefeller family guest house, New York, 1950; Asia House, New York, 1959). The network of relationships is very complex. See also Chapter III, note No. 98.

32. See Karl E. Meyer, *The Art Museum, Power, Money, Ethics*, New York, 1979, pp. 238—242.

33. Mumford, *The Culture of Cities*, p. 447.

34. *Ibid.*, p. 263.

35. *Ibid.*, pp. 263—264.

36. Cited in Calvin Tomkins, *Merchants and Masterpieces*, London, pp. 214—215.

37. Thomas Hoving, *The Second Century*, The Comprehensive Architectural Plan for the Metropolitan Museum of Art, with a statement by August Heckscher, New York, 1971.

38. The source of this exhibition with its nationalistic message can be traced in the ancestral gallery of distinguished families and the early national collections. See Wittlin, *The Museum*, p. 40.

39. André Malraux, *Museum Without Walls*, New York, 1967. The original French edition of *Le Musée Imaginaire* was published in 1965.

40. *Ibid.*, p. 10.

41. *Ibid.*, p. 12.

42. Cited in Norman Reid, *Official Guide to the Tate Gallery*, London, 1970.

43. According to Malraux
Like the reading of a play as distinct from seeing it performed, or listening to a phonograph record as distinct from hearing the same piece in a concert hall... there is now appearing outside the walls of the museum and distinct from its contents, the broadest artistic domain man has even known, the first heritage of all history — including history as yet unknown.
Museum Without Walls, p. 157.

44. Raymond Durgnat, "Musée Imaginaire," *Art and Artists*, Vol. 4, No. 10, January 1970, pp. 22—25.

45. Malraux, *Museum Without Walls*, p. 232.

46. *Ibid.*, p. 12.

47. *Ibid.*, p. 222.

48. See Roy Perrott, "Brazil's Reckless Dash for Tomorrow," *Observer Magazine*, 30th April, 1972.

49. That Malraux and perhaps MOMA may have been influenced by the *musée populaire* of the late 1930's and the 1940's was brought to my attention by Professor R. Banham. *Le Musée Vivant* was the bulletin of the Association Populaire des Amis de Musées (L'APADAM) established in 1937. The following typical quotation is taken from the tenth volume of the bulletin (No. 5, p. 8): "Pour que les musées deviennent ces lieux d'éducation que nous souhaitons, il reste beaucoup à faire... Il faut multiplier le production et imprimer, au verso, comme on le fait en U.R.S.S. une note succinte sur l'artiste et l'oeuvre..." (In order for the museum to become the centers of learning we wish them to be, there remains a great deal to be done. It is necessary to reproduce the work of art and print on the back, as they do in the U.S.S.R., a brief note on the artist and the work.) The *musée populaire* organized conducted tours of Paris of the kind that the London Museum and New York City Museum later offered to their visitors. In 1946, for example, *Le Musée Vivant* organized tours

in various parts of Paris. Starting in town and not at the museum the visits focussed on different aspects of urbanism like "l'habitation urbaine, le quartier historique, les problèmes de la circulation urbaine, la rue et son décor, la vie sociale de l'homme, les espaces vertes, les jardins et la respiration d'une grande ville, etc." (urban housing, historic neighborhoods, problems of urban traffic circulation, the street and its setting, the social life of man, green spaces, parks and the respiration of a large city, etc.) In connection with exhibitions on contemporary art *Le Musée Vivant* arranged for introductory lectures and visits to artists' studios. The programs were also linked with the Centre des Etudes Cinématographiques.

50. Malraux, *Museum Without Walls*, p. 224.

For a highly critical review of this and other ideas of Malraux, see Ernst H. Gombrich's review of the *Voice of Silence* in the *Burlington Magazine*, 1957. Reprinted in *Meditations on a Hobby Horse and Other Essays on the Theory of Art*, London, 1963, pp. 78—85.

CHAPTER II. THE SOCIAL ASPECT OF THE MODERN MUSEUM — TEMPLE OR SHOWROOM?

1. Robert Rosenblum, *Transformation in Late Eighteenth Century Art*, Princeton, 1967, p.137.

2. This suggests, of course, the by now almost legendary article by Erwin Panofsky, "The Ideological Antecedents of the Rolls Royce Radiator," *Proceedings of the American Philosophical Society*, Vol. 107, No. 4, August 1963, pp. 237—238.

3. Henry Russell Hitchcock also noted other examples of the relation between Philip Johnson and Schinkel in his introduction to *Philip Johnson Architecture 1949—1965*, London, 1966, pp. 16—17. At the Utica Museum of Art, Munson-Williams-Proctor Institute (1960), Hitchcock pointed out, "in the double staircase leading to the upper floor and in the importance of the *pièce centrale*, the glass-roofed court, there are recollections not really of the Beaux Arts Museums of the later nineteenth and twentieth century, but of those of 1810—40, the early heyday of museum architecture. This is even more evident at Fort Worth (Amon Carter Museum of Western Art, 1961); there the actual edifice is more literally, to use a classical term, a stoa than was Schinkel's Altes Museum of 1924—28 in Berlin.

4. For the relation of Mies van der Rohe to Schinkel, see Jack Paul, "German Neo-Classicism and the Modern Movement," *The Architectural Review*, Vol. CLII, No. 907, September 1972, pp. 176—180.

> Mies went to extraordinary lengths to symbolize the plan... of the Neo-classical Altes Museum. A comparison of the plans reveals a striking similarity in the placement and attitude of staircases and walls especially in those gallery walls near the center of the rotunda, the massing of the gallery also pays tribute. The entrance floor's monumental peristyle states the scale (as did Schinkel's colonnade) and recreates the centrality of Durand's museum appropriate to an island site.
>
> Schinkel searched for "...an antique model that justified him in his esthetic preference for permitting the triglyphs to return around the corner," in the design of the new Guard House. Mies's roof designs from the 'fifties on, reveal similar preoccupation with the problem. He strove to obtain the centrality of roof plan that alone could justify similarity of expression on all facades. In the gallery his central egg-crate roof justifies the two-way beams and hence radiates the web-stiffening 'triglyphs' he displays on the roof 'entablature.' To employ the German idiom the Gallery is a 'Mal' or remembrance for the Altes Museum and beyond it to Schinkel.

5. It suggests in a way Turner's request to exhibit one of the paintings he left to the nation next to a painting by Claude Lorrain. "It was his ambition to reach if not surpass the celebrated landscape paintings of Claude Lorrain." Ernst Gombrich, *The Story of Art*, London, p. 373.

6. See Ludwig Glaeser's catalogue of the MOMA exhibition of *Architecture of Museums* (1968). Glaeser wrote that Etienne Boullée's Museum, which has at its center a temple of fame, is "in idea and form a secular pantheon. Indeed, that Roman monument became as much the prototype for the interiors of the Classicist museums as did the Greek temple fronts for their otherwise plain exteriors." Glaeser added that "Boullée's 1783 design for a museum as visionary as most of his other schemes, projected contemporary ideas and aspirations on a monumental scale. The first museums actually built embody these ideas; the Glypothek in Munich and the Altes Museum in Berlin follow Boullée's square symmetrical plan organized around interior courts and circular domed halls." See also Helmut Seling, "The Genesis of the Museum," *The Architectural Review*, Vol. CXLI, No. 840, February 1967, pp. 105ff and p. 110. It is interesting to note that J. Russell Pope, P. Johnson, and L. Mies van der Rohe returned to early examples of the public museum and not to the endless later examples of Neo-classical temples of art.

7. Frank Lloyd Wright, *The Guggenheim Museum*, New York, 1960, p. 18.

8. The income-producing apartment tower designed by Cesar Pelli will emphasize the commercial aspect of museum building. See Paul Goldberger, "Townhouse to Tower," *Artnews*, Vol. 78, No. 8, October 1979, pp. 180—182. See Pl. 17.

9. The Design Centre, London, was designed by Robert and Roger Nicholson (interior design) in association with the Council of Industrial Design, Exhibition Section. The shopfront was conceived with the help of Ward and Austin. See *Design*, The Council of Industrial Design, No. 89, May 1967, The Design Centre Special Issue.

10. Many times the location of the museum is determined by the availability of space and funds, since centrally located sites have become increasingly more expensive and difficult to find. Often it also depends on the availability of publicly owned land, so that not in every case is the museum located according to the wishes of the museum staff or the architect. In the case of cultural centers which include an art museum, the location problem is more complex. In some instances the center creates a separate cultural island. As such, it is very close to the "park museum."

11. When I asked Kevin Roche in the summer of 1971 whether he considered the Oakland Museum more as a downtown museum or a park museum, his answer was, "I had imagined it as a downtown museum."

12. See the following discussion on the Metropolitan Museum of Art, New York, for example.

13. *The Architectural Review: For the Artists and Craftsmen*, Vol. 9, 1901, pp. 129—131, pointed out that

> the narrowness of the only frontage into which the exit and entrance have to be contrived, prevents the display of much architectural talent and it is only by the ingenuity in the arrangement and disposition that one can estimate the architectural value of the building...

14. One can learn from the diagrams in the catalogues of the first years that the exhibition installation started straight from the central hall without a transit corridor.

15. For the illustration of the mosaic design by Walter Crane, see *The Architectural Review*, Vol. 9, p. 129 or *Architectural Design*, Vol. 50 nos. 1—2, 1980, p. 2 and pp. 48—50. It was intended to be 25 feet long and 13 feet high. It is interesting to note that Ludwig Glaeser, Curator of the Mies van der Rohe Archives at the Museum of Modern Art, suggested a large mural in his privately circulated design recommendations for the Musée d'Art Haitien (July 1970). He felt that such an exterior mural would not only "prevent the wall from being defaced by unwanted posters, but it would, by its existence alone, advertise the museum in a most direct and effective manner." Robert Venturi pushed this idea to the extreme in his project for a Football Hall of Fame of 1968. The huge neon light billboard flashing out scores and images is much bigger than the museum behind. (For illustrations see Charles Jencks, *Architecture 2000, Predictions and Methods*, London, 1971, p. 114, Ill. 104, 105.)

16. See *The Museum News*, The American Association of Museums, "Brooklyn Museum Makes Important Changes in Building'" Vol. XII, No. 8, October 15, 1934, p. 1, and *The Museums News*, Vol. XIII, No. 11, December 1, 1935, p. 1. Also Laurence V. Coleman, *Museum Buildings*, American Association of Museums, Washington, 1950, pp. 64—65.

17. The facade of the slightly later design for Asia House (1960) is somewhat similar, but the tinted glass windows of Asia House hardly allow any view of the inside.

18. See John Jacobus, *Twentieth Century Architecture, The Middle Years, 1940—1965*, New York, 1966, p. 158.
Philip Johnson told me that he prefers the temple concept and opposes the showroom museum, but at the Museum of Modern Art he followed the museum policy of an open wall since it was only an addition to an existing museum. According to him the front facade was always translucent. Johnson's use of dark glass as well as the recess of the windows in the ground level continue the approach of the first architects. This somewhat ambiguous stance in relation to the street suggests Labrouste's Bibliothèque Nationale in Paris (1858—68). According to Giedion, "Labrouste had the audacity that was needed in his day to erect a large glass screen in the opening" (of the *magasin central*)' "so that the magazine of books stored in the stacks could be glimpsed from the reading room. This was an early use on a large scale of transparent areas so dear to modern architects. Labrouste, afraid of his own daring, partially covered his glass screen with heavy red drapery..." Sigfried S. Giedion, *Space, Time and Architecture*, fifth edition, Cambridge, Mass., 1971, pp.227.

19. Coleman, *Museum Buildings*, p. 49.

20. Museum Boymans-van Beuningen, Rotterdam, *Nieuwe Vleugel, erst fase*, architect A. Bodin, Rotterdam, 1972, p. 10.

21. Robert Hughes, *Time* magazine, New York, April 26, 1971.

22. Hoving, *The Second Century*, p. 39.
Similarly, the architect hoped that the garden of the Oakland Museum would be open to the public after the museum closed for the day, but the museum director did not pursue this policy.

23. *Ibid.*, p. 44.

24. Lawrence Alloway wrote that, "as the pavilions are occasional architecture they are more demonstrative than buildings put up for continuous use..." He divides pavilions that were built and rebuilt at various periods into categories of folkloristic, classicizing, and international, although he feels, "all pavilions are, to some extent, folkloristic." Lawrence Alloway, *The Venice Biennale, 1895—1968*, From Salon to Goldfish Bowl, London, 1969 (Quotations from p. 17 and p. 19).

25. *Ibid.*, Nos. 1, 2, 3, p. 57. The austere colonnade of 1932 was left unchanged in the late 1960's.

26. According to Hitchcock, the processional walk in the MOMA garden resembles the processional element of other museums designed by Philip Johnson in the 1960's such as in Utica and Fort Worth. The core of the garden has hardly been changed "...but the processional path, so to call it, has been much clarified and prolonged actually and visually. Now the circulation leads straight through the center of the original building into the western half of the house."
The visitor

> can turn left to the restaurant terrace and thenceforth merely follow with his eyes the further stages, or he can proceed to the right among the pools, the sculpture and the trees. Always ahead is the challenge of the tall staircase — tall but gently sloping — rising diagonally across the blank marble wall of the museum at the latest wing of the garden. At the top of the stairs, the processional way comes to an end on the wide marble paved terrace which is closed to the east by a row of trees across the rear of Canada House and on the south by the wide wall of St. Thomas' Church. The goal now proved to be the view backwards and downwards as at an Italian villa across the garden that has been left behind.

Hitchcock's introduction to *Philip Johnson's Architecture, 1949—1965*, pp. 15—16.

27. In this case the social awareness of a trustee prevented the hermetic enclosure of the garden. According to Philip Johnson, Rockefeller thought that the public would be outraged if the garden gates were replaced by bricks. Johnson, who did not want the doors at all, designed very deep grills so that the view both ways is restricted. The cafeteria walls continue the garden brick walls, while the glass screen wall ensures favorable climatic conditions year round.

28. Marcel Breuer, "The Architect's Approach to the Design of the Whitney Museum" (privately circulated). Discussed in more detail in the fourth chapter on the formal aspect.

29. According to Professor Prown, Louis Kahn enthusiastically endorsed the idea of commercial space. But Karl Meyer emphasizes that it was the local officials who demanded the shops' presence in order to compensate the city for the loss of tax-producing land.
See Jules Prown, *The Architecture of the Yale Center for British Art*, New Haven, 1977, p. 15, and Meyer, *The Art Museum*, p. 160.

30. Charles Jencks argues that "the Getty Museum is a passable, if unintended example of Post-Modernist building," "Don't Panic!, J. Paul Getty Museum Malibu California," *The Architectural Review*, Vol. CLXIII, No. 972, February 1978, pp. 83—85.

31. Malraux, *Museum Without Walls.*

32. Robert Goldwater, *Primitivism in Modern Art,* Revised Edition, New York, 1967, p. 13.

33. *Ibid.,* see Appendix, Summary Chronology of Ethnographical Museums and Exhibitions, pp. 273–277.

34. *Ibid.,* p. 8.

35. *Ibid.,* p.9.

36. The Chairman of the Administrative Committee of the new Department of Primitive Art was Professor Robert Goldwater, the former chairman of the committee of the former Museum of Primitive Art and an art historian of modern Western art who wrote the pioneering study on *Primitivism in Modern Art* in 1938. The Consultative Chairman was Dudley Easby, the former secretary of the Board, who, according to Tomkins, "never wholly gave up hope that the Met. might one day recall its loaned specimens and restore them to favor." (Tomkins, *Merchants and Masterpieces,* pp. 358–359.)

37. Robert Goldwater discussed the child cult in his book, *Primitivism in Modern Art,* pp. 192–225, focussing mainly on Klee and Dubuffet.

38. See Samuel Cauman, *The Living Museum: Experience of an Art Historian and Museum Director — Alexander Dorner,* New York, 1958, pp.88–91.
   Dorner rearranged the collection in chronological order.

>The atmosphere rooms were quite different from period rooms. A period room is a presentation of a specific style in a variety of manifestations; these are to be contemplated, or perhaps used to provide models for interior decoration. An atmosphere room was meant to provide insight into the vision of an earlier day; it conveyed in visual terms our modern understanding of the past as a process of creative growth. This display philosophy Dorner came eventually to see as evolutionary psychology in action integrating art and art history with scientific thinking." (p. 88)

The objects of each period were displayed in rooms with different backgrounds "shaped and coloured to suggest the corresponding historic visions of reality." The Medieval rooms, for example, were painted in dark colors, since most Medieval churches did not have light interiors. The Renaissance rooms had clear white or grey walls and ceilings to correspond with the new conception of "the clearly defined volume of space-cubes and hemispheres — with structural elements framing the defining frame. Perspective in Renaissance painting was used to make this geometrical picture of reality plain to the senses. The clear light walls of the Renaissance galleries emphasized the cubic character of the rooms. The pictures were like views lit into the walls; their frames played the part of window frames." Red velvet framed in gold, was the background of the Baroque galleries since "the picture space lost its clear definition." (p. 89)

39. *Ibid.,* p. 109.

40. *Ibid.,* p. 110.

41. The Brooklyn Children's Museum, New York, founded in the second decade of the twentieth century, and the one in Jamaica Plain, Boston, are among the first. See Alma S. Wittlin, *Museums: In Search of a Usable Future,* Cambridge, Massachusetts, 1970, Appendix: Museums and Children, or Children's Museums, pp. 235–240. For further bibliography (by Helen V. Fisher, A.E. Parr, Molly Harrison and Barbara R. Winstanely), see note 2, p. 294.

42. See Tomkins, *Merchants and Masterpieces,* pp. 291–292.

43. Ayala Gordon, "The Museum's Junior Wing," *Ariel,* A review of the Arts and Sciences in Israel, Israel Museum Issue, Jerusalem, No. 10, Spring 1965, pp. 49–53; see also *The Israel Museum News* No. 13, 1978, pp. 7–20.

44. E.L.L. Wilde, "Notes on the Role of a Museum of Modern Art," *Art and Artists,* Vol. 4, No. 10, January 1970, p. 14.

45. *The Museum of Modern Art Biennial Report,* 1967–69, p.24.

46. *The Museum of Modern Art Bulletin,* New York, Fall–Winter 1954–55, Vol. XXII, No. 1–2.

47. *The Museum of Modern Art Biennial Report,* 1976–78.

48. Katherine S. Dreier, *Collection of the Société Anonyme: Museum of Modern Art 1920,* Yale University Gallery, New Haven, 1950, p. XIV.

49. *Ibid.*

50. *Ibid.,* p. XVII.

51. *Architectural Forum,* Vol. 135, No. 4, November 1971, p. 28.

52. The catalogue list of Arno Press includes more than 40 reprinted catalogues of the Museum of Modern Art in New York.

53. Clarence Stein, "The Art Museum of Tomorrow," *Architectural Record,* Vol. 67, No. 1, January 1930, pp. 5–12,
   Idem, "Making Museums Function," *Architectural Forum,* Vol. XVI, No. 6, June 1932, pp.609–616.
   Idem, "Study Storage — Theory and Practice," *The Museum News,* Vol. XXII, No. 12, December 15, 1944, pp. 9–12.

54. Stein, "The Art Museum of Tomorrow," p. 5.

55. Clarence Stein believed, on the other hand, that the casual visitor "...wants inspiration first, instruction later," *Ibid.,* p. 5. In discussing the public museum, his first statement was: "The casual visitor goes to a museum to enjoy himself. (Explanation will not help him!)"

56. Stein, "The Art Museum of Tomorrow," p. 5.

57. Stein, "The Art Museum of Tomorrow," p. 9.

58. *Ibid.* See also Stein, "Making Museums Function," p. 609.

>The appearance of the books in the stocks of a library is not the essential, it is the ease with which a student can obtain and use the books. The material in the study collections is working material and requires different arrangement from the display material in the public galleries. The material should be arranged and lighted so as to facilitate research and comparison.

59. *Muséographie,* Architecture et Aménagement de Musées d'Art, Conférence International d'Études, Société des Nations, Office International des Musées, Institut International de Cooperation

Intellectuelle, Madrid, 1934, Vol. I, pp. 22—26 (Ill. p. 23).

60. *Masterpieces in the Victoria and Albert,* Forward by Sir Leigh Ashton, London, 1952.

61. Tomkins, *Merchants and Masterpieces,* p. 215.

62. According to Laurence Coleman, science museums anticipated the trend towards allocating generous proportion of space to the reserve collection. He observed a steady increase in the ratio between live storage space and curatorial offices on the one hand, and exhibition areas on the other. The first wing of the American Museum (1877—1909) has one floor of study-storage space and four of exhibits. At the National Museum (1911), the proportion was two floors for exhibition to two floors of study reserve. The Chicago Natural History Museum of 1921 originally had more study and curatorial space than exhibition area, while the new wings of the American Museum, opened to the public in 1935, increased study space from 20 percent to nearly 70 percent in the new units. Coleman concluded in 1950 that "Science museums generally now tend to have as much curatorial space as exhibition space." Coleman, *Museum Buildings,* pp. 16—17 and p. 179.
In terms of floor area Philip Johnson has advocated a proportion of one-third for primary exhibition to two-thirds for services including the study collection. Brawne, *The New Museum,* p. 14.

63. *Director's Report,* The National Gallery, January 1967 — December 1968, London 1969, pp. 15—16.

64. *L'Oeil,* No. 197, May 1971, pp. 2—7.

65. *The Museum News,* The American Association of Museums, "Frick Collection Opened to the Public," Vol. XII, No. 3, January, 1936, p. 4.

66. Interview with Michael Compton and "Hayward Building Revisited," *Architectural Journal,* Vol. 153, No. 5, February 3, 1971, pp. 243—255.

CHAPTER III. THE FUNCTIONAL ASPECT.

1. For these circulation schemes see Lorimer Rich, "Planning Art Museums," *The Architectural Forum,* Vol. 47, No. 6, December 1927, pp. 553—580 and Coleman, *Museum Buildings,* pp. 141—143.

2. Benjamin Ives Gilman, "Aims and Principles of the Construction and Management of Museums of Fine Art: A Syllabus," *Museum Journal,* July 1909, reprinted in his *Museums, Ideas of Purpose and Method,* Cambridge, Mass., 1918, p. 399.

3. Although the word helix is used as a synonym for spiral, Professor R. Banham drew my attention to the difference between the two terms. According to the Oxford Dictionary, "The spiral has sometimes been distinguished from the helix... spiral in architectural sculpture, etc. is a curve that ascends, winding about a cone... by this it is distinguished from the helix which winds... around a cylinder," (*A New English Dictionary of Historical Principles,* James A.H. Murray, ed. Vol. IX, p. 613, Chambers, quote No. 1728). In other words, unlike the helix, which is an open form, the spirla is a finite form which expands in one direction and terminates in the other. Le Corbusier's museums terminate in the central hall, they are complete spirals, while the Guggenheim Museum, according to this definition, is only part of a complete spiral (the parking garage ramp, for example, is a double helix).

4. Troels Andersen and others, *Vladimir Tatlin,* Moderna Museet, Stockholm, 1968, pp. 7—8 and 52—67.

5. K.G. Pontus Hulten, *The Machine as seen at the end of the Mechanical Age,* The Museum of Modern Art, New York, 1968, p. 136, Nickel Construction, p. 132, Kinetic Construction. See also Laszlo Moholy-Nagy, *The New Vision: From Material to Architecture,* New York, 1930, p. 102. Moholy-Nagy valued Raoul Franche's idea that nature could be looked upon as an infinite collection of variations on a limited number of formal themes. One of them is the spiral. See also Christopher K. Green, M.A. Thesis on *Naum Gabo in England,* Courtauld Institute of Art, London, 1967.

6. *Bulletin de l'Effort Moderne,* No. 17, July 1925. See also short text by Kiesler in issue no. 11, January 1925. The illustration of the stage model is reprinted in John Golding and Christopher Green's *Léger and Purist Paris,* Tate Gallery, London, 1970, p. 77.

7. Arthur Drexler, *The Drawings of Frank Lloyd Wright,* London,1962, Ill. pp. 106—113. Project for Gordon Strong Automobile Objective and Planetarium, Sugar Loaf Mountain, Maryland, 1925.

8. Green, *Naum Gabo in England.*

9. Le Corbusier, *L'Art Decoratif d'Aujourd'hui,* Collection de l'Esprit Nouveau, Nouvelle édition augmentée, Paris, 1959, p. 184 (section drawing). *Idem, The City of Tomorrow,* London, 1929, p. 197. The title of the photograph is "The above might well be taken as an image of perfect harmony."

10. Lewis Mumford, *Technics and Civilization,* London, 1934. Illustration facing p. 324, "Nature and the Machine," No. 1. "Roentgen photograph of Nautilus by J.B. Polak. Nature's use of the spiral in construction. The X-ray, like the microscope, reveals a new esthetic world." This photograph is compared with another illustration called, "Section of modern hydro-turbine spiral form dictated by mechanical necessity."

11. Francis Henry Taylor, *Babel's Tower, the Dilemma of the Modern Museum,* New York, 1945.

12. Willy Boesiger and Hans Girsberger, *Le Corbusier 1910—1965,* London, 1967; Museum of Contemporary Art, Paris, 1931, p. 235; The Museum of Unlimited Extension, Philippeville, 1939, p. 238; Cultural Center of Ahmedabad, 1954, pp. 242—245; The Tokyo Museum, 1959, pp. 246—251. For the Museum and Art Gallery at Chandigarh, 1964—68, see Willy Boesiger, ed., *Le Corbusier: Last Works, Oeuvre Complète,* Vol. VIII, London, 1970, pp. 92—96.

13. A circulation scheme and system of space organization similar to that of the Paris World Exhibition of 1867 can be found in a project for the earlier London exhibition of 1862. It was proposed in the *Builder,* Vol. 19, No.941, 16 February, 1861, pp. 106—108, III, by E.J. Pyne who designed the structure and George Maw who suggested the system of classification. The suggested circulation patterns were circular (or elliptical, according to the chosen form) together with a double system of intersecting avenues (Pl. 71).
Unlike the Paris exhibition, this arrangement was to be constructed all under one roof, as a single space subdivided by display blocks. The organization of exhibited material received more emphasis than circulation. As such, the plan is closer to library designs such as the project for a circular

royal library in Paris (Benjamin Dellessert, 1835), the revised Parisian project of 1938 with an oval reading room, and the round reading room of the British Museum. But instead of radiating bookshelves or desks, this project would have been arranged in concentric circles and transverse paths similar to the circular reading room of the Library of Congress, Washington, D.C. (finished 1897). For a discussion of circular reading rooms, see Crook, *The British Museum*, pp. 151–193.

14. According to Le Corbusier and Pierre Jeanneret, the expositions of the (then) recent past have fallen into an architecture of imitation seeking to limit the reality of houses or palaces constructed "authentically". Their idea was, on the contrary, to take up once more the grand tradition of the universal exhibitions of the 19th century (iron and glass) and to create "places of exhibition" that would be favorable to visibility and circulation and elicit an architectural feeling owing to the frankness of the proposed solution. Such was the project at hand, executed in electrically soldered tôle d'acier.

   Max Bill, ed., Le Corbusier and Pierre Jeanneret, *Oeuvre Complète*, Vol. III, 1934–38, Zurich, 1939, p. 173.

   For the Paris Exhibition of 1867 see: *L'Exposition Universelle de 1867*, illustrée, publication internationale autorisée par la commission imperiale, Paris, 1867;
   A. Hirsch, *Remarques sur le plan et dessins d'Architecture à L'Exposition Universelle de 1867*, Paris, 1869;
   Giedion, *Space, Time and Architecture, The Growth of a New Tradition*, pp. 260–264.

15. Coleman, *Museum Buildings*, p. 144.

16. Willy Boesiger and O. Stonorow, eds., Le Corbusier and Pierre Jeanneret, *Oeuvre Complète*, Vol. I, 1910–1929. Zurich 1937, pp. 192–193, and W. Boesiger and H.G. Girsberger, *Le Corbusier 1910–1965*, London, 1967,pp. 234–235.

17. Arthur Drexler also notes the connection between the Automobile Objective of 1925 and the Guggenheim Mseum in his book, *The Drawings of Frank Lloyd Wright*, p. 300 (Pls. 106–113).
   Pyramidal compositions were basic to Wright's work from the earliest prairie houses on, but it has not always been realized that the circle, which makes its appearance as an element of the plan around 1938 with the Jester House and culminates in the spiral of the Guggenheim Museum of 1943–1957 was very much in Wright's mind as early as 1925. The Guggenheim Museum is in fact the Sugarloaf Mountain Automobile Objective turned inside out.

18. For the criticism of Lewis Mumford, Peter Blake, and Vincent Scully, see the following chapter.

19. I am grateful fo Professor Edgar Kaufmann Jr., for valuable information on the Guggenheim Museum acquired in his seminar on F.L. Wright at Columbia University and to Louise Averill Svendsen, Curator, the Guggenheim Museum. Needless to say, they are not responsible for any of the opinions expressed here and in the chapter on the formal aspect.

20. Lewis Mumford feels that, "The worst feature of the old-fashioned museum was the continuous corridor and it is not improved here by being made spiral. It remains for some pious machine-minded disciple of Wright's to go one step further and place the pictures on a moving belt so that the spectator may remain seated." Lewis Mumford, *The Highway and the City*, "What Wright hath Wrought," New York, 1964, p. 142. For a moving display of pictures, see Brawne, *The New Museum*, p. 13. Brawne cites Lina Bo Bardi's suggestion of revolving drums and Cicero Diaf's design for a mechanical display of pictures. Albini and Bonfante in fact designed a mechanized display of photographs for the 1961 Labor Exhibition in Turin. The photographs were displayed on panels that moved vertically and horizontally.

21. Mumford, *The Highway and the City*, p. 136.

22. Suzanne Stephens, "Big Deals and Bitter Endings: The Hirshhorn Museum and Sculpture Garden," *Artforum*, Vol. XIII, No. 6, February 1975, pp. 56–62.

23. The wider spiral is not used for a more flexible display than at the Guggenheim. In this case the central space is walled up and used as a separate conical space which dramatically frames the Mexican Constitution. The comparison between this museum and the Guggenheim demonstrates how much more successful, as well as more impressive is the manipulation of space at the Guggenheim.

24. "It is like putting the Guggenheim spiral inside the Corbu scheme and filling the centre space of the Guggenheim with water," observed the architect, Ivan Chermayeff.

   C.R.S. (C. Ray Smith), "Boston's Underwater Environment," *Progressive Architecture*, Vol. L, No. 12, December 1969, p. 100.

25. Irene Nicholson, Criticism: "Anthropological Museum, Mexico City," *The Architectural Review*, Vol. 140, No. 834, August 1966, pp. 118–125. (Note especially p. 120).

26. Michael Webb, *Architecture in Britain Today*, London, 1969, pp. 239–247.

27. Grace Gluek, "Capital Gallery Shows Plan for Wing," *New York Times*, May 6, 1971, p. 52.

28. Carter Ratcliff, "Modernism for the Ages," *Art in America*, Vol. 66, No.4, July-August 1978, p. 53.

29. J. Benjamin Townsend assisted by Ruth M. Peton, *100, The Buffalo Fine Arts Academy, 1862–1962*, Buffalo, 1962.

30. Externally the raised long podium and the glass and metal cube suggest Mies van der Rohe's later Neue Nationalgalerie, Berlin, 1962–68, and the related earlier projects.

31. "The Tate Gallery was designed by Sidney R.J. Smith, an unfortunate choice, and in view of Smith's other buildings, no doubt Sir Henry Tate's. He used the accepted late Victorian grand manner, but neither with discretion nor with originality."
   Nikolaus Pevsner, *The Buildings of England, London*, Vol. 1, Third Edition revised by Bridget Cherry, Harmondsworth, 1978, p. 518.

32. Norman Reid, Director's Report, *The Tate Gallery 1964–65*, London, 1966, p. 3.

33. *Idem*, Director's Report, *The Tate Gallery, 1968–70*, London, 1971, pp. 7–13.

34. For the rush of art museum construction throughout Texas, see Ann Holmes, "From Panhandle to the Gulf Coast: The Museum Boom in Texas," *Artnews*, May 1973, pp. 34–36.

35. W. Sandberg, A. Mansfeld, D. Gad, I. Noguchi, "About the Israel Museum, Jerusalem," *Architecture in Israel*, No. 4, October-December 1966, pp. 4–33.

36. *Architectural Forum*, "Umbrellas for Chandigarh," Vol. 135, No. 2, September 1971, pp. 26–27.

37. For an illustration see A. Drexler, *Ludwig Mies van der Rohe*, New York and London, 1960, Ill. 6.

38. The result of this solution, according to the architects,

> ...is the appearance of two architectural expressions on the site, rather than three: one, the original 1916 building, and two, the 1958 wing and new education wing architecturally unified... The new striated and textured wall plane also wraps around the east side of the 1958 wing. This unifying measure reflects the conviction that the esthetic of the total museum demands a merging into one architectural language of the rather related contemporary buildings. Parallelling the unification of the wall surfaces is a balancing of building heights and masses with the original 1916 wing. The architectural 'bridge' with the 1916 wing on the east is accomplished by means of a bridge grille which is designed to admit daylight to the interior spaces it veils.

Marcel Breuer and Hamilton P. Smith, "A New Wing for the Cleveland Museum of Art, 1967—71" *Architects' Report,* January 1971 (privately circulated).

39. *Architectural Forum,* "Education in the Arts," Vol. 135, No. 2, September 1971, p. 20.

40. Hoving, *The Second Century,* pp. 4—61.
See also Tomkins, *Merchants and Masterpieces.*

41. Boesiger and Girsberger, *Le Corbusier 1910—1965,* p. 236, and Willy Boesiger, ed., *Le Corbusier, Oeuvre Complète,* Vol. III, Last Works, London, 1970, p. 95.

42. Green, *Naum Gabo in England,* p. 23 (see Note No. 5).

43. Germain Bazin, *The Museum Age,* New York, 1967, pp. 178—180.
Hubert Robert created several paintings illustrating his ideas for the Main Gallery (and views of its opening in 1793). The plan was partially carried out in the Empire style but was not finally completed until 1949. See Ills. 91 and 92.
For Hubert Robert's project for lighting the Grande Galerie by means of a vault and for dividing it without obstructing the long view, see Christian Aulanier, "Histoire de la Grande Galerie," *La Revue du Louvre et des Musées de France,* XXII, 1972, pp. 123—124. For an illustration of the gallery in 1826, still without a skylight, see p. 124.
See also Marie-Catherine Sahut, *Le Louvre d'Hubert Robert,* Paris, 1979.

44. According to Helmut Seling,

> ...d'Angivillers suggested in 1755 that the Grande Galerie of the Louvre should be used and the idea of skylighting was contemplated. Designs were asked for it from Soufflot, Clerisseau de Wailly and two others, but none was accepted. The Salon Carré received skylighting shortly after 1789, the Grande Galerie only in 1938, although Hubert Robert had painted it about 1802 with a large curved skylight, following the shape of the tunnel vaults. The idea came in all probability from Boullée's drawings for the National Library which has just this motif. Percier and Fontaine used high side lighting instead...

Helmut Seling (abridged version of a Ph.D. Thesis shortened and translated by N. Pevsner), "The Genesis of the Museum," *The Architectural Review,* Vol. CXLI, No. 840, February 1967, p. 109.

45. *Ibid.,* Skylighting "...had already been done in Palais Royale and Cassel. This was also the method used for the Royal Academy in the Strand range of Somerset House, that is, about 1780." (p.109). "Sir John Soane designed the gallery with five main rooms, all lanternlit on the pattern of the Royal Academy in Somerset House" (p. 111).

46. *Ibid.,* p. 114.

> The (Alte) Pinakothek, set, behind its neo-Renaissance facades, the standard for the internal arrangement of nineteenth century picture galleries in a long row of skylit main rooms and even larger number of small accompanying cabinets with side light. With this and the Glyptothek to his credit, even if Schinkel was the greater architect, Klenze must be acclaimed as the most important of all designers of museums.

47. Coleman, *Museum Buildings,* p. 92.

48. Le Corbusier used monitor lights for the museum in Tokyo. There the lighting galleries are glazed and they also include artificial light. Another recent example of the use of monitors is Aalto and Baruel's North Jutland Museum of Art, Denmark. In this case natural light comes through an asymmetrical monitor light which permits the direct penetration of sunlight.
Michael Brawne, criticism, *Architectural Review,* Vol. CLIII, No. 913, March 1973, pp. 162—164.

49. Examples of top side lighting are Duveen Gallery, National Gallery, London and the Marlay Gallery at the Fitzwilliam Museum, Cambridge. See Coleman, *Museum Buildings,* pp. 97—99.

50. *Ibid.,* p. 93.

51. *Ibid.,* p. 79.

52. Stein, "The Art Museum of Tomorrow," p. 12, and "Making Museums Function," p. 615.

53. Coleman, *Museum Buildings,* p. 91.

54. Coleman and Stein did not object to the use of skylight where it did not dictate a low building.

55. George Howe, *A Modern Museum,* Howe and Lescaze, Architects, New York and Philadelphia, Springdale, Conn., privately printed, 1930. See also Howe and Lescaze: "A Proposed Museum of Contemporary Art for New York City, *The Architectural Record,* Vol. 30, No. 1, July 1936, pp. 43—50.
Robert Stern believes that "Had not John D. Rockefeller Jr. donated the house on West Fifty-third Street, which served as the museum's headquarters between 1932 and 1938, some variant of Scheme Six or one of its predecessors would most likely have become the first Museum of Modern Art." Stern also suggests relationships among Howe's Scheme Six, Wright's Guggenheim and Stone's Huntington-Hartford Gallery of Modern Art. Robert Stern, *George Howe, Towards a Modern Architecture,* New Haven, 1975, pp. 104—106.

56. Howe, *A Modern Museum,* p. 48 "Light is of such paramount importance in a museum that it had dictated block form of scheme 4. In order to obtain direct and satisfactory lighting for each gallery, some potential building space has been given over to provide an efficient distribution of light."

57. The main reason for the dramatic sculptural ceiling of Yale Art Gallery is the expression of the structural system. It was a "...radical structural innovation... — the tetra-hedral concrete space-frame floor structures spanning between fairly widely set concrete columns..." Reyner Banham, *The New Brutalism, Ethic or Aesthetic?,* London 1966, p. 44.
According to John Jacobus,

> Kahn found that the crux of the matter was in the slab which formed both floor and ceiling, as its tensile quality determined the wide separation of vertical supports. Having established

the structural challenge, Kahn then proceeded to realize it in the form of a tetrahedron which, in his view, could have been constructed in a much lighter more elegant shape than the one his engineers insisted upon. Thus the entire spatial effect is governed by the sole permanent interior feature, the slab of tetrahedrons.
Jacobus, *Twentieth Century Architecture, the Middle Years, 1940–65*, p. 120.
Scully believes that in designing the ceiling Kahn was most probably influenced by Buckminster Fuller. The gallery was conceived by Kahn as a concrete space frame and

> ...since the slab for each floor was poured across the apices of those shapes, a continuous horizontal void resulted through which Kahn ran channels and ducts for flexible lighting and ventilation from the central service core. The mechanical equipment was now an integral part of the building's hollow fabric.

Vincent Scully, Jr., *Louis I. Kahn*, New York, 1962, pp. 20–21.

58. Garry Thomson, "A New Look at Colour Rendering, Level of Illumination and Protection from Ultra-violet Radiation in Museum Lighting," *Studies in Conservation,* Vol. 6, Nos. 2 and 3, August 1961, pp. 49–70.

59. See W.A. Allen, "The Museum in Lisbon for the Gulbenkian Collection, A New Approach to Illumination," *The Museum Journal,* Vol. 71, No. 2, September 1971, pp. 54–58.

60. Thomson, "A New Look at Colour Rendering," p.51.

61. Garry Thomson, "Hayward Gallery, Assessment," *The Architect's Journal,* Vol. 148, No. 27, 3 July, 1968, p.63.

62. *The Architect's Journal,* "Hayward Building Revisited," Vol. 153, No. 5, 3 February, 1971, p. 252 (pp. 243–255).

63. Marcel Breuer and Hamilton P. Smith, "Architect's Report," A New Wing for the Cleveland Museum of Art, 1967–71. In Cleveland, however, the architects did attempt to compensate for the building's northern exposure by alternating dark and light grey granite bands. The position of the color bands changes from one wall to the next so that a light course on a wall surface facing north is a dark course when the wall turns to face east or west and vice versa (Pl. 97). These alternating strips suggest Joseph Albers's works from the Bauhaus period and his murals in later buildings designed by Gropius: the Harvard Graduate Center and the Pan American Building. It is also curiously similar to the black strips in the house for Josephine Baker (1928) planned by Adolf Loos.

64. Edward Larrabee Barnes, "Walker Art Center," 1971, *Design Quarterly,* No. 81, 1971. The lobby of the Art Center is connected to the Guthrie Theater. It is illuminated by a large pyramidal skylight. Most galleries are windowless; Gallery 3's primary source of illumination is standard incandescent and quartz lights but it has in addition a single corner window, set at a 45 degree angle from the north wall.

65. As early as 1923, Luckeish and Holliday reported that initial construction costs for natural lighting were 80 to 180 percent higher than for artificial illumination, while operating costs for daylight were approximately 135 percent higher. Luckeish and Holliday, "The Cost of Daylight," *Transaction of the Illuminating Engineering Society,* 1923, pp. 130–133.
Coleman, *Museum Buildings,* p. 99.
Laurence S. Harrison determined in 1948 the high cost of daylight at the Metropolitan Museum of Art, New York. "Counting the lost investment income at four percent in lieu of depreciation estimates, the present day added annual cost of glass skylights installed and maintained is approximately $ 550 per sq. ft. of roof area." See Coleman, *Museum Buildings,* p. 99. As energy prices continue to rise, it appears that these financial calculations have now been reversed.

66. Michael Levin, "Philip Johnson's Positives-Negatives, The Thirtieth Anniversary of the Glass House," *Architectural Design,* Vol. 49, No. 2, 1979, pp. 52–53.

67. Michael Brawne, "North Jutland Museum of Arts, Aalborg, Denmark," Criticism, *The Architectural Review,* Vol. CLIII, No. 913, March 1973, p. 163. See also Ill. Nos. 7, 8, 10, pp. 160–161.

68. Richard Padovan, "Kröller–Müller Art Gallery, Otterlo, Holland," Criticism, *The Architectural Review,* Vol. CLXIII, No. 972, February 1978, pp. 74–82.

69. Manfred Lehmbruck, "Museum Architecture," *Museum,* Vol. XXVI, No. 3/4, 1974, p. 213.

70. Coleman, *Museum Buildings,* p. 199.

71. *The Museum News,* "Frick Collection Opened to the Public," Vol. XIII, No. 31, January 1936.

72. W.A. Cartwright, *Guide to Art Museums in the United States,* New York, 1958, p. 56.

73. *The Architects' Journal,* Vol. 153, No. 5, 3 February 1971, pp. 252 & 254.

74. Thomson, "Hayward Gallery, Assessment," p. 62.

75. *Ibid.,* p. 62.

76. Thomson, "A New Look at Colour Rendering," p. 60.

77. *Ibid.,* p. 50.

78. Thomson, "Hayward Gallery Assessment."

79. Lehmbruck, "Museum Architecture," pp. 212–215.

80. See Coleman, *Museum Buildings,* 1950, Table II, Floor Area Distribution, pp. 33–36.

81. *Ibid.*

82. For the relationship between gallery space and total museum space in museums constructed between 1950–1979, see Meyer, *The Art Museum,* Appendix A, pp. 271–284.

83. Christopher Hobhouse, *1851 and the Crystal Palace,* London 1937.

84. Henry Russell Hitchcock, *Early Victorian Architecture in Britain,* New Haven, 1954, p. 542.

85. *Idem, Early Victorian Architecture,* pp. 533–534.

86. *Ibid.,* p.545.

87. *Ibid.,* p. 557.

88. Hitchcock, *Architecture; Nineteenth and Twentieth Centuries,* p. 186.

89. *The Builder,* Vol. XIII, September 1, 1855, p. 416.

90. Giedion, *Space, Time and Architecture,* pp. 256–59, figures 148–152.

91. *Ibid.,* pp. 270–271.

92. A. Anderson, "The Paris Exhibition Buildings," *The Architectural Review,* Vol. VII, January 1900,

pp. 28—37.

93. Ian Jeffcott, "Thoughts on the Foundation of the Building Exhibition," *The Architectural Review*, Vol. LXXVI, July 1932, pp. 72—78.

94. Hitchcock, *Early Victorian Architecture*, p. 547.

95. Klaus Franck, *Exhibitions, A Survey of International Designs*, London, 1961.

96. Hitchcock, *Early Victorian Architecture*, p. 567.
   > It is true that Sir William Cubitt was supposed to be concerned in an advisory capacity but seemed to have had little or nothing to say about the particular form the building took — and perhaps cared less. Cole's architect friends, Owen Jones and Wyatt, so closely associated with the educational work of the department in industrial design, were also conspicuously absent as consultants on this structure.

97. Sir Leigh Ashton, *The Centenary of the Victoria and Albert Museum*, London, 1952.

98. Board of Education, South Kensington, *A Brief Guide to the Collections in the Bethnal Green Branch of Victoria and Albert Museum*, South Kensington, London, 1902.

99. The photograph was taken after the museum was modernized by the Department of the Environment in collaboration with Stefan Buzas and Alan Irvine. See also *Design*, No. 278, February 1972.

100. Stein, "Making Museums Function," p. 615. Stein formulated his ideas on flexibility in "The Art Museum of Tomorrow," (January 1930). But in his later article, "Making Museums Function," (June 1932), he developed his ideas in greater detail. "Museums are not even so flexible as a loft or office building in which walls and partitions are rearranged to meet the need of each new tenant." p. 616.

101. *Ibid.*, p. 614.

102. For illustration, see *Ibid.*, p. 608.
   The principal requirements for the partition system, according to Clarence Stein are:
   1. Ease and simplicity of installment.
   2. Unit system easily changed to new localities.
   3. Minimum alteration of parts.
   4. Maximum salvage.
   5. Fireproof, moisture-proof, dustproof.
   6. Rigidity.
   7. Durability.
   8. Good appearance.
   9. Ease of redecoration.
   10. Good nailing or fastening surface.
   11. Ease of storing of surplus parts.
   Ibid., p. 616.

103. The Department of Architecture and Design was named after Philip Goodwin, a trustee of the Museum of Modern Art and an art collector. The associate architect, Edward Durrell Stone, was a popularizer of the International Style and designed, among other buildings, a house in this style for Richard H. Mandel in 1933 and another private house for A. Conger Goodyear (the President of the MOMA Board of Trustees) at Old Westbury, New York, 1938. According to Russell Lynes, it was Nelson Rockefeller who proposed that Edward Durrell Stone be associated with Philip Lippincott Goodwin in designing the Museum of Modern Art. Stone had worked as the principal designer under Raymond Hood and Wallace K. Harrison on the Radio City Music Hall and the Center Theater. He had also worked on displays for the Museum of Science and Industry which Nelson Rockefeller was organizing in the RCA Building in Rockefeller Center. "It was evident to the Building Committee that Goodwin alone was not the man to design a modern structure that would be a lesson and an example and a declaration of faith in the new forms all in one, and Goodwin was unquestionably as aware of this as they."
   Russell Lynes, *Good Old Modern, An Intimate Portrait of the Museum of Modern Art*, New York, 1973, pp. 190—193.
   It was impossible then to predict that in his later years Stone would design a version of the Venetian Doge's Palace for Huntington Hartford's Gallery of Modern Art, New York (1964) and later a structure suggesting a wedding cake for the J.F. Kennedy Cultural Center.

104. Edward Durrell Stone, *The Evolution of an Architect*, New York, 1962. pp. 35—36.
   Alfred Barr thought that only five architects could be considered to design the Museum of Modern Art: Wright, Le Corbusier, Oud, Gropius, and Mies. As it seemed impossible to work with the first two, he suggested the last three to the Building Committee. Since the decision to engage Goodwin with Stone as his associate was made while Barr was in Europe, he declined to take part in the Committee's official consultations, but appointed John McAndrew to represent his views. Barr wished to preserve the open space which the museum enjoyed in its first location, and he wanted the facade mainly of glass instead of white marble, to allow diffused daylight into the galleries. See Russell Lynes, *Good Old Modern*, pp. 190—195.

105. P. Francheaux, "Ville de Paris, Musée d'Art Moderne," *L'Architecture d'Aujourd'hui*, No. 163, Août—Septembre, 1972, pp. 98—102.

106. Alfred Mansfeld and Dora Gad, "About the Israel Museum," *Architecture in Israel*, No. 4, November—December, 1964, p. 4.

107. Betty Bradford, "The Brick Palace of 1862," *The Architectural Review*, Vol. 132, No. 785, July 1962, pp. 14—21.

108. For example, the projects for Court Houses 1931—38, a project for the Resor House, Jackson Hole, Wyoming, and the 1942 project for a concert hall. See James S. Speyer, *Mies van der Rohe*, Chicago, 1968, pp. 50, 56, 61, and Ludwig Glaeser, *Mies van der Rohe, Drawings from the Collection of the Museum of Modern Art*, New York, 1968.

109. Frederick Kolper, catalogue entry in A. James Speyer's *Mies van der Rohe*, p. 58. For an explanatory text on Mies's project, see *Architectural Forum*, No. 78, May 1943, pp. 84—85.

110. The museum was first called "Twentieth Century Art Gallery" as it was intended for the twentieth century art collection of the city of Berlin. In 1965 this collection was merged with the collection of the Nationalgalerie of the Foundation, "Preussicher Kulturbesitz." Hence its new name: Neue Nationalgalerie Berlin.

111. Charles Jencks, *Modern Movements in Architecture*, p. 99.

112. Peter Blake, "Mies' Berlin Museum," *Architectural Forum*, Vol. 129, No. 3, October 1968, p. 40.

113. Werner Blaser believes that the great hall of the George Shäfer Museum can be used for many different purposes. He claims that,
> The fact that the users proposed to insert a concert hall into the building on a free floor plan irrespective of the structure shows that the hall is almost infinitely flexible in the functions it can serve. In size these spacious halls are comparable to the large industrial buildings constructed by engineers: structurally they are of general validity.

Werner Blaser, *Mies van der Rohe, The Art of Structure, Modern Movements in Architecture*, p. 99.

114. Giedion, *Space, Time and Architecture*, p. 593, Ill. 355.

115. Brian O'Doherty, "Inside the White Cube: Notes on the Gallery Space," *Artforum*, Vol. XIV, No. 7, March 1976, pp. 24—30.

116. Wolfgang Peht, *German Architecture 1960—1970*, London, 1970, p. 170.

117. Hitchcock's comparison between Philip Johnson's Museum and Schinkel's Altes Museum in Berlin and other early nineteenth century museums has already been mentioned (see note II—3). He finds references to these museums in the double staircase leading to the upper floor and in the importance of the *"pièce centrale*, the glass roofed court." Hitchcock's introduction to *Philip Johnson Architecture* 1949—1965, p.17. Jürgen Joedicke points out that it is difficult to analyze the particular influences affecting Johnson's work. At times Johnson's own explanations seem calculated to confuse rather than to clarify. One thing, however, is certain. He derives inspiration from his thorough knowledge of architectural history.
> This does not imply eclecticism in the sense of an acceptance of established forms as we find to some extent in the second half of the nineteenth century, but an assimilation of certain principles of order and spatial organization. Even a building like the Museum of the Munson-Williams-Proctor Institute at Utica, New York (1957—1960), which reveals in its structural articulation obvious influences from Mies van der Rohe is definable historically in its spatial treatment as a self-contained continuum. But in the same building a deliberate formal dichotomy also occurs: the basement story is open to the outside.

Jürgen Joedicke, *Architecture Since 1945, Sources and Directions*, London, 1969, p. 141.

118. Leo Krier, "Speaking of the Sainsbury Center," *Architectural Design*, Vol. 49, No. 2, 1979, A.D. Profile 19, p. 28.

119. Peter Cook, "Sainsbury Center for the Visual Arts, Criticism," *The Architectural Review*, Vol. CLXIV, No. 982, December 1978, p. 356.

120. Reyner Banham, "Centre Pompidou, Paris, Enigma of the rue de Renard, Criticism," *The Architectural Review*, Vol. CLXI, No. 963, May 1977, pp. 277—278.

121. O'Doherty, "Inside the White Cube."

122. Willy Boesiger, *Le Corbusier Last Works, Oeuvre complète*, Vol. VIII, London, 1980, pp. 142—157.

CHAPTER IV. THE FORMAL ASPECT OF MUSEUM DESIGN

1. Ada Louise Huxtable, "Architecture of Museums," *The Museum News*, Vol. 47, No. 3, November 1968, pp. 18—19, reprinted from *The New York Times*.

2. See Hitchcock, *Architecture: Nineteenth and Twentieth Centuries*, p. 292.
"Townsend remained a 'fellow traveller' rather than a member of the international Art Nouveau group for a decade."

3. Should architecture decorate the museum? Ought it (the museum form) to be conceived as a work of art independent of the museum's contents or rather as a simple machine for displaying the objects? Until the end of the 19th century, as has been observed, the first concept was predominant. Some theoreticians are today in favor of the second approach.
Conference International d'Études, Société des Nations, Office International des Musées, Institut de Cooperation Intellectuele, *Muséographie, Architecture et Aménagement des Musées d'Art*, Madrid 1934, Vol. I, pp. 33—36.

4. As mentioned before in the section on flexibility, in Mies's project for a Museum for a Small City, 1942, a pencil drawing of the interior included a photograph of Picasso's *Guernica* (Pl. 131). Claiming that his design for the Guggenheim answered the need for flexibility, Frank Lloyd Wright argued that in the upper floor, "...painting as big as the Guernica could be seen." Wright, *The Guggenheim Museum*, pp. 18—19.

5. Conference International, *Muséographie*, pp. 33—36.

6. "Dorner rearranged the Hanover collection in chronological order with consecutive phases of art set in background shaped and colored to suggest the corresponding historic visions of reality. The background effect was that of a series of stages set for different dramas."
Cauman, *The Living Museum*, p. 88. See also Chapter II.

7. Roberto Aloi, *Musei, Architettura — Technica*, Milan, 1962, p. 176.

8. C. Ray Smith, "The Great Museum Debate," *Progressive Architecture*, Vol. L, No. 12, December 1969, pp. 76—85.

9. Brawne, *The New Museum*, from the text appearing on the inside cover.

10. *Ibid.*, p. 10.

11. *Ibid.*, p. 10.

12. Mumford, "What Wright Hath Wrought," *The Highway and the City*, pp. 132—146.

13. Peter Blake, *Frank Lloyd Wright*, Architecture and Space, Harmondsworth, 1960, p. 120.

14. A visit usually takes about an hour and most visitors are not tired at the end of the visit, according to the museum's curator, Dr. Louise Averill Svendsen.

15. Mumford, *The Highway and the City*, p. 143.

16. Scully, *Frank Lloyd Wright*, New York, 1960, p. 31.

17. William Hennessey believes that the design for the Guggenheim Museum was influenced by Hilla Rebay's insistence that Wright give form to the ideas of the abstract painter Rudolph Bauer, who in turn was inspired by Frederick Kiesler.

See William Hennessey, "Frank Lloyd Wright and the Guggenheim: A New Perspective," *Arts Magazine*, Vol. 52, No.8, April 1978,pp. 128–133.

18. Drexler, *The Drawings of Frank Lloyd Wright*, note and commentary, p. 308.

19. Peter Blake, Criticism, "The Guggenheim: Museum or Monument," *Architectural Forum*, Vol. III, No. 6, December 1959, p. 92.

20. Thomas M. Masser, et al., "The Growing Guggenheim," *Art in America*, Vol. 53, June 1965, p. 30.

21. This is probably only one of the sources of the white walls. For the studio-type whitewash and its vernacular sources, see Reyner Banham, *Theory and Design in the First Machine Age*, London, 1970, pp. 217–219. Reviewing the architectural section of the 1922 salon d'Automne in L'Esprit Nouveau, Le Corbusier stated that "Whitewash is absolute, on it everything stands out, inscribes itself absolutely..." Already in the late nineteenth century, Whistler's house, designed by Edward Godwin, had white walls (White House, Tite Street, Chelsea, London, 1878).

22. Louise Averill Svendsen, *The Solomon R. Guggenheim Museum Collection*, a brief history, New York, n.d.

23. According to Malraux,

> with the advent of Impressionism, painters began to find it increasingly difficult to reconcile their work with frames. The curators of museums have found it even more difficult, and now enclose the Van Goghs in Amsterdam in slender strips of wood or imbed the Monets of the Louvre in the wall to free them from Louis XV or Second Empire confections which once framed them, and whose use for this purpose becomes incomprehensible if we forget that they were attempting ingenuously to provide a link between modern painting and ancient rooms. Braque and Rouault sometimes painted their own frames, thereby making them into an annex to the picture; a reversal of the practices of the past which tends only to isolate the painting while concealing its basic framework — something that could be accomplished by the most inconspicuous strip of wood, when the wall is white and unbroken.

In art books the frame is replaced by the margin of the page which was inherited from engravings and reproductions but is "also formed by the white walls of the present day museums and galleries." Malraux, *Museum Without Walls*, p. 219.

24. For an illustration of the Guggenheim Museum of Non-Objective Painting, see Coleman, *Museum Buildings*, Washington, 1960, p. 103.

25. Peter Blake, "The Guggenheim: Museum or Monument," p. 92.

26. Lewis Mumford, *The Highway and the City*, p. 144.

27. *Architects' Journal*, "Hayward Gallery Appraisal," p. 56.

28. Norman Engleback, "South Bank Arts Centre, Architecture," *Arup Journal*, Vol. 1, No. 5, p. 20.

29. See the *Architectural Record*, "Denver Art Museum: Spirited and Unconventional," Vol. 151, No. 3, March 1971, pp. 87–92.

30. Huxtable, "Architecture of Museums" *Museum News*, Vol. 47, No. 3, November 1968, pp. 18–19, reprinted from *The New York Times*. According to Peter Blake, in comparison to the Guggenheim Museum, Mies's 1942 project for Museum for a Small City "...is in some respects the realization of every museum director's dreams; it is a large, open space — infinitely flexible," *op cit.*, p. 89.

31. Harald Szeemann (ed. interpreter), "Problems of Museums of Contemporary Art in the West, Exchange of Views of a Group of Experts," *Museum*, Vol. XXIV, No. 1, 1971, p. 29. The group of experts included Pierre Gaudibert (deputy curator, Musée d'Art Moderne de la Ville de Paris et ARC), Pontus Hulten (former director of Modern Museet, Stockholm), Jean Leymarie (director, Musée National d'Art Moderne, Paris), François Mathey (chief curator, Musée des Arts Decoratifs), George Henry Rivière (permanent advisor to the International Council of Museums, member of board of editors of *Museum*), Harald Szeeman (former director of Kunsthalle, Bern) and Edward de Wilde (director of Stedelijk Museum, Amsterdam).

32. Barnes, "Walker Art Center."

33. Jacobus, *Twentieth Century Architecture, The Middle Years 1940–1965*, p. 64.

34. Mumford, *The Highway and the City*, p. 139.

35. Notes for Marcel Breuer's comments when presenting the project on November 12, 1963.

36. This proves again that the designers of the Lisbon museum chose the right approach. They resisted the temptation to design a specific building for the fixed collection. Instead the policy was "...to treat it in principle as a simple enclosure." Allen, "The Museum in Lisbon," p. 54.

37. For an interesting comparison between the Guggenheim and the Whitney see Martin Engle, "The Circle and the Square," *Arts in Society*, Vol. 8, No. 1, Spring–Summer 1971, pp. 359–372. "If Wright's Guggenheim is the romantic circle, Breuer's Whitney is the classic square," (p. 364). "For structures consciously set into the city the Whitney, referred to by critics as an upside down ziggurat, is too much an isolated sculptural block, too much at variance with its neighbors, too dramatic an architectural statement to be part of Bauhaus variety functional style." (p. 365). According to Engle, there is no contact between the Whitney and the street.

> The Guggenheim, being a public structure, does not use windows in the main building at all but, like the Whitney, carefully excludes the outside. In other words, both the Guggenheim and the Whitney rejected the world outside, their focus is inward. If the glass of the basement level and first floor implies openness, the endless wall surfaces which dominate the viewer's eye clearly contradict their openness. The trapezoidal windows of the upper floors play no role except to affirm the romanesque massive walls by their sculptural shape and seemingly random size and placement." (p. 366).

As far as the contact with the street is concerned, I have tried to demonstrate the Whitney's openness to the street in the second chapter.

38. The Guggenheim also has a large window which opens to the street, but the museum is still a self-contained sculptural structure.

39. Notes for Marcel Breuer's comments.

40. John Morris Dixon, "The Whitney: Big for its Size," *The Architectural Forum*, Vol. 125, No. 2, September 1966, p. 81.

41. See Drexler, The Drawings of Frank Lloyd Wright, Ill. 276, p. 193, Note 307.

42. Marcel Breuer and Hamilton Smith, *Architect's Report, Whitney Museum of American Art*, p. 2.

43. *Idem*, "A New Wing for the Cleveland Museum of Art 1967–1971."

44. *The Architectural Forum*, "Syracuse, Spatial Diversity Within a Giant Space," Vol. 130, No. 5, June 1969, p.56.
The director of the Everson Museum, Max S. Sullivan, felt that vast anonymous space would be unsuitable for the museum's needs.

CHAPTER V. FULFILLMENT AND CHALLENGE

1. Hitchcock, *Architecture: Nineteenth and Twentieth Centuries, p. 397,* dates the Whitechapel Art Gallery to 1898—99, while Nikolaus Pevsner's dates are 1897—99, *Pioneers of the Modern Movement,* London, 1963, pp. 154—155, but according to *The Architectural Review,* Vol. 9, 1901, pp. 123—131, it was opened on March 12, 1901.

2. Frank Anderson Trapp, "The Armory Show: A Review," *The Art Journal,* Vol. XXIII, No. 1, Fall 1963, pp.2—9.

3. In 1941 Gallatin refused to give his collection to MOMA since he did not approve of the Museum's progressive taste. "It would have been like putting a good apple in a barrel of rotten ones." Instead, the collection was given to the Philadelphia Museum of Art in 1943. The collection of the Société Anonyme was given to Yale University Art Gallery in 1941; most probably since the Museum of *Modern Art fulfilled the original aims of the Société Anonyme and had more resources to achieve* these goals. Lynes, *Good Old Modern,* pp. 48—49.
In the 1950 catalogue of the Société Anonyme Collection, Katherine Dreier explained that many well known artists are represented only by a lithograph or an etching "...since we were a small organization with little means at our disposal in a field which demands untold resources, we were naturally limited." Dreier, Collection of the Société Anonyme: Museum of Modern Art 1920, p. XV.

4. For L'Enseigne de Gersaint, see G. .Bazin, *The Museum Age,* pp. 106—107. This can be compared with paintings illustrating picture galleries in traditional museums such as Joseph Castiglione's "Le Salon Carré" in 1865, the Louvre Museum, Paris, *ibid.,* p. 219.

5. *The architectural Forum,* "The Smithsonian Gallery of Art Competition," Vol. 71, No. 1, pp. I—XVI.

6. Joshua C. Taylor, *Futurism,* New York, 1961, pp. 124—25.

7. Peter Plagens, "West Coast Blues," *Artforum,* Vol. IX, No. 6, February 1971, p. 52.

8. "I would like to see art productions appear in the city, in the city's most lively places, and not (have them) confined in sinister museums... The museums are morgues of embarrassment, citadels of mandarin culture. The very name with its reference to the imbecilic Greek and Latin notion of the *muses* says sufficiently what wind moves it. I am strongly convinced of the sterilizing effect of cultural pomp."
Dubuffet in a letter to the Musée des Arts Decoratifs explaining the reasons for donating his work to the Museum.

9. "As things actually stand now, and as much as I watch for it, there is in the living city no place for the production of art and minds are so perfectly indoctrinated that productions of art presented other than in a museum do not have the least chance that I — in spite of it all — decided to hang them nonetheless at last in a museum." *Ibid.*

10. See Arturo Schwarz, *The Complete Works of Marcel Duchamp,* London, 1969, p. 513.

11. See Michel Ragon, "Mathias Goeritz," *Cimaise,* Art et Architecture Actuels, Vol. 20, No. 106 mars—avril—mai 1972, pp. 27—40 and Olivia Zuñiga, *Mathias Goeritz,* Mexico, D.F., 1963, pp. 30—35.

12. Claes Oldenburg, *Store Days,* New York, 1967, reprinted in John Russell and Suzi Gablik's *Pop Art Redefined,* London, 1969, pp. 97—99.

13. *Documenta 5,* Befragung der Realitat Bildwelten Heute, Kassel, 1972, Section 13, "Museen von Kunstlern," p. 7.

14. Angela Westwater Reaves, "Claes Oldenburg, An Interview," *Artforum,* Vol. XI, No. 2, October 1972, pp. 36—39.

15. See cover design for *Studio International,* Vol. 179, No. 923, June 1970.

16. See Judith Russi Kirshner, The Mouse Museum, The Ray Gun Wing / Two Buildings by Claes Oldenburg, Chicago, 1977.

17. Peter Killer, *Introduction to Herbert Distel,* The Museum of Drawers, Zurich, 1978, pp. 17—19.

18. Michael Kustow, "Profiles and Situations of Some Museums of Contemporary Art," *Museum,* Vol. XXIV, No. 1, 1972, p. 42.

19. For Heizer's "Double Negative" and Smithson's "Spiral Jetty," ("Art is nature rearranged"), see Philip Leider, "How I Spent my Summer Vacation or Art and Politics in Nevada, Berkeley, San Francisco and Utah," *Artforum,* Vol. IX, No. 1, September 1970, pp. 40—49.
According to Heizer, "Our alternative to the museum enclosure is to go beyond it. Both art and the museums are victims of the city, which demands compliance with its laws and limits. Anything is only part of where it is." See Michael Heizer, "The Art of Michael Heizer," *Artforum,* Vol. 8, December 1969, p. 37. Robert Smithson believes that "The museums and parks are graveyards above the ground — congealed memories of the past that act as a pretext for reality. This causes anxiety among artists insofar as they challenge, compete and fight for the spoiled ideals of lost situations," Robert Smithson, "Culture Confinement," *Artforum,* Vol. 11, No. 2, October 1972, p. 39.

20. William S. Rubin, *Christo Wraps the Museum,* The Museum of Modern Art, New York, 1968, Ill. No. 1.

21. For an illustration see *Museum,* Vol. XXIV, No. 1, 1972, Ill. No.19.

22. See Jean-Marie Benoist, "de l'Anti-Oedipe a l'anti-musée," *Chronique de L'Art Vivant,* No. 35, p. 15.

23. Hilton Kramer, "Playing the Gracious Host — But to What?" *The New York Times,* Sunday, March 7, 1971, p. 21.

24. Guy Brett, "How Professional?" *The Times,* Tuesday, December 14, 1971.

25. Harald Szeeman, ed., "Problems of the Museums of Contemporary Art," p. 30.

26. A few visitors were injured in the Tate exhibition which was damaged by the public and had to close only a few days after it was opened. For the Whitney exhibition, see Annette Michelson, "Three Notes on an Exhibition as a Work," *Artforum,* Vol. VIII, No. 10, June 1970, pp. 62–64, and Carter Ratcliff, "New York Letter," *Art International,* Vol. XIV, No. 6, Summer 1970, pp. 136–37.

27. I do not judge, I inform.
    Pierre Schneider, "Spectacles, Les parking d'art modern," *L'Express,* No. 1017, 4–10 janvier, 1971, p. 41.

28. Michael Kustow, "Profiles," p.35 and p. 46.

APPENDIX – SCULPTURE GARDENS

1. See Chapter II, and Hitchcock's observation of a line of procession, Note No. 22.

2. An architectural historian before he became an architect, Philip Johnson is very conscious of historical sources, particularly those linked to the classical tradition. He was, most probably, familiar withthe publications and lectures of Ackerman on the reconstruction of Bramante's project for the Cortile del Belvedere. See James S. Ackerman, "Belvedere as a Classical Villa," *Journal of the Warburg and Courtauld Institutes,* Vol. 14, pp. 70–91, January 1951, the summary of his thesis in *Marsyas,* No. 6, and *The Cortile del Belvedere,* Studi e Documenti per la Storia del Palazzo Apostolico Vaticano, Vol. III, Rome, 1954.
    However, Johnson, who tends to suggest many historical sources for his designs, did not recall in an interview in 1974 reading anything by Ackerman on the Cortile del Belvedere.
    In the second design phase for the MOMA garden two levels were introduced with stairs leading to the upper part which also provides a general view of the sculpture garden. The architect avoided a totally symmetrical arrangement by locating the garden entrance in the center of the original building, but at the side of the garden.

3. For these sources as well as others (Wright, Poussin, Dali, and Lewis Carroll), see Elizabeth Kassler, "The Sculpture Garden," *MOMA,* No. 4, Summer 1975.

4. See *Illustrated London News,* "Battersea Park as an Open Air Sculpture Garden," Vol. 212, May 22, 1948, pp. 588–89.

5. The partitions in Billy Rose Art Garden are similar, in a way, to the temporary walls of the original MOMA garden, which was designed just prior to the opening of the 1939 building. See *Architectural Forum,* "Museum of Modern Art," Vol. 71, No. 2, pp. 115–118.

6. Glaeser, *Architecture of Museums,* pp. 15–16.

Selected Bibliography

I. General

1. Banham, Reyner. *Megastructure,* Urban Futures of the Recent Past, London: Thomas and Hudson, 1976.

2. *The New Brutalism, Ethic or Aesthetic?* London: The Architectural Press, 1966.

3. *Theory and Design in the First Machine Age,* London: The Architectural Press, 1960.

4. Bastlund, Kund. *José Louis Sert, Architecture, City Planning, Urban Design,* with an introduction by Sigfried Giedion, Zurich: Verlag für Architektur (Artemis), 1967.

5. Besset, Maurice. *Who Was Le Corbusier?,* Geneva: Skira, 1968.

6. Bill, Max, ed. Le Corbusier and Pierre Jeanneret, *Oeuvre Complète,* Vol. III, 1934—38, Zurich: Verlag für Architektur (Artemis), 1939.

7. Blake, Peter. *Le Corbusier, Architecture and Form,* New York, 1960 Harmondsworth: Penguin Books, 1968.

8. *Frank Lloyd Wright, Architecture and Space,* Harmondsworth: Penguin Books, 1968.

9. Boesiger, Willy & Stonorow, Oscar, eds. Le Corbusier and Pierre Jeanneret, *Oeuvre Complète,* Vol. I, 1910—1929, Zurich: Verlag für Architektur (Artemis), 1937.

10. Boesiger, Willy, ed. Le Corbusier Last Works, *Oeuvre Complète,* Vol. VIII, London: Thames and Hudson, 1970.

11. Drexler, Arthur. *Ludwig Mies van der Rohe,* New York: Braziller, 1960.

12. *The Drawings of Frank Lloyd Wright,* London: Thames and Hudson, 1962.

13. Giedion, Sigfried. *Space, Time and Architecture, The Growth of a New Tradition,* Cambridge, Mass.: Harvard University Press, fifth revised edition, 1967.

14. Girsberger, H.G. *Le Corbusier 1910—1965,* London: Thames and Hudson, 1967.

15. Goldwater, Robert. *Primitivism in Modern Art,* 1938; revised edition, New York: Vintage Books, 1967.

16. Gombrich, Ernst H. *Meditations on a Hobby Horse* and Other Essays on the Theory of Art, London: Phaidon, 1963.

17. Greenberg, Clement. *Art and Culture,* Critical Essays, 1961. Boston: Beacon Press, 1965.

18. Hatje, Gerd et al. *Encyclopedia of Modern Architecture,* London: Thames and Hudson, 1963.

19. Hitchcock, Henry Russell. *Architecture: Nineteenth and Twentieth Centuries,* Harmondsworth: Penguin Books, 1958, 3rd ed., 1971.

20. *Early Victorian Architecture in Britain,* 2 vols., New Haven and London: Yale University Press, 1954.

21. Hitchcock, Henry Russell & Johnson, Philip. *The International Style, Architecture Since 1922,* New York, 1932, 2nd ed., New York: Norton, 1966.

22. Huxtable, Ada Louise.	*Kicked a Building Lately?* New York: Quadrangle Books, 1978.
23. Jacobus, John M., Jr.	*Philip Johnson,* New York: Braziller, 1962.
24.	*Twentieth Century Architecture, The Middle Years: 1940–1965,* New York: Praeger, 1966.
25. Jencks, Charles.	*Architecture 2000, Predictions and Methods,* London: Studio Vista, 1971.
26.	*Modern Movements in Architecture,* Harmondsworth: Penguin Books, 1973.
27. Joedicke, Jürgen.	*Architecture Since 1945, Source and Directions,* London: Pall Mall, 1969.
28. Johnson, Philip.	*Philip Johnson Architecture 1949–1965,* with an introduction by Henry Russell Hitchcock, New York: Holt, Rinehart and Winston, 1966.
29. Levin, Michael.	"Philip Johnson's Positives-Negatives, The Thirtieth Anniversary of the Glass House," *The Architectural Design,* Vol. 49, No. 2, 1979, pp.52–53.
30. Mumford, Lewis.	*The Culture of Cities,* London: Secker and Warburg, 1938.
31.	*The Highway and the City,* New York: The New American Library, 1964.
32. Ortega Y Gasset, José.	*The Dehumanization of Art,* and Other Essays of Art, Culture and Literature, 1948, Princeton: Princeton University Press, 1968.
33. Papachristou, Tician.	*Marcel Breuer, New Buildings and Projects 1960–1970* and works in Retrospect 1921–1960, London: Thames and Hudson, 1970.
34. Paul, Jack.	"German Neo-classicism and the Modern Movement," *Architectural Review,* Vol. CLII, No. 907, September 1972, pp. 176–180.
35. Pehnt, Wolfgang.	*German Architecture 1960–1970,* London: The Architectural Press, 1970.
36. Pevsner, Nikolaus.	*A History of Building Types,* London: Thames and Hudson, 1976.
37. Rosenblum, Robert.	*Transformations in Late Eighteenth Century Art,* Princeton: Princeton University Press, 1967.
38. Sahut, Marie-Catherine.	*Le Louvre d'Hubert Robert,* Paris: Edition de la Réunion des Musées nationaux, 1979.
39. Scully, Vincent, Jr.	*Frank Lloyd Wright,* New York: Braziller, 1960.
40.	*Louis I. Kahn,* New York: Braziller, 1962.
41. Speyer, A. James.	*Mies van der Rohe,* Catalogue Entries by Frederick Koeper, Chicago: Art Institute of Chicago, 1968.
42. Stone, Edward Durrell.	*The Evolution of an Architect,* New York: Horizon Press, 1962.
43. Webb, Michael.	*Architecture in Britain Today,* London: Country Life, 1969.
44. Zuñiga, Olivia.	*Mathias Goeritz,* Mexico D.F.: Editorial Intercontinental, 1963.

II. Museums and Museology.

45. A.D. Profiles.	No. 2, "Centre Pompidou," n.d.
46. Allen, W.A.	"The Museum in Lisbon for the Gulbenkian Collection, A New Approach to Illumination," *The Museum Journal,* Vol. 71, No. 2, September 1971, pp. 54–58.
47. Alloway, Laurence.	*The Venice Biennale, 1895–1968, from Salon to Goldfish Bowl,* Greenwich, Conn.: New York Graphic Society, 1968.
48. Aloi, Roberto.	*Musei, Architettura–Technica,* with an essay by Carlo Bassi, Milan: Ulrico Hope, 1962.
49. *The Architectural Forum.*	"Museum of Modern Art," Vol. 71, No. 2, August 1939, pp. 115–128.
50.	"Syracuse: Spatial Diversity with a Giant Sculpture," Vol. 130, No. 5, June 1969, p. 56.
51. *The Architectural Review.*	"The Pompidolium," Vol. CLXI, No. 693, May 1977, pp. 271–294.
52. *L'Architecture d'Aujourd'hui.*	"Centre Pompidou," No. 189, 1977.
53. *The Architect's Journal.*	"Building Illustrated, Hayward Gallery Appraisal," Vol. 148, No. 28, 10 July 1968, pp. 56–60.
54.	"Burrell Collection Competition," Vol. 156, No. 12, March 1972, pp. 590–603.
55.	"Hayward Building Revisited," Vol. 153, No. 5, February 3, 1971, pp. 243–255.
56. *Artforum.*	"Validating Modern Art: The Impact of Museums on Modern Art History," Vol. VX, No. 5, January 1977, pp. 36–43.
57. *Art in America.*	Special Museum Issue with contributions by Brian O'Doherty, Linda Nochlin, John E. Bowlt, Ernest van den Haag, Bryan Robertson, Thomas W. Leavitt, Edward F. Fry, Grace Glueck, John R. Spencer, Max Kozloff, Hugh Kenner, Vol. 59, No. 4, July–August, 1971.
58. Banham, Reyner.	"Centre Pompidou, Paris," *The Architectural Review,* Vol. CLXI, No. 693, May 1977, pp. 273–278.
59. Barnes, Edward Larrabee.	"Walker Art Center," *Design Quarterly,* No. 81, Minneapolis, 1971.
60. *Baumeister.*	Prahistorische Staatssammlung in München, Vol. 74, No. 3, March 1977, pp. 222–225.

61. Bazin, Germain. *The Museum Age,* Brussels, 1967, New York: Universe Books, 1967.

62. Blake, Peter. "Architecture is an art and MOMA is its prophet," *Artnews,* Vol. 78, No. 8, October 1979, pp. 67–101.

63. Criticism, "The Guggenheim: Museum or Monument," *Architectural Forum,* Vol. III, No. 6, December 1959, pp. 86–92.

64. "Mies' Berlin Museum," *Architectural Forum,* Vol. 129, No. 3, October 1968, pp. 35–47.

65. Boymans-van Beuningen Museum, Rotterdam Nieuwe Vleugel, eerste fase, Rotterdam: Boyman-van Beuningen Museum, 1972.

66. Bradford, Betty. "The Brick Palace of 1862," *The Architectural Review,* Vol. 132, No. 785, July 1962, pp. 15–21.

67. Breckenridge, J.P. "Lateranus Redivivus," *The Art Bulletin,* Vol. LIV, No. 1, March 1972, pp. 69–72.

68. Brawne, Michael. *The New Museum,* London: The Architectural Press, 1965.

69. "North Jutland Museum of Arts, Aalborg, Denmark, Criticism," *The Architectural Review,* Vol. CLIII, No. 913, March 1973, pp. 162–64.

70. Breuer, Marcel & Smith, Hamilton. *The Architects' Approach to the Design of the Whitney Museum of Art, 1967–71,* (privately circulated), New York, 1963.

71. *The Architect's Report, A New Wing for the Cleveland Museum of Art, 1967–71,* Revised January 1971 (privately circulated).

72. Burt, Nathaniel. *Palaces for the People: A Social History of the American Art Museum,* Boston and Toronto: Little, Brown, 1977.

73. Canati, Cesare; Robers, Richard; Piano, Renzo; and Rice, Peter. (Symposium) "Centre Pompidou," *Domus,* No. 566, January 1977, pp. 5–19.

74. Cantor, Jay. "Temples of Art," *The Metropolitan Museum of Art Bulletin,* Vol. XXVIII, No. 81, April 1970, pp. 331–354.

75. Cauman, Samuel. *The Living Museum,* Experience of an Art Historian and Museum Director — Alexander Dorner, with an introduction by Walter Gropius, New York: New York University Press, 1958.

76. *Chronique de L'Art Vivant.* "Le Musée en Question," No. 35, Decembre 1972 — Janvier 1973.

77. Coleman, Lawrence. *Museum Buildings,* I, A Planning Study, Washington, D.C.: The American Association of Museums, 1950.

78. *The Museum in America,* A Critical Study, 3 vols., Washington, D.C.: The American Association of Museums, 1939.

79. Coleman A.D. "Photography: 'No other institution comes close,'" *Artnews,* Vol. 78, No. 8, October 1979, pp. 102–105.

80. Conférence International d'Étude, Société des Nations, Office International de Musées, Institut International de Cooperation Intellectuelle, Muséographie, Architecture et Aménagement de Musées d'Art, 2 Vols., Madrid, 1934.

81. Cook, Peter. "Sainsbury Center for the Visual Arts." *The Architectural Review,* Vol. CLXIV, No. 982, December 1978, pp. 355–356.

82. Crook, J. Mordaunt. *The British Museum,* London: Allen Lane, The Penguin Press, 1972.

83. DeWit, Wim. "The new wing of the Kröller-Müller Museum at Otterlo. A Building by Wim G. Quist," *Dutch Art and Architecture Today,* No. 2, December 1977, pp. 70–78.

84. Dixon, John Morris. "The Whitney: Big for its Size," *The Architectural Forum,* Vol. 125, No. 2, September, 1966, p. 81.

85. Dreier, Katherine S. *Collection of the Société Anonyme: Museum of Modern Art, 1920,* New Haven: Yale University Gallery, 1950.

86. Durgnat, Raymond. "Musée Imaginaire," *Art and Artists,* Vol. 4, No. 10, January 1970, pp. 22–25.

87. Engle, Margin. "The Circle and the Square," *Arts in Society,* Vol. 8, No. 1, Spring — Summer 1971, pp. 358–372.

88. Engleback, Norman. "South Bank Arts Centre Architecture," *Arup Journal,* Vol. 1, No. 5, pp. 20–24.

89. Etablissement Public du Centre Beaubourg. *Rapport du Jury, Concours International pour la Réalisation du Centre Beaubourg,* Paris, 1972.

90. Finlay, Ian. *Priceless Heritage,* The Future of Museums, London: Faber and Faber, 1977.

91. Framer, Margaret & Lifchez, Raymond. "Building Types: Museum," *The Architectural Record,* Vol. 145, No. 7, June 1969, pp. 175–190.

92. Francheaux, Pierre. "Ville de Paris, Musée d'Art Moderne," *L'Architecture d'Aujourd'hui,* No. 163, août-septembre, 1972, pp. 98–102.

93. Franck, Klaus. *Exhibitions,* A Survey of International Designs, London: The Architectural Press, 1961.

94. Gilman, Benjamin Ives. Museum Ideals of Purpose and Method, Cambridge, Mass.: Museum of Fine Arts, Boston, Riverside Press, 1918.

95. Giraudy, Daniele & Bouilhet, Henri. Le Musée et la Vie, Paris: La Documentation Francaise, 1977.

96. Glaeser, Ludwig. *Architecture of Museums,* New York: The Museum of Modern Art, 1968.

97. Goldberger, Paul. "The New MOMA: Mixing Art with Real Estate," *The New York Times Magazine,* November 4, 1979, pp. 46–56.

98.   "Townhouse to Tower," *Artnews*, Vol. 78, No. 8, October, 1979, pp. 180–182.

99. Goldin, Amy & Smith, Roberta. "Present Tense: New Art and the New York Museum," *Art in America*, Vol. 65, No. 5, September–October, 1977, pp. 92–104.

100. Gordon, Ayala. "The Museum's Junior Wing," *Ariel*, No. 10, Spring 1965.

101. Greater London Council Press Office. "Hayward Gallery Electrical Services," 5 June 1968.

102. Gruen, John. "The Artist Speaks: Isamu Noguchi," *Art in America*, Vol. LVI, No. 2, March–April 1968, pp. 28–31.

103. Hallmark Neff, John. "How Contemporary is Modern?", MOMA at 50: Directions, *Artnews*, Vol. 78, No. 8, October 1979, pp. 170–177.

104. Hennesey, William. "Frank Lloyd Wright and the Guggenheim: A New Perspective," *Arts Magazine*, Vol. 52, No. 8, April 1978, pp. 128–133.

105. Hobhouse, Christopher. *1851 and the Crystal Palace*, London: John Murray, 1937.

106. Holmes, Ann. "From Panhandle to the Gulf Coast: The Museum Boom in Texas," *Artnews*, Vol. LXXII, No. 5, May 1973, pp. 34–36.

107. Hoving, Thomas. "Advanced Crisis or Coming of Age?" *Artnews*, Vol. 71, No. 7, November 1972, pp. 34–35.

108.   *The Second Century*. The Comprehensive Architectural Plan for the Metropolitan Museum of Art, with a statement by August Heckscher, New York, 1971.

109. Howe, George. "A Modern Museum, Howe and Lescaze Architects, New York and Philadelphia, Springdale, Conn., (privately printed) 1930.

110. Howe, George & Lescase, H. "A Proposed Museum of Contemporary Art for New York City," *The Architectural Record*, Vol. 80, No. 1, July 1936, pp. 43–50.

111. Hudson, Kenneth. *Museums for the 1980's*. London: UNESCO and Macmillan, 1977.

112. Huxtable, Ada Louise. "Architecture of Museums," *The Museum News*, Vol. 47, No. 3, November 1968, pp. 18–19 (reprint from *The New York Times*).

113. Jehle Schulte Strathaus, Ulrike. "Von der ästhetischen Kirche zu Fabrik ästhetischen Informationen," Werk, Bauen und Wohnen, Nr. 12, December 1980, pp. 19–23.

114. Jencks, Charles. "Don't Panic!, J. Paul Getty Museum Malibu California," *The Architectural Review*, Vol. CLXIII, No. 972, February 1978, pp. 83–85.

115. Jordy, William H. "Kimbell Art Museum, Library, Philips Exeter Academy, Criticism," *The Architectural Review*, Vol. CLV, No. 928, June 1974, pp. 330–335.

116. J.T.B., P/A Observor (Burns, James T. Jr.) "Whitney Opens," *Progressive Architecture*, Vol. 47, No. 10, October 1966, pp. 238–241.

117. Kassler, Elizabeth. "The Sculpture Garden," *MOMA*, A Publication for Members of the Museum of Modern Art, No. 4, Summer, 1975.

118. Katz, Karl, Kahne, P.P., & Broshi, Magen. *From the Beginning*, Archeology and Art in the Israel Museum, Jerusalem, with an introduction by Philip Hendy, London: Weidenfeld and Nicholson, 1968.

119. Kustow, Michael. "Profiles and Situations of Some Museums of Contemporary Art," *Museum*, Vol. XXIV, No. 1, 1972, pp. 33–57.

120. Lee, Sherman, E., ed. *On Understanding Art Museums*, Englewood Cliffs, N.J.: Prentice Hall, 1975.

121. Lehmbruck, Manfred. "Museum Architecture," *Museum*, Vol. XXVI, No. 34, 1974, pp. 129–267.

122. Leitner, Bernhard. "A Master Plan, the Met Plans its Second Century," *Artforum*, Vol. 9, No. 2, October 1970, pp. 64–68.

123. Little, David B. "The Misguided Mission: A Disenchanted View of Art Museums Today," *Curator*, Vol. X, No. 3, September 1967, pp. 221–226.

124. Low, Theodor L. *The Museum as a Social Instrument*, New York, 1942.

125. Lueddeckens, Ernst. "The Abstract Cabinet of El Lissitsky," *Art Journal*, Vol. XXX, No. 3, Spring 1971, pp. 265–266.

126. Lynes, Russell. *Good Old Modern*, An Intimate Portrait of the Museum of Modern Art, New York: Atheneum, 1973.

127. Malraux, André. *Museum Without Walls, The Voices of Silence*, Garden City: Doubleday, 1967.

128. Meyer, Karl E. *The Art Museum, Power, Money, Ethics*, New York: William Morrow, 1979.

129. Newsom, Barbara Y. & Silver, Adele Z. eds. *The Art Museum as Educator: A Collection of Studies as Guides to Practice and Policy*, Los Angeles and London: University of California Press, 1978.

130. Nicholson, Irene. "Criticism: Anthropological Museum, Mexico City," *The Architectural Review*, Vol. 140, No. 834, August 1966, pp. 118–125.

131. Norman, Geraldine. "America's Art Behind Closing Doors," *The Times*, Saturday Review, London, December 16, 1972, p. 7.

132. O'Doherty, Brian. "Inside the White Cube: Notes on the Gallery Space" (Part I), *Artforum*, Vol. XIV, No. 7, March 1976, pp. 24–30.

133. Oille, Janifer, "Washington: Capital and Culture," *Art Monthly*, No. 23, February 1979, pp. 3–5.

134. Padovan, Richard. "Kröller-Müller Art Gallery, Otterlo, Holland, Criticism," *The Architectural Review*, Vol. CLXIII, February 1978, No. 972, pp. 74–82.

135. Papademetriou, Peter C. "Varied reflections in Houston, Contemporary Arts Museum, Houston, Texas," *Progressive Architecture*, Vol. LVI, No. 3, March 1975, pp. 52—57.

136. Peckham, Andrew et al. "A.D. Profiles 19: Foster Associates' Sainsbury Center," *Architectural Design*, Vol. 49, No. 2, 1979, pp. 1—34.

137. Pevsner, Nikolaus. "British Museum: Some Unsolved Problems of its Architectural History," *The Architectural Review*, Vol. 113, No. 675, March 1953, pp. 179—182.

138. Plagens, Peter. "West Coast Blues, A Museum in Berkeley, A West Coast Show in Omaha," *Artforum*, Vol. 9, No. 6, February 1971, pp. 52—57.

139. *Progressive Architecture* Museums; Museum as monument; Too little from Tange; Varied reflections in Houston; Moma Italian style; The art of high art; A touch of De Stije, Vol. LVI, No. 3, March 1975, pp. 41—71.

140. Prown, Jules. *The Architecture of the Yale Center for British Art*, New Haven: Yale University Press, 1977.

141. Pyne, E.J. & Maw, George. "Design for an Exhibition Building, Embracing a Suggestion for a Method of Classifying the Proposed Exhibition of 1862, *The Builder*, Vol. 19, No. 941, 16 February, 1861, pp. 106—108.

142. Ratcliff, Carter. "Modernism for the Ages," *Art in America*, Vol. 66, No. 4, July—August, 1978, pp. 50—54.

143. Ripley, Dillon. *The Sacred Grove*, Essays on Museums, New York: Simon and Schuster, 1969.

144. Rosenblatt, R. "Architects and Museums," *The Metropolitan Museum of Art Bulletin*, Vol. XXVIII, No. 8, April 1970.

145. Sandberg, Willem. "The Israel Museum in Jerusalem," *Museum*, Vol. XIX, No. 1, 1966.

146. Noguchi, Isamu, Mnasfeld, Alfred, Gad, Dora, "Israel Museum Jerusalem," *Architecture in Israel*, No. 4, 1966, pp. 5—33.

147. Sandler, Irving. "When MOMA met the Avant-garde," *Artnews*, Vol. 78, No. 8, October 1979, pp. 114—118.

148. Santon, Corrin Hughes. "Museums — and How to Make the Most of Them," *Design*, No. 278, February 1972, pp. 25—29.

149. Schneider, Pierre. "Spectacle, Les Parkings de l'art Moderne," *L'Express*, No. 1017, 4—10 janvier 1971, pp. 40—41.

150 S.C. "New Wing for the Vatican Museum, Rome," *The Architectural Review*, Vol. CLI, No. 899, January 1972, pp. 35—40.

151. Schulz, Franz. "The East Building: Trapezoid Triumphant," *Art in America*, Vol. 66, No. 4, July—August, 1978, pp. 55—63.

152. Seling, Helmut. "The Genesis of the Museum," *The Architectural Review*, Vol. CXLI, No. 840, February 1967, pp. 103—114.

153. Shapiro, Meyer. "Democratize the Board of Trustees," (part of an inquiry, The Metropolitan Museum 1870—1970—2001), *Artnews*, Vol. 68, January 1970, p. 29.

154. Smith, C. Ray. "Boston's Underwater Environment," *Progressive Architecture*, Vol. L, No. 12, December 1969, pp. 96—107.

155. "The Great Museum Debate," *Progressive Architecture*, Vol. L, No. 12, December 1969, pp. 76—85.

156. Stein, Clarence. "The Art Museum of Tomorrow," *Architectural Record*, Vol. 67, No. 1, January 1930, pp. 5—12.

157. "Making Museums Function," *Architectural Forum*, Vol. LVI, No. 6, June 1932, pp. 609—616.

158. "Study-Storage — Theory and Practice," *The Museum News*, Vol. XXII, No. 12. December 15, 1944, pp. 9—12.

159. Stephens, Suzanne. "Big Deals and Bitter Endings: The Hirshhorn Museum and Sculpture Garden," *Artforum*, Vol. XIII, No. 6 February, 1975, pp. 56—62.

160. "Museum as Monument, Hirshhorn Museum and Sculpture Garden, Washington, D.C.," *Progressive Architecture*, Vol. LVI, No. 3, March 1975, pp. 42—47.

161. Svendsen, Louise Averill. "The Solomon R. Guggenheim Museum Collection," a brief history, New York.

162. Szeeman, Harald, and Hulten, Pontus; Kustow, Michael; Leymarie, Jean; Mathey, Francois; Rivière, George Henry; Szeeman, Harald, and de Wilde, Edouard. "Problems of the Museum of Contemporary Art in the West, Exchange of Views of a Group of Experts," *Museum*, Vol. XXIV, No. 1, 1972, pp.5—33.

163. Taylor, Francis Henry. *Babel's Tower, The Dilemma of the Modern Museum*, New York: Columbia University Press, 1945.

164. *The Taste of Angels:* A History of Art Collection from Ramses to Napoleon, Boston: Little, Brown, 1948.

165. Thomson, Garry. "Hayward Gallery, Assessment," *The Architect's Journal*, Vol. 148, No. 27, 3 July 1968, p. 63.

166. "A New Look at Colour Rendering, Level of Illumination and Protection from Ultra-Violet Radiation in Museum Lighting," *Studies in Conservation*, Vol. 6, Nos. 2 and 3, August 1961, pp. 49—70.

167. Tomkins, Calvin.   *Merchants and Masterpieces,* The Story of the Metropolitan Museum of Art, London: Longman, 1970.

168. Townsend, Benjamin & Peyton, M. Ruth.   *100, The Buffalo Fine Arts Academy, 1862—1962,* Albright-Knox Gallery, Buffalo, N.Y.: The Buffalo Fine Arts Academy, 1962.

169. Wilde, E.L.L.   "Notes on the Role of Modern Art," *Art and Artists,* Vol. 4, No. 10, January 1970, pp. 14—15.

170. Wittlin, Alma S.   *The Museum,* Its History and Its Tasks in Education, London: Routledge and Kegan Paul, 1949.

171.   *Museums:* In search of a Usable Future, with a foreword by S. Dillon Ripley, Cambridge, Mass.: The MIT Press and London, 1970.

172. Wolfe, Ruth.   "Noguchi: Past, Present, Future, A Picture Survey," *Art in America,* Vol. LVI, No. 2, March—April 1968, pp. 32—45.

173. Wright, Frank Lloyd.   *The Solomon Guggenheim Museum,* with an introduction by Harry F. Guggenheim, New York: Guggenheim Museum, 1960.

174. Yee, Roger.   "A touch of De Stije, Vincent van Gogh Museum, Amsterdam, Netherlands," *Progressive Architecture,* Vol. LVI, No. 3, March 1975, pp. 68—71.

Index